shelve in AGN 3/2016
OCT 2 2012

D1194781

interiorae

fantagraphics books
7563 lake city way ne
seattle, wa 98115

——

Edited and Translated by Kim Thompson
Designed by Alexa Koenings
Production by Paul Baresh
Lettered by Ben Horak
Associate Publisher: Eric Reynolds
Published by Gary Groth and Kim Thompson

This material originally appeared (in a slightly different version) in four issues of the "Ignatz" series *Interiorae*, edited by Igort. This book was lettered in the "NADIR" font created by Patrick Doan.

Special thanks to Thomas Gabison of Actes Sud BD, Jacques Leng, Jaso Miles, Kristy Valenti, and Lorenzo Mattotti.

All characters, stories, and artwork © 2012 Gabriella Giandelli. U.S. translation © 2012 Kim Thompson. Introduction © 2012 Lorenzo Mattotti. All rights reserved. Permission to quote or reproduce material for reviews or notices must be obtained from the author or Fantagraphics Books.

To receive a free catalog of comics, call 1-800-657-1100 or write us at
Fantagraphics Books, 7563 Lake City Way NE, Seattle, WA 98115.

Distributed in the U.S. by W.W. Norton and Company, Inc. (800-233-4830)
Distributed in Canada by Canadian Manda Group (800-452-6642 x862)
Distributed in the United Kingdom by Turnaround Distribution (44-(0)20-8829-3002)
Distributed to comics shops in the U.S. by Diamond Comic Distributors (800-452-6642 x215)

Visit the Fantagraphics website at www.fantagraphics.com
Visit Gabriella Giandelli's website at www.gabriellagiandelli.com

First printing: April, 2012.

ISBN: 978-1-60699-559-4

Printed in Hong Kong.

Gabriella Giandelli

—

interiorae

—

Fantagraphics Books

SPRINGDALE PUBLIC LIBRARY
405 South Pleasant
Springdale, Arkansas 72764

Introduction by Lorenzo Mattotti

—

In Milan, within these identical apartment complexes, there is a wealth of mysteries — the mysteries each one of us carries inside: our dreams, our fears, our petty cruelties, our woes, our loves, our labors…

And there are people in whom magic is particularly strong, who can sense the mysteries within everyone else.

Gabriella is one of those people.

Like that woman gazing out of her window, lost within that vast façade, Gabriella observes…

But she does much more than observe. She intuits and experiences the lives of others, she ventures into their apartments and, with bottomless empathy and compassion, she tells the stories of the silences, and of the colors within those silences. Gabriella never resorts to spectacle, and she works without shouting, without bizarre distortions; she eschews the smoke and mirrors that can be used to dazzle the reader.

Restrained and quiet, Gabriella, like a tiny ant, is busily building a vast body of work — personal, lyrical, and powerful in its chronicling of weakness, insecurity, and hope.

She puts us under her spell with the gentle gaze she levels at the world.

Gabriella always manages to imbue her drawings with an intimate, everyday mood. Every object, every plant, every animal seems as if it belongs to her, or as if she has pulled it from her own trunk, photo album, or closet.

Even when she draws a big city, Gabriella knows every window, every gutter, every brick; she manages to make them her own — takes them over, if you will.

Gabriella is never cynical, cold, or calculated. Her characters are magical — never caricatured or grotesque, nor excessively sweet. Observing them with affectionate detachment, she strives to accept them in their smallness, their day-to-day lives. They are like wonderful toys in the hands of a Child of Destiny, playing with them on a carpet of stars.

Gabriella does not follow any fashion: Those who wish to enjoy her marvelously delicate stories must put aside the cynicism, the distance that nowadays comprises a "normal" outlook on the world. Sometimes I think entering Gabriella's drawings requires extra effort: The reader must adjust his own temperament, cleanse himself of his distrust. Such is the purity and honesty of feeling in her drawings — devoid of calculation, deceit, or any striving for success or acceptance — so sweetly does she gaze upon these living creatures, that it is as if she is asking us, her readers, to become more pure, more open — ultimately, better.

For my Father.

TUESDAY, DECEMBER 19

35 hours, 52 minutes, 36 seconds

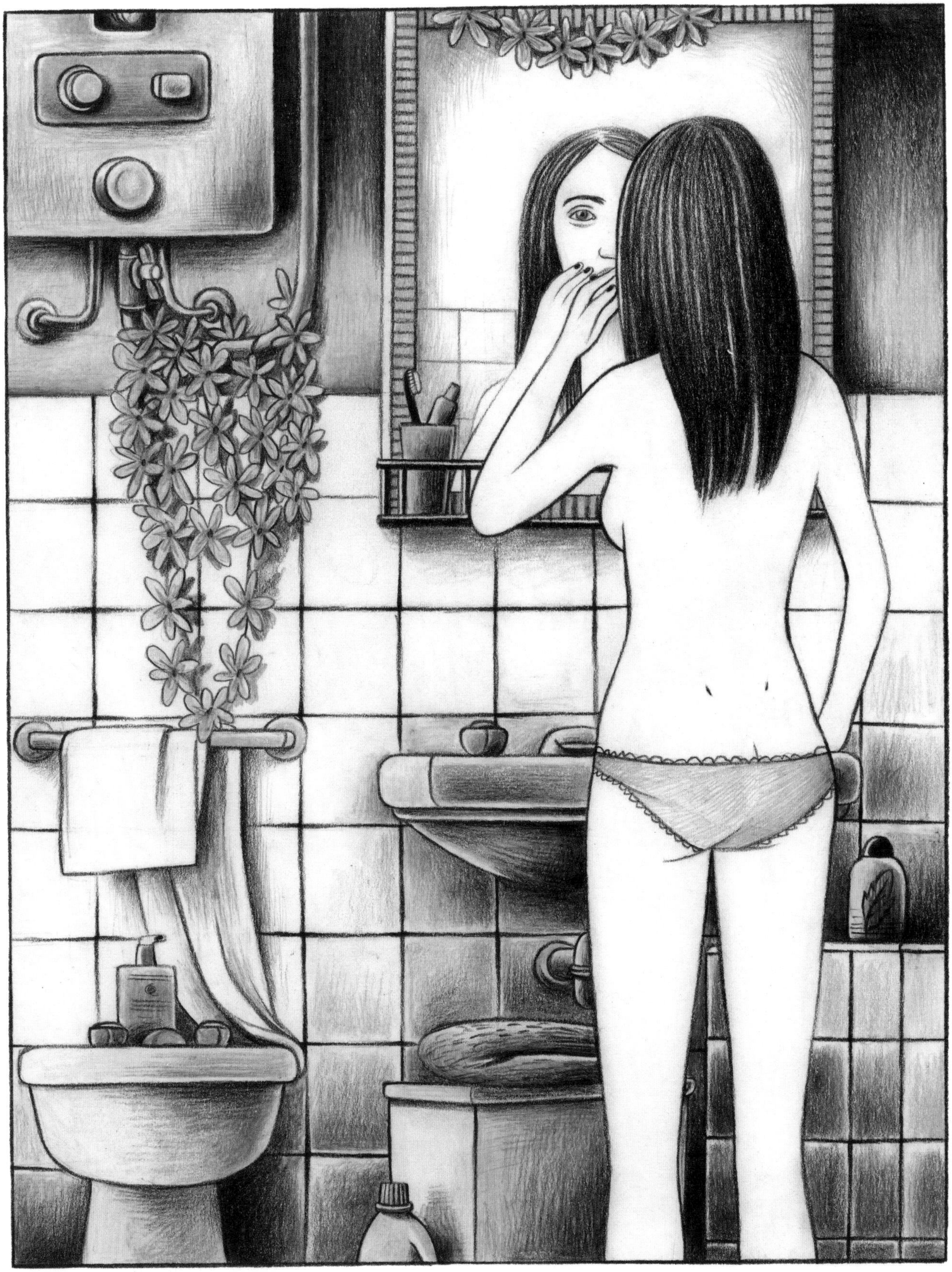

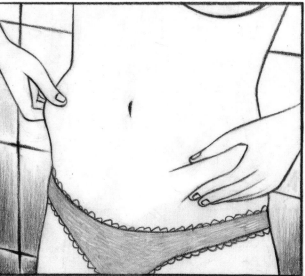

DRIIIIN

Oh, hi...

No... I just need to finish up here, pack my suitcase and answer some e-mails...

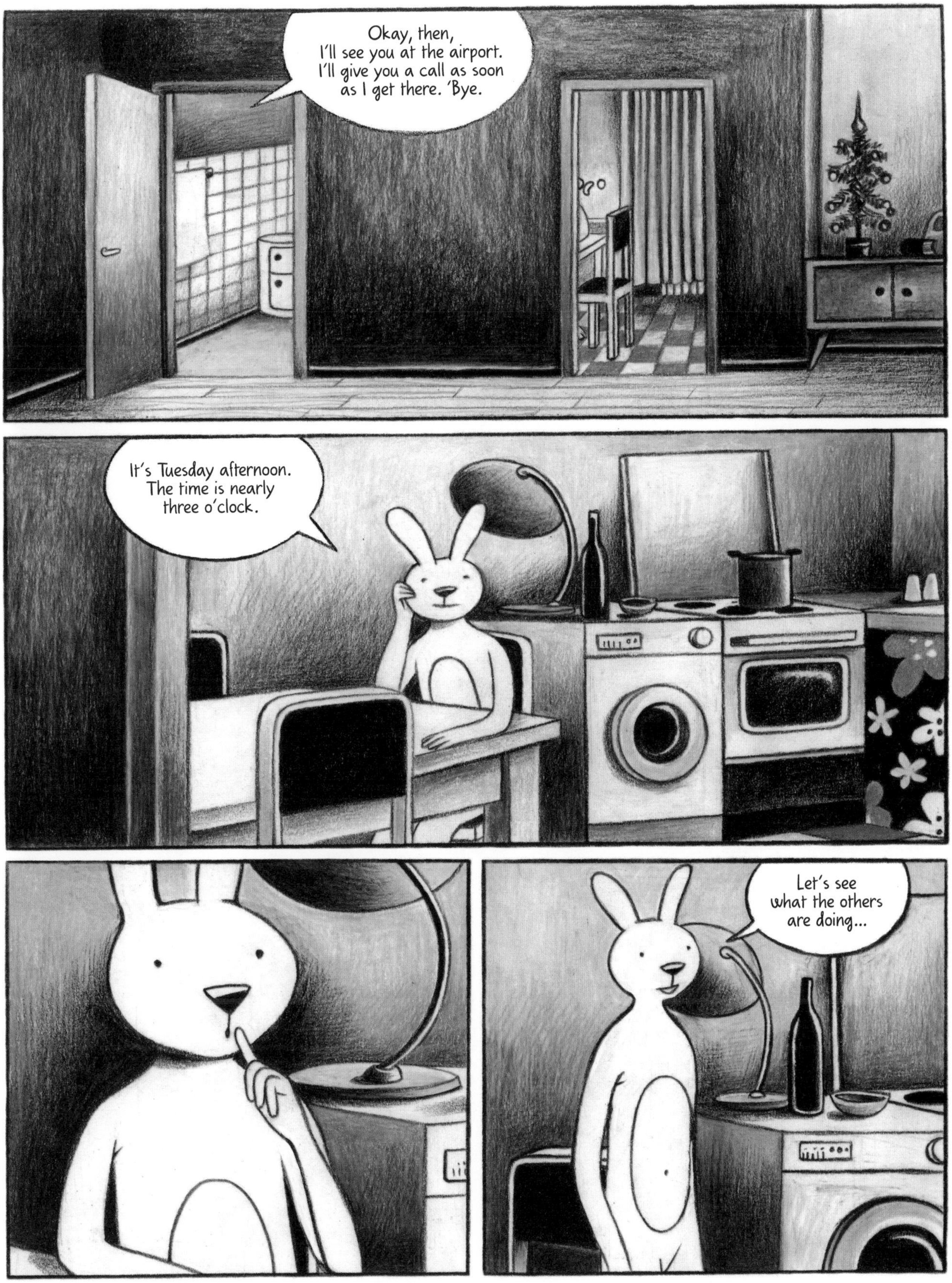
Okay, then, I'll see you at the airport. I'll give you a call as soon as I get there. 'Bye.
It's Tuesday afternoon. The time is nearly three o'clock.
Let's see what the others are doing...

I can go wherever I want. I move through things.

No one can see me.

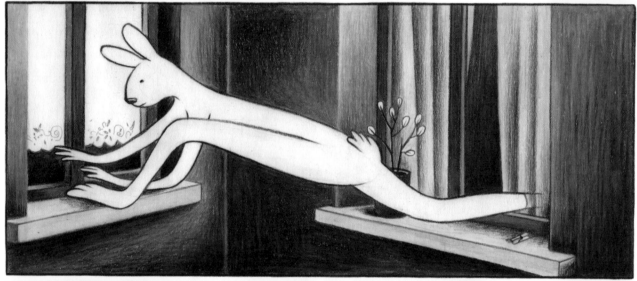

12

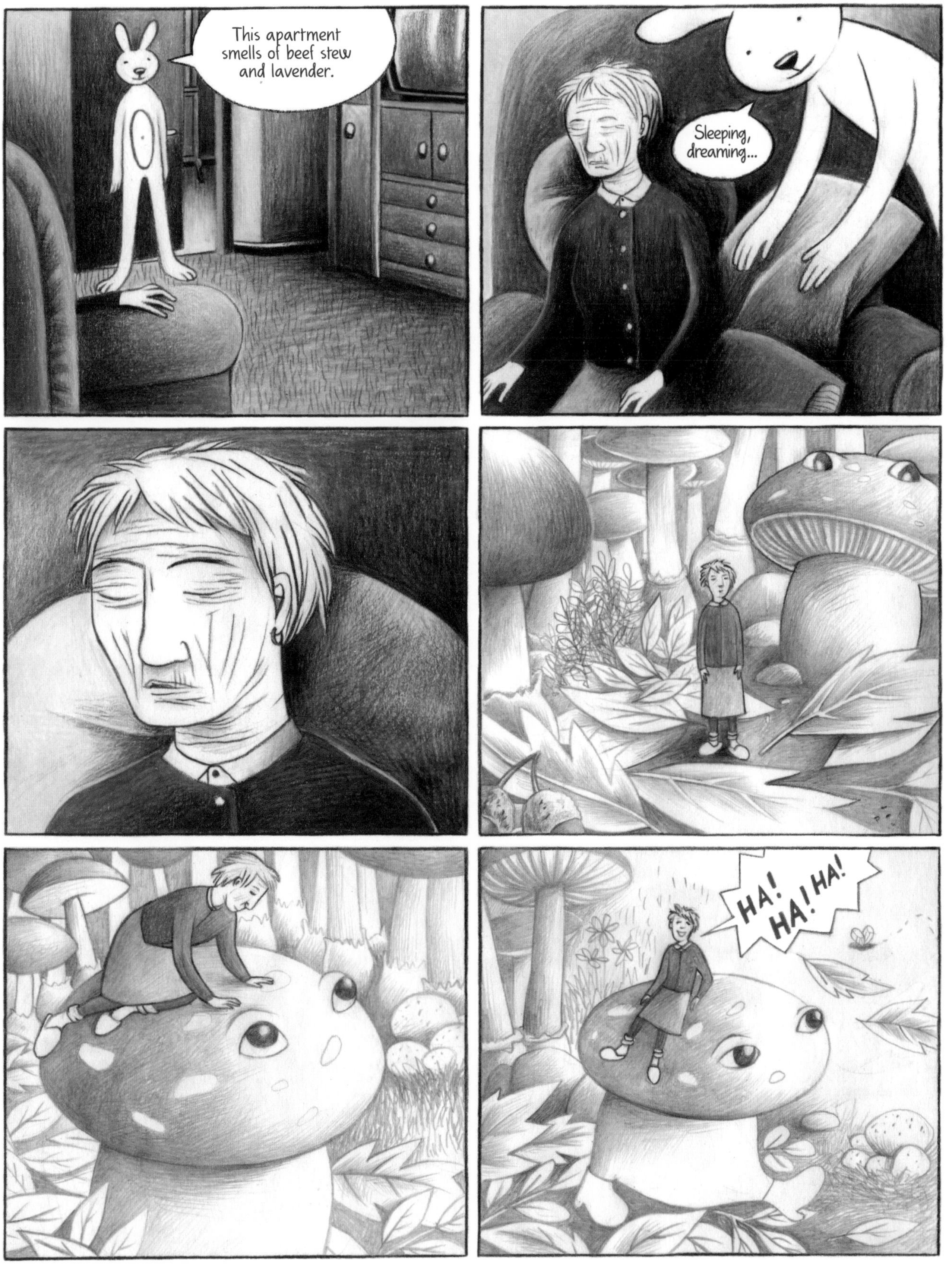
This apartment smells of beef stew and lavender.
Sleeping, dreaming...
HA! HA! HA!

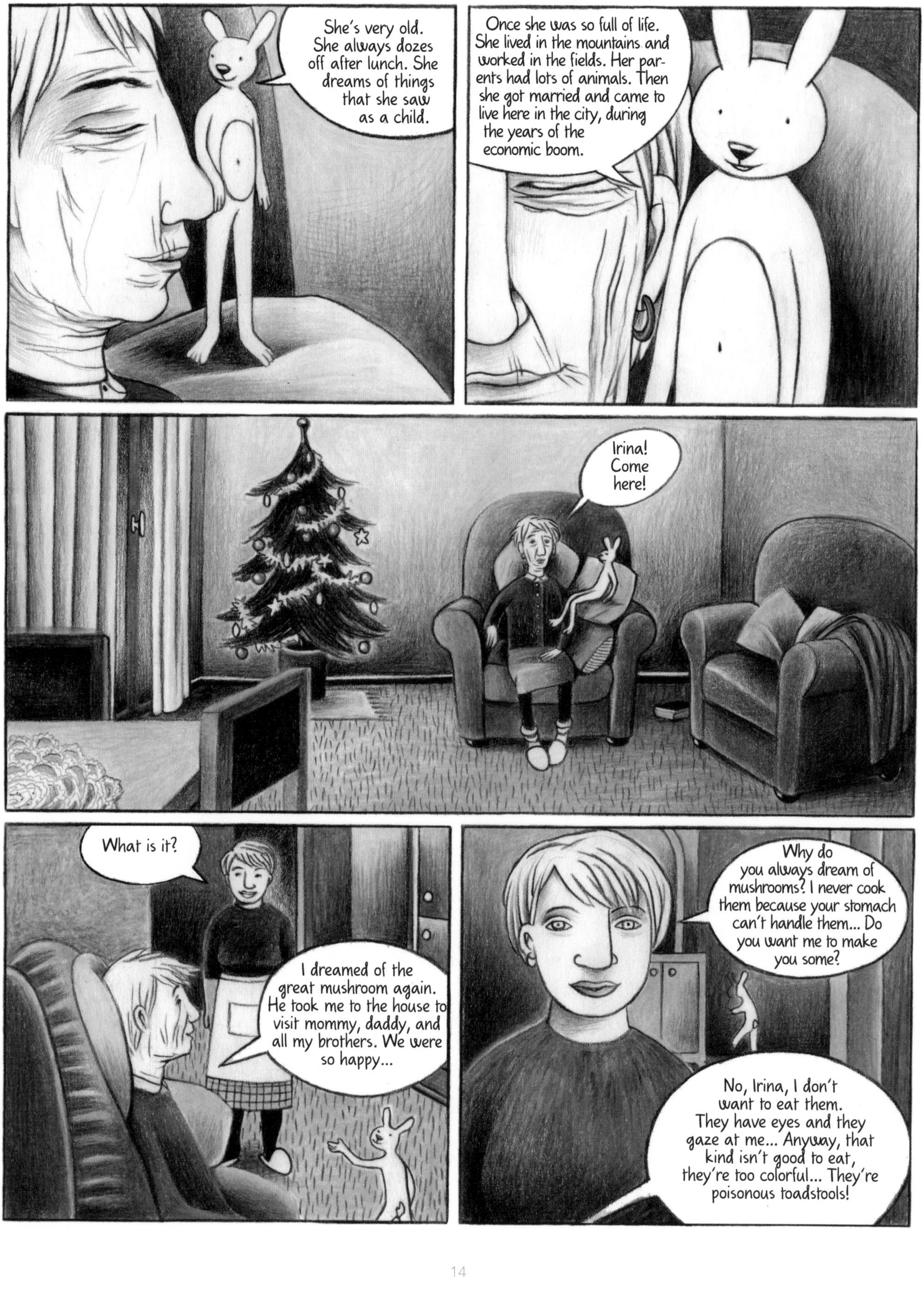
She's very old. She always dozes off after lunch. She dreams of things that she saw as a child.
Once she was so full of life. She lived in the mountains and worked in the fields. Her parents had lots of animals. Then she got married and came to live here in the city, during the years of the economic boom.
Irina! Come here!
What is it?
I dreamed of the great mushroom again. He took me to the house to visit mommy, daddy, and all my brothers. We were so happy...
Why do you always dream of mushrooms? I never cook them because your stomach can't handle them... Do you want me to make you some?
No, Irina, I don't want to eat them. They have eyes and they gaze at me... Anyway, that kind isn't good to eat, they're too colorful... They're poisonous toadstools!

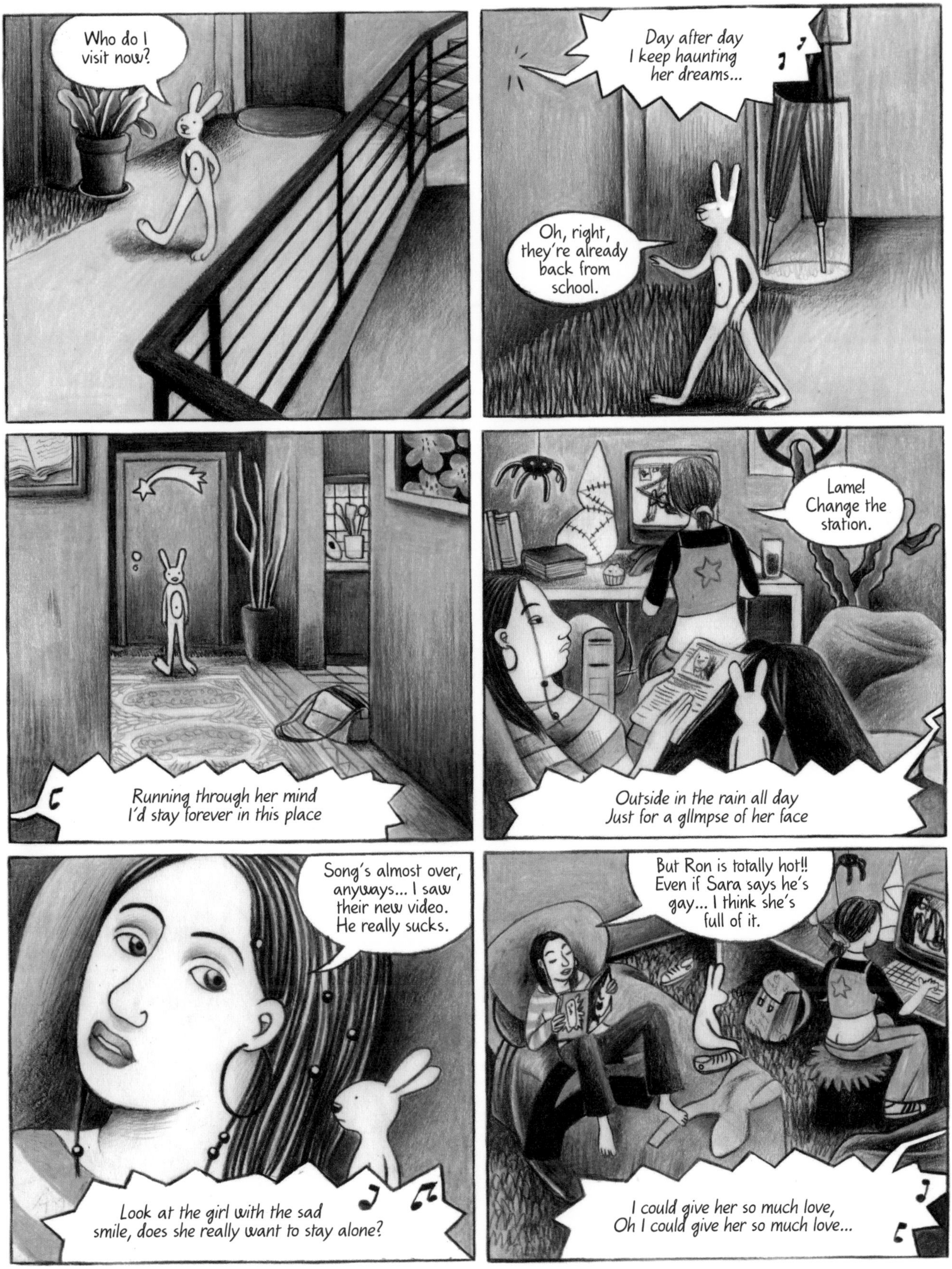

Who do I visit now?
Day after day I keep haunting her dreams...
Oh, right, they're already back from school.
Running through her mind I'd stay forever in this place
Lame! Change the station.
Outside in the rain all day Just for a glimpse of her face
Song's almost over, anyways... I saw their new video. He really sucks.
Look at the girl with the sad smile, does she really want to stay alone?
But Ron is totally hot!! Even if Sara says he's gay... I think she's full of it.
I could give her so much love, Oh I could give her so much love...

Whatever! 'sides, if he's gay, who cares? It's not like you're gonna bump into him...

Come to my window, fly into my heart, let peace flow from me to you, I know you've been waiting so long...

Eh, I'd just like to know that he isn't! ...And meeting him, it could happen, if we go to London this summer... I love rock stars...

It may not always be rainbows and butter-flies...

Me, I think it's better to just focus on real boys. Like your brother's friend...

But that's okay...

Who, him?! When he comes here he treats me like I'm retarded! Anyway, I'm sorry, but in dreams everything is prettier. You can totally make stuff up and pretend everything's perfect...

Soon Christmas vacation will be here... long, white, boring afternoons... They're so cute, I love listening to them. They make me feel like I'm in the right place... exactly where a white rabbit ought to be!

With real guys, there's always something wrong, like, he's a bastard or whatever...

And they smell good, too. Their dreams are among my master's favorites... In fact, I probably ought to go give him a report...

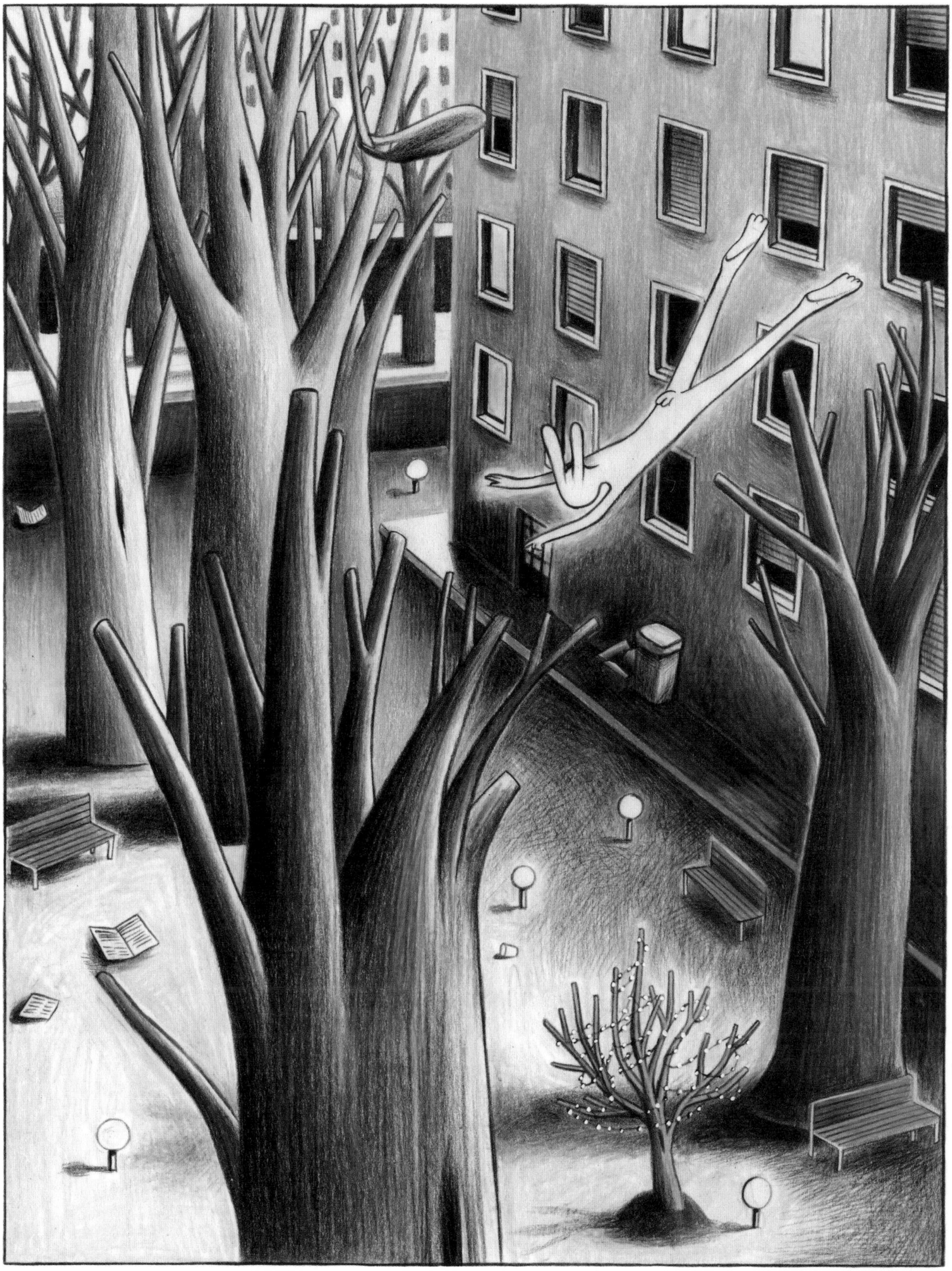

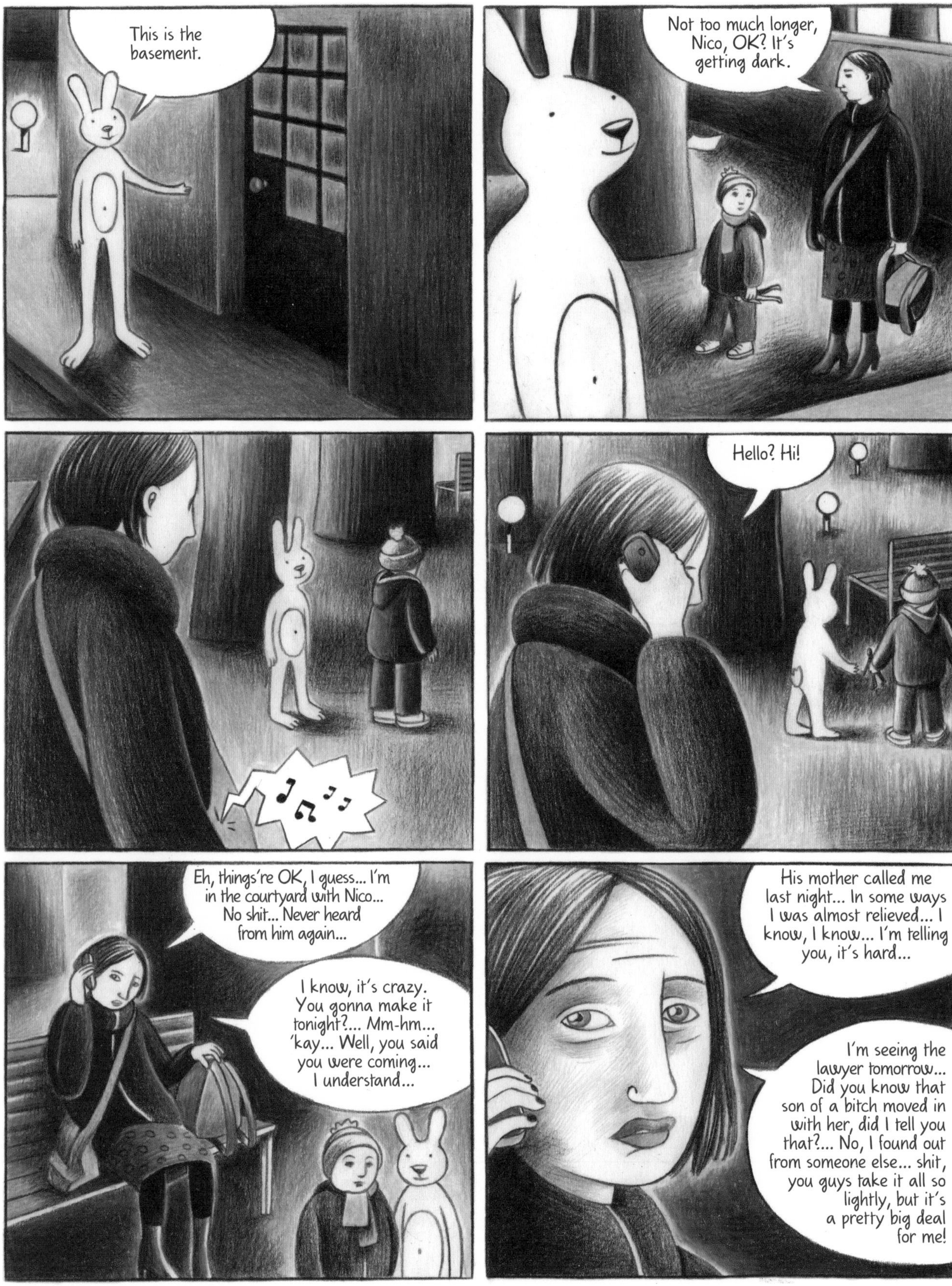
This is the basement.
Not too much longer, Nico, OK? It's getting dark.
Hello? Hi!
Eh, things're OK, I guess... I'm in the courtyard with Nico... No shit... Never heard from him again...
I know, it's crazy. You gonna make it tonight?... Mm-hm... 'kay... Well, you said you were coming... I understand...
His mother called me last night... In some ways I was almost relieved... I know, I know... I'm telling you, it's hard...
I'm seeing the lawyer tomorrow... Did you know that son of a bitch moved in with her, did I tell you that?... No, I found out from someone else... shit, you guys take it all so lightly, but it's a pretty big deal for me!

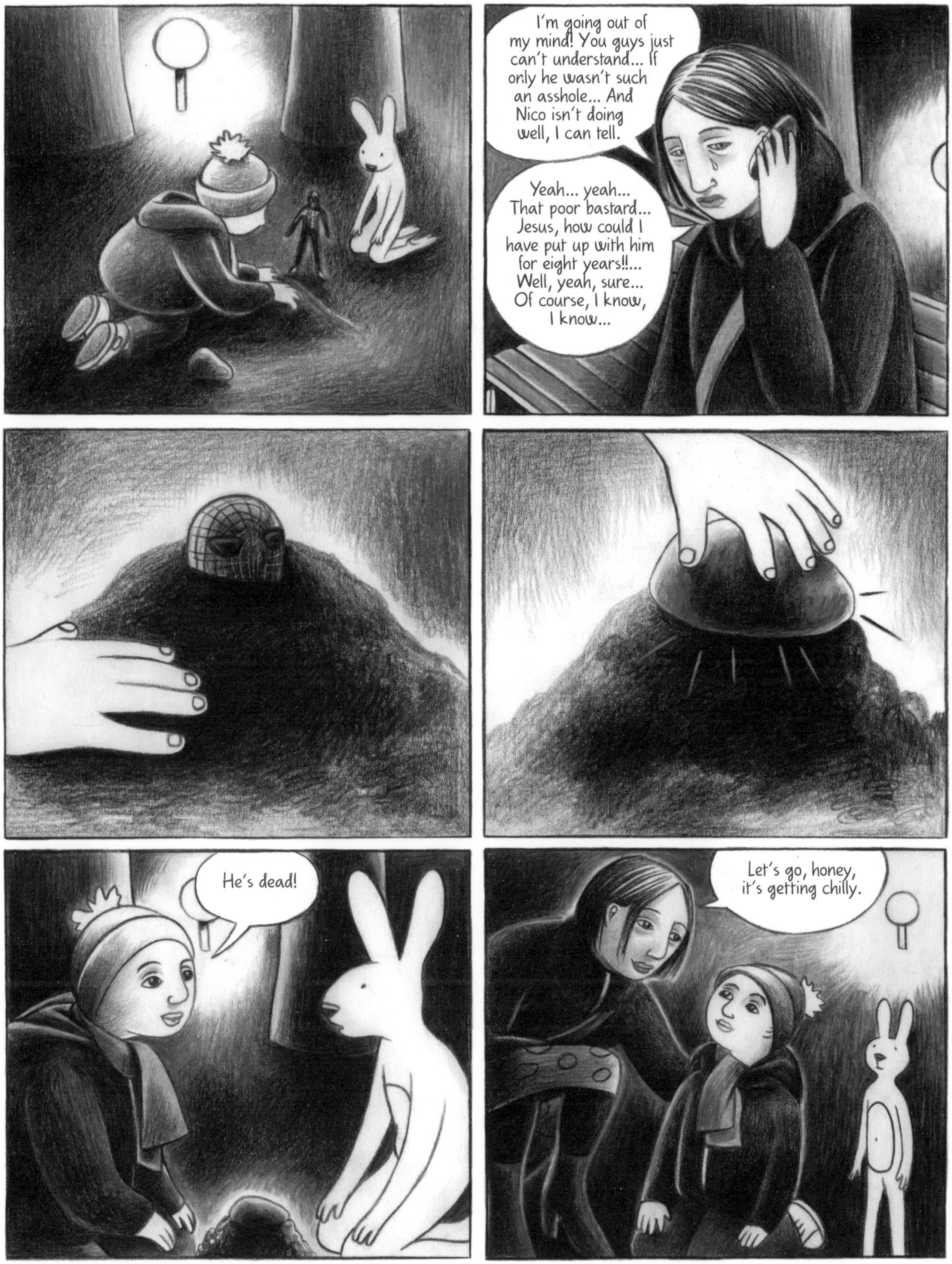
I'm going out of my mind! You guys just can't understand... If only he wasn't such an asshole... And Nico isn't doing well, I can tell.
Yeah... yeah... That poor bastard... Jesus, how could I have put up with him for eight years!!... Well, yeah, sure... Of course, I know, I know...
He's dead!
Let's go, honey, it's getting chilly.

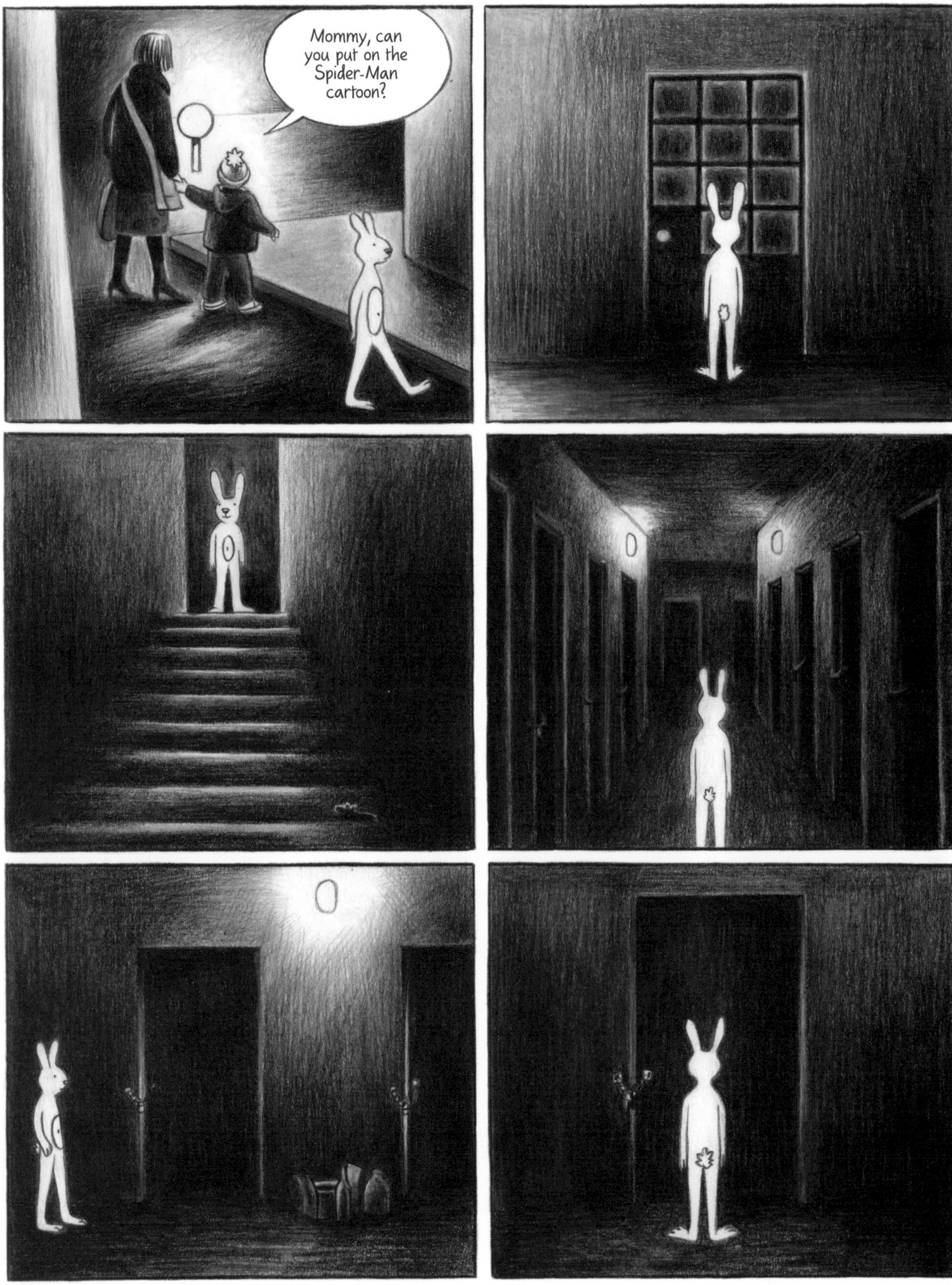
Mommy, can you put on the Spider-Man cartoon?

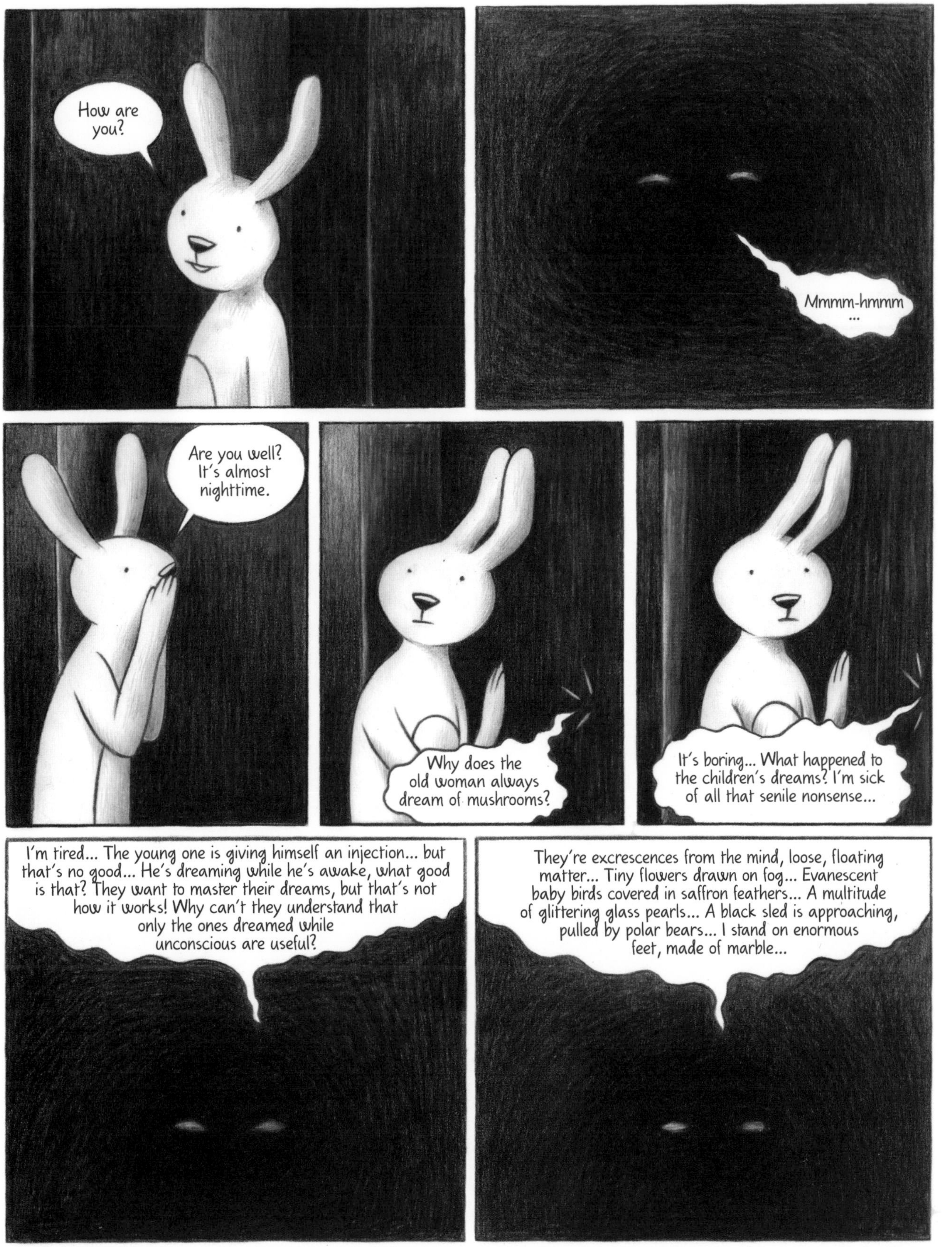
How are you?
Mmmm-hmmm ...
Are you well? It's almost nighttime.
Why does the old woman always dream of mushrooms?
It's boring... What happened to the children's dreams? I'm sick of all that senile nonsense...
I'm tired... The young one is giving himself an injection... but that's no good... He's dreaming while he's awake, what good is that? They want to master their dreams, but that's not how it works! Why can't they understand that only the ones dreamed while unconscious are useful?
They're excrescences from the mind, loose, floating matter... Tiny flowers drawn on fog... Evanescent baby birds covered in saffron feathers... A multitude of glittering glass pearls... A black sled is approaching, pulled by polar bears... I stand on enormous feet, made of marble...

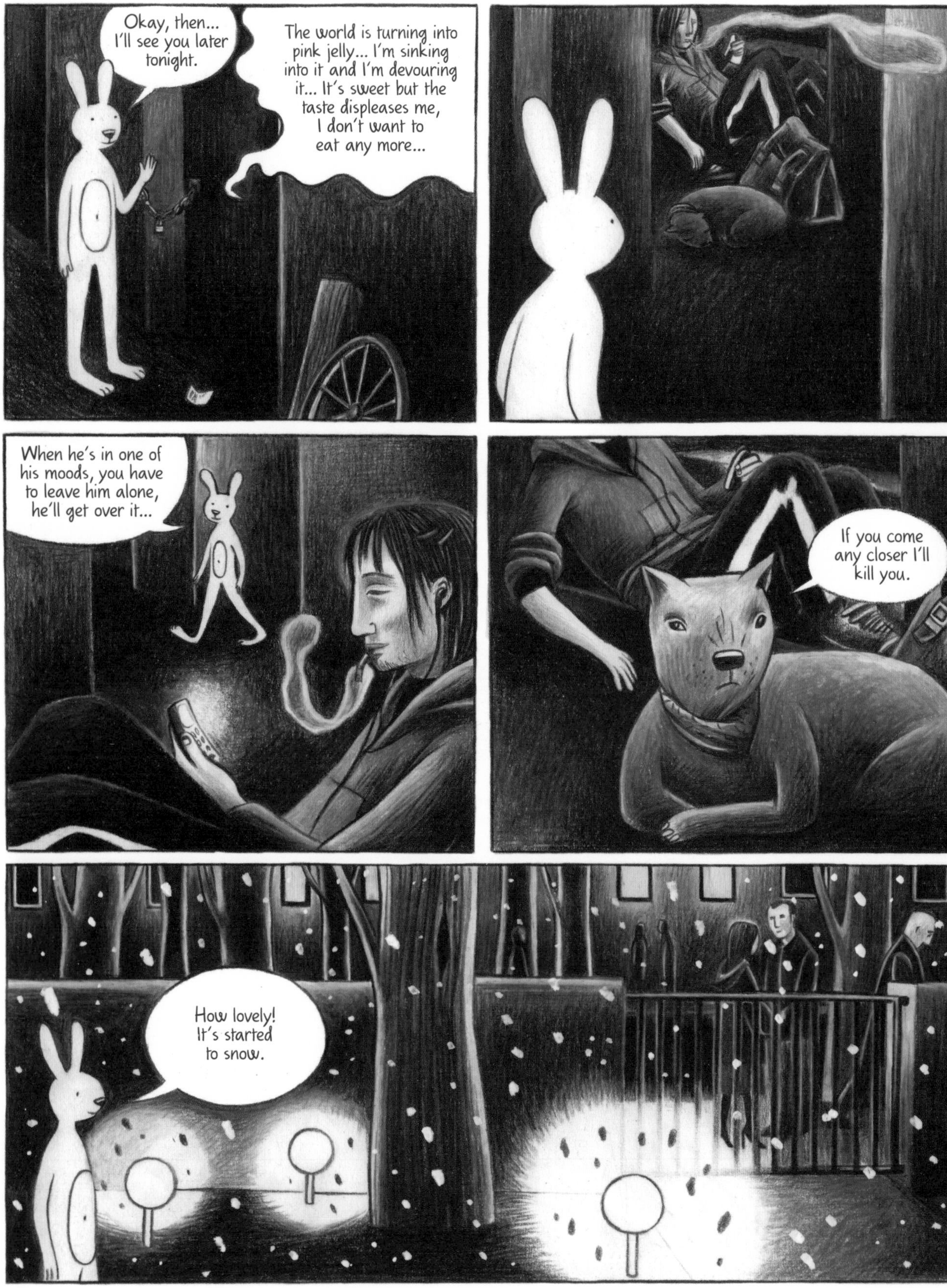
Okay, then... I'll see you later tonight.
The world is turning into pink jelly... I'm sinking into it and I'm devouring it... It's sweet but the taste displeases me, I don't want to eat any more...
When he's in one of his moods, you have to leave him alone, he'll get over it...
If you come any closer I'll kill you.
How lovely! It's started to snow.

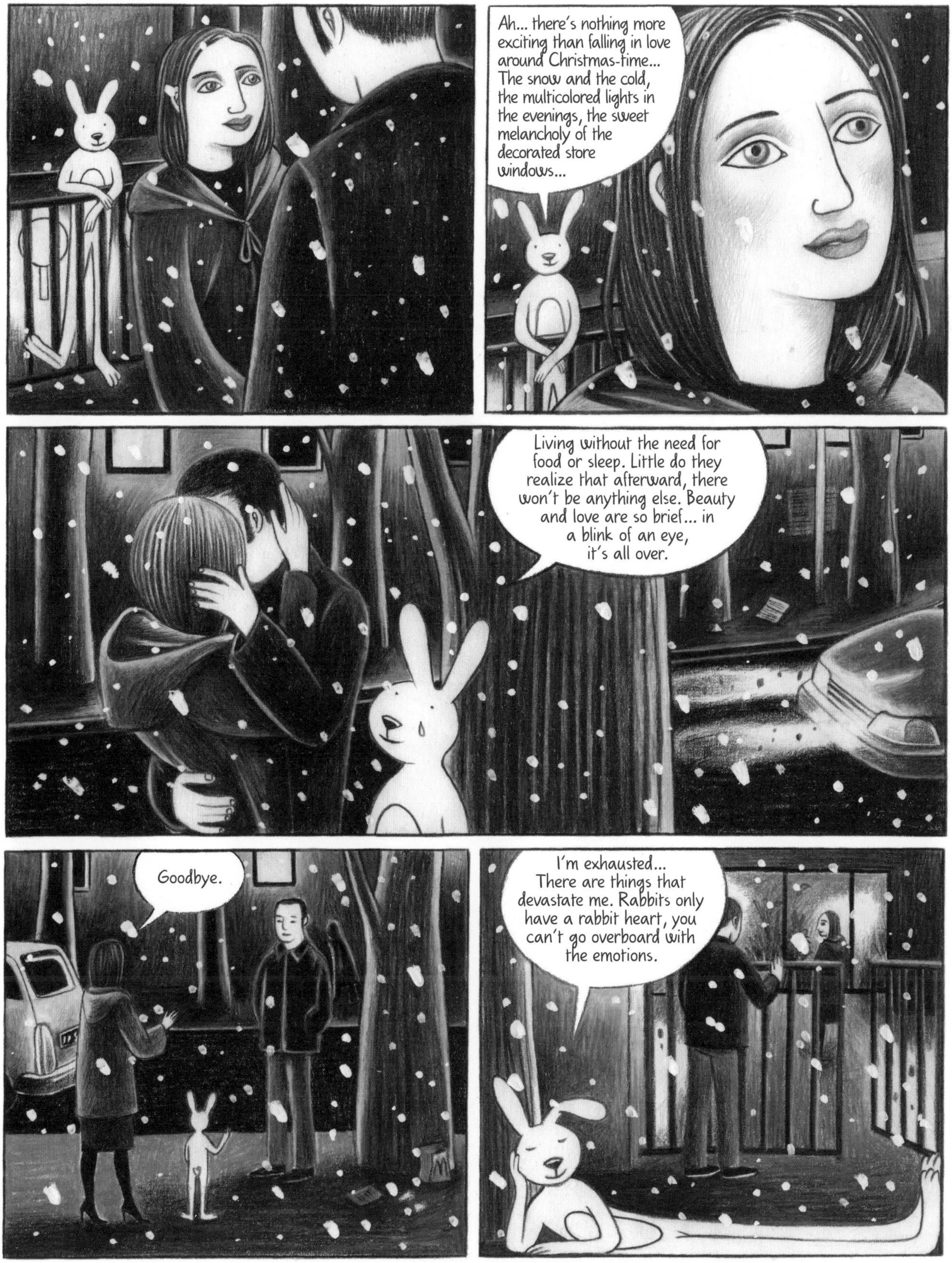
Ah... there's nothing more exciting than falling in love around Christmas-time... The snow and the cold, the multicolored lights in the evenings, the sweet melancholy of the decorated store windows...
Living without the need for food or sleep. Little do they realize that afterward, there won't be anything else. Beauty and love are so brief... in a blink of an eye, it's all over.
Goodbye.
I'm exhausted... There are things that devastate me. Rabbits only have a rabbit heart, you can't go overboard with the emotions.

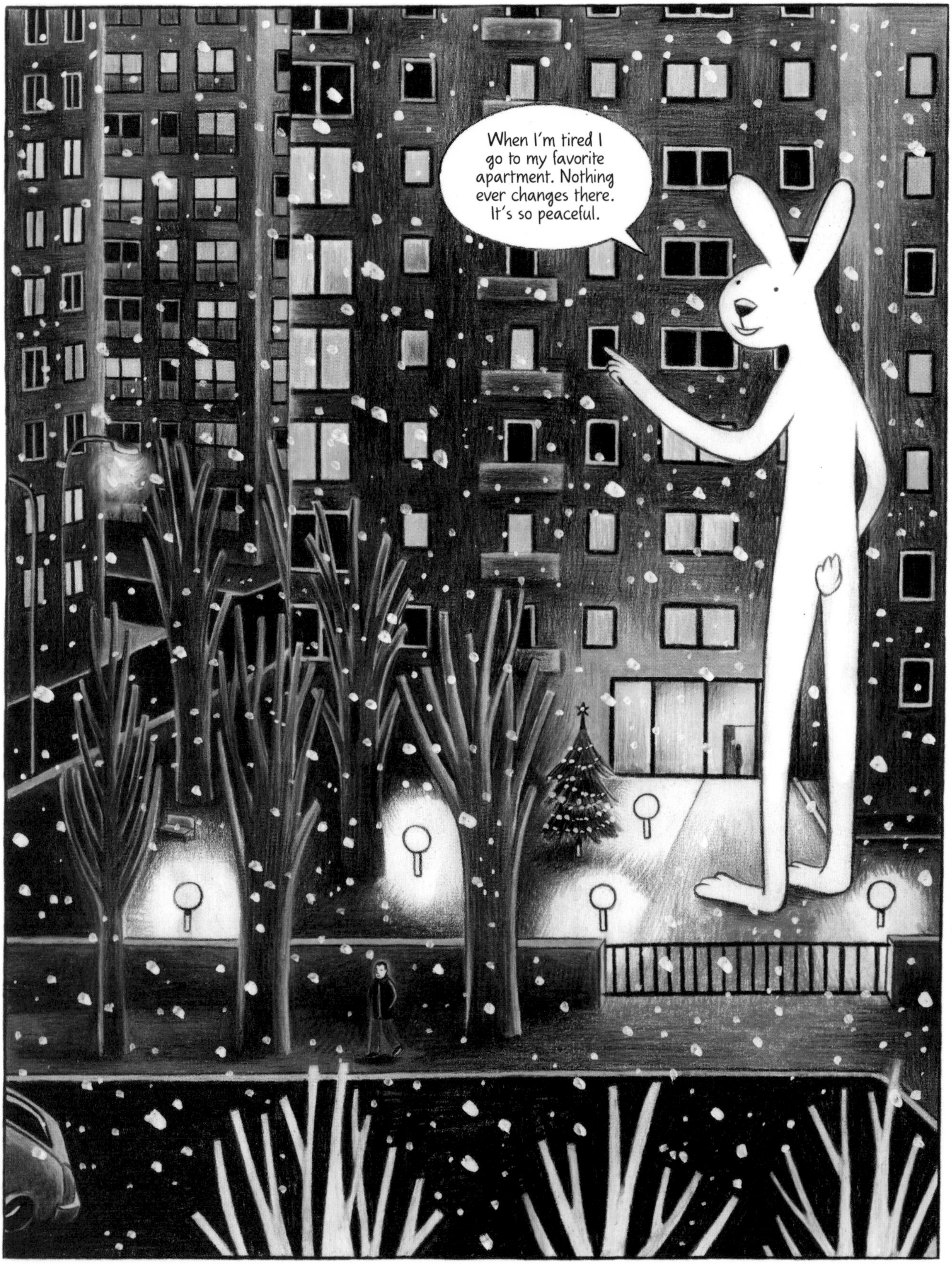
When I'm tired I go to my favorite apartment. Nothing ever changes there. It's so peaceful.

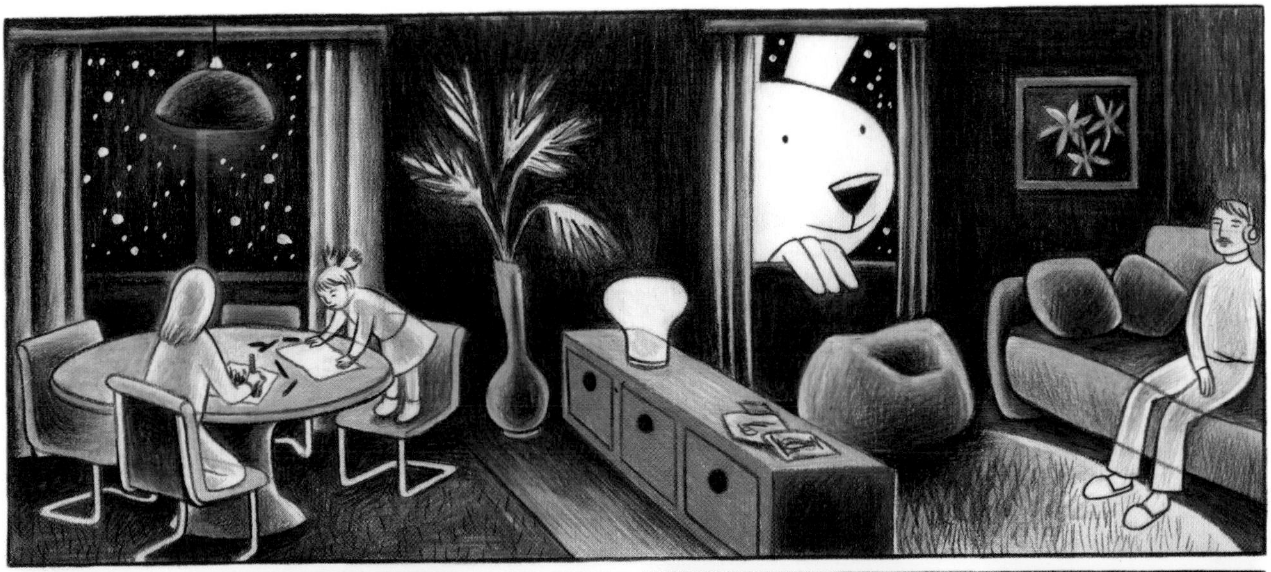

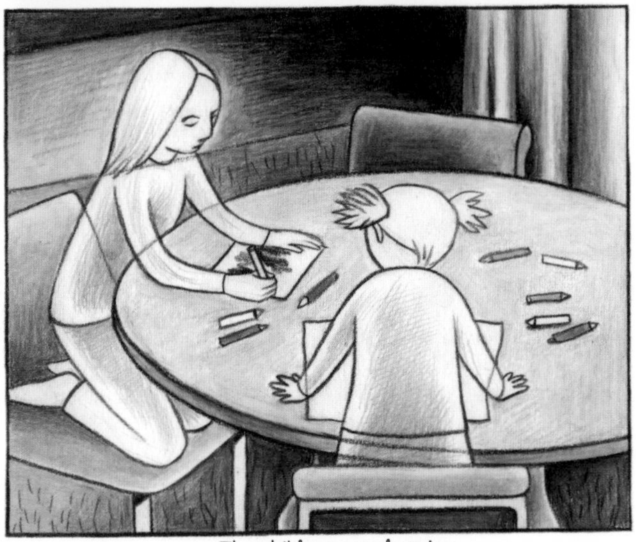

The children are drawing.

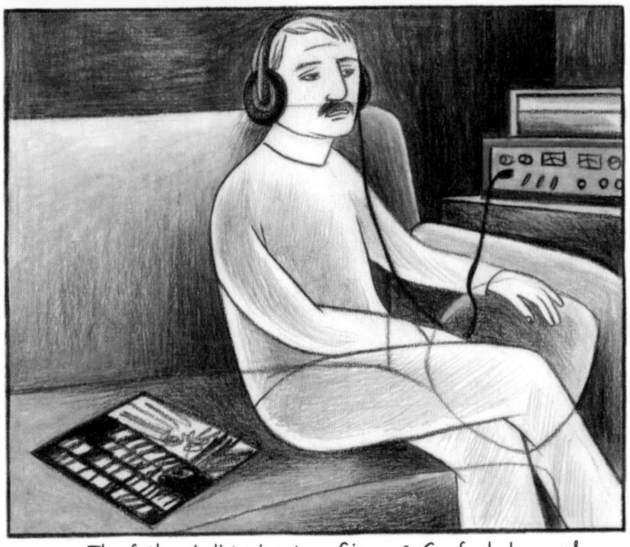

The father is listening to a Simon & Garfunkel record.

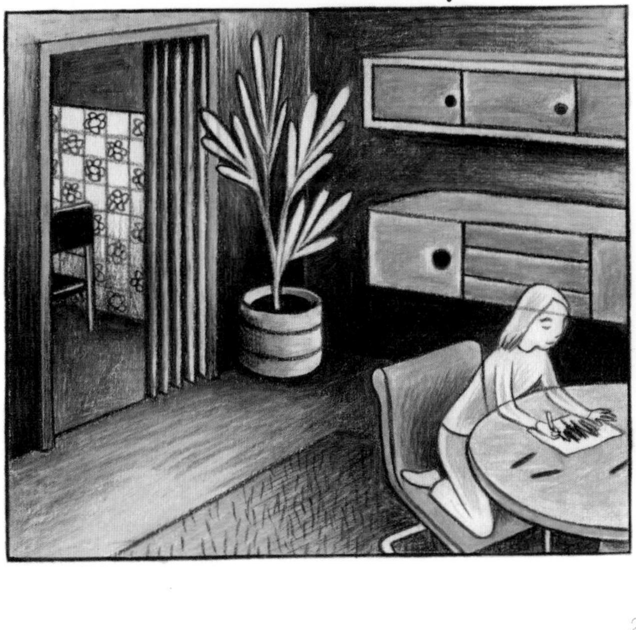

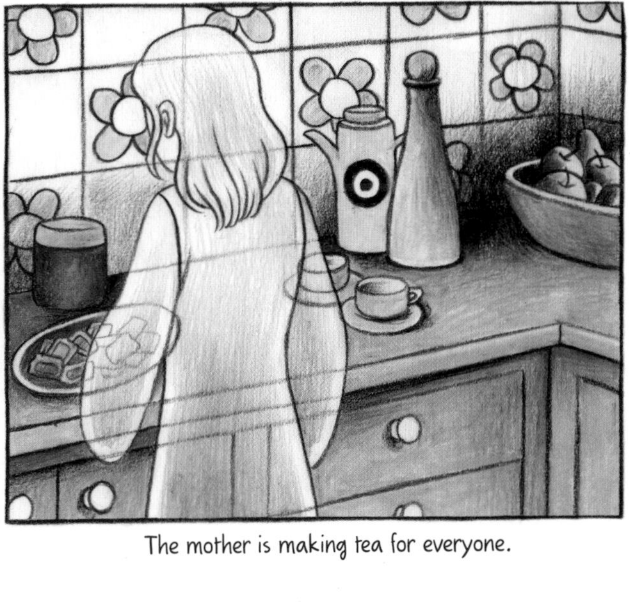

The mother is making tea for everyone.

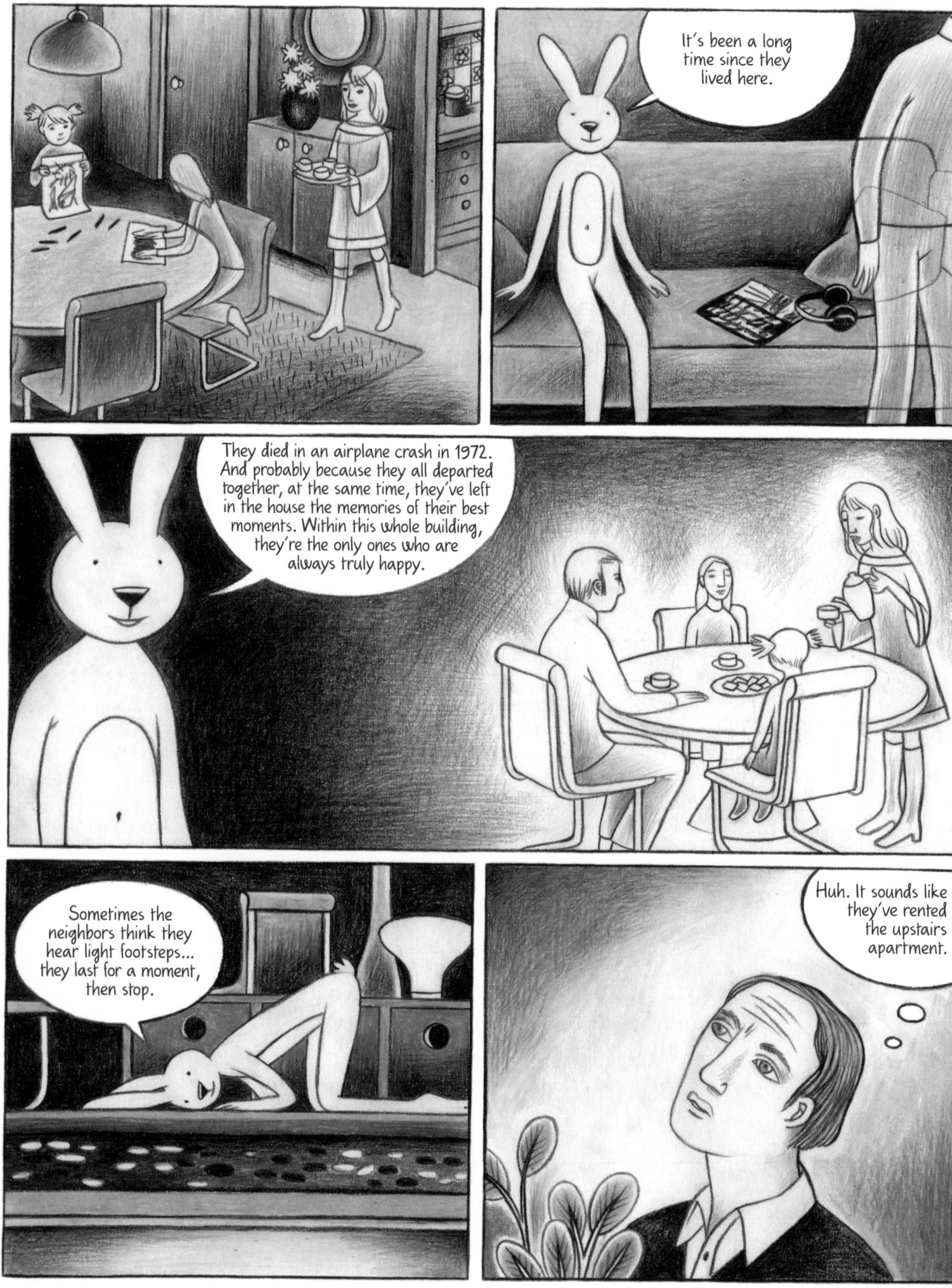
It's been a long time since they lived here.
They died in an airplane crash in 1972. And probably because they all departed together, at the same time, they've left in the house the memories of their best moments. Within this whole building, they're the only ones who are always truly happy.
Sometimes the neighbors think they hear light footsteps... they last for a moment, then stop.
Huh. It sounds like they've rented the upstairs apartment.

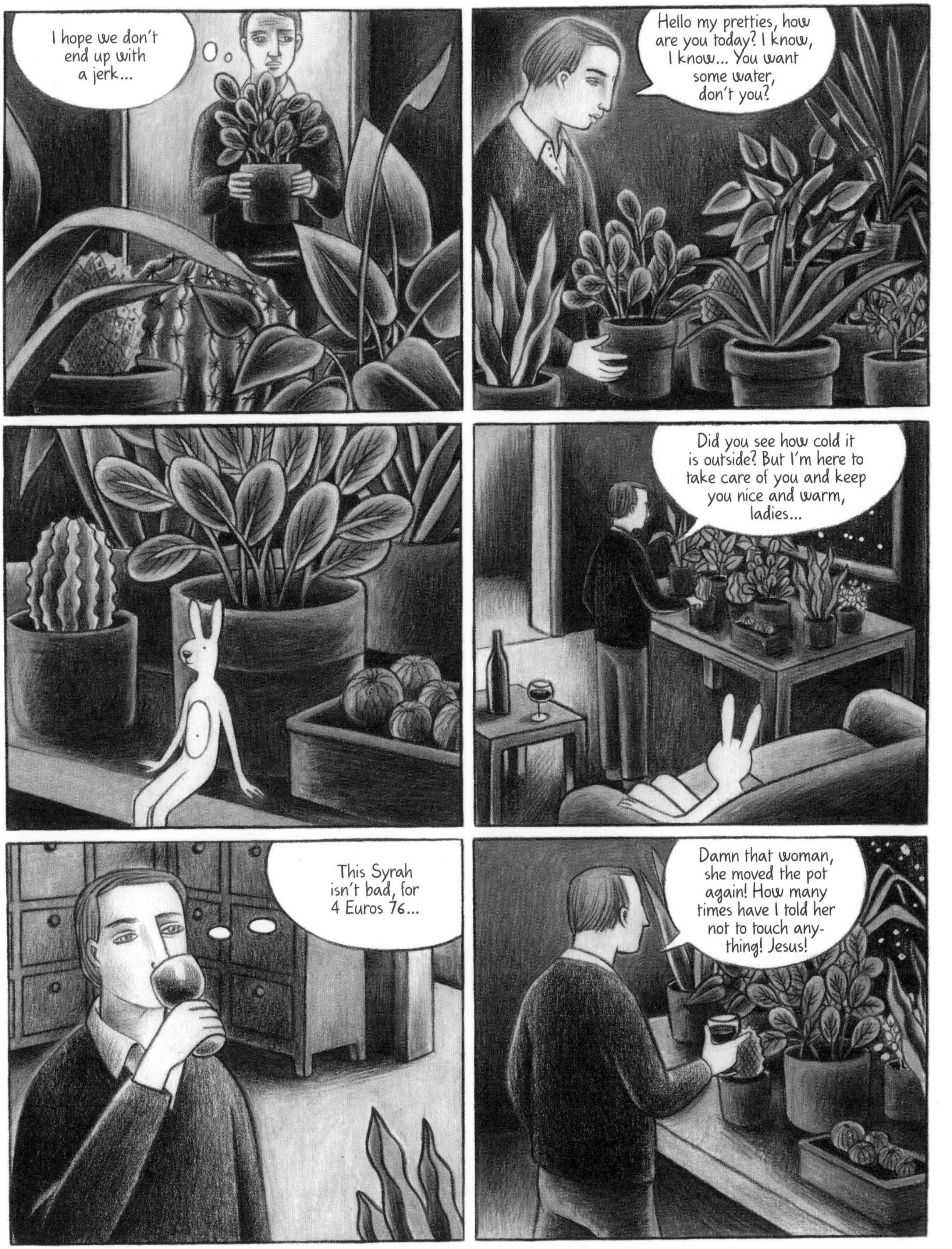

I hope we don't end up with a jerk...
Hello my pretties, how are you today? I know, I know... You want some water, don't you?
Did you see how cold it is outside? But I'm here to take care of you and keep you nice and warm, ladies...
This Syrah isn't bad, for 4 Euros 76...
Damn that woman, she moved the pot again! How many times have I told her not to touch any-thing! Jesus!

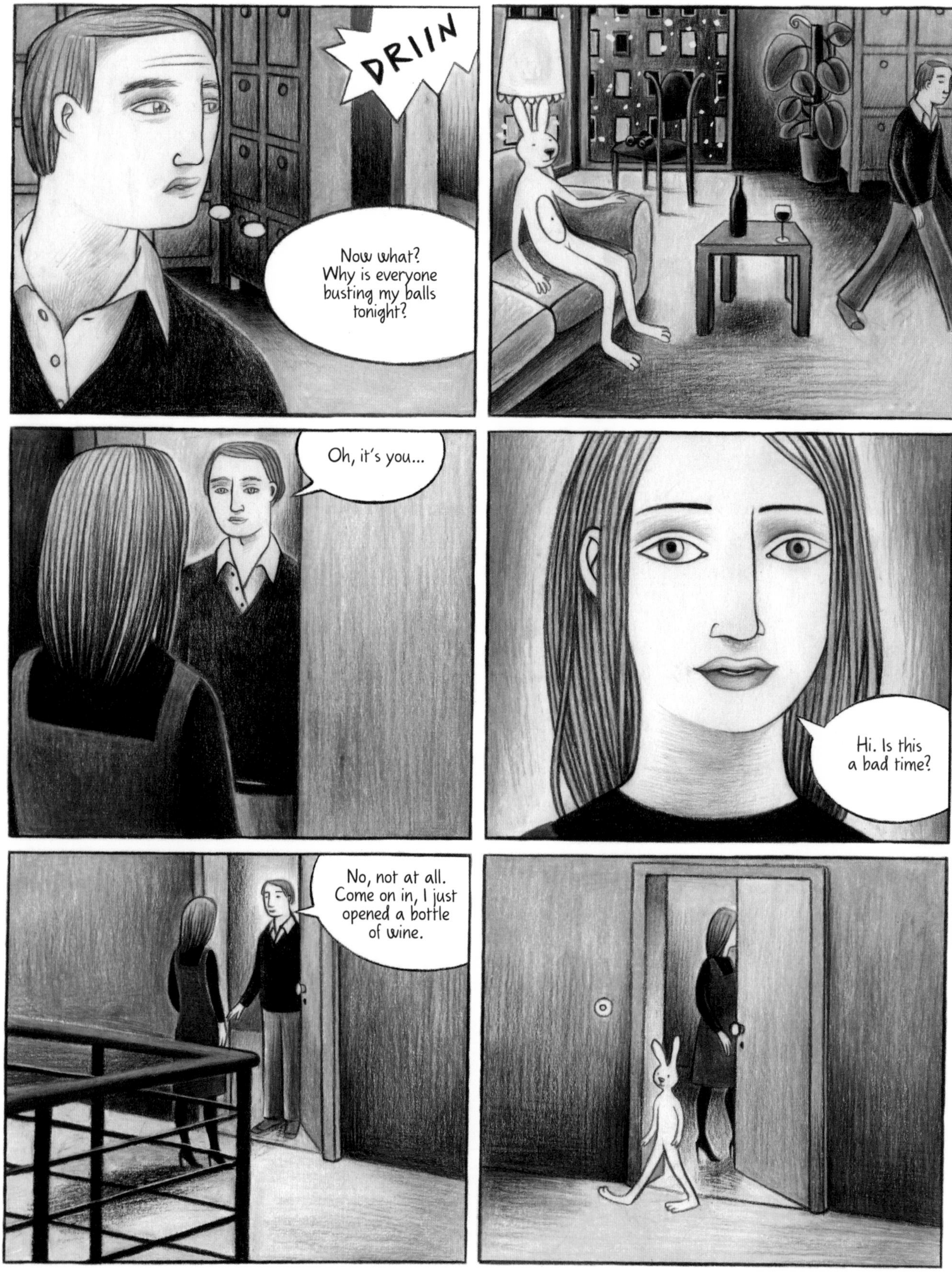
DRIIN
Now what? Why is everyone busting my balls tonight?
Oh, it's you...
Hi. Is this a bad time?
No, not at all. Come on in, I just opened a bottle of wine.

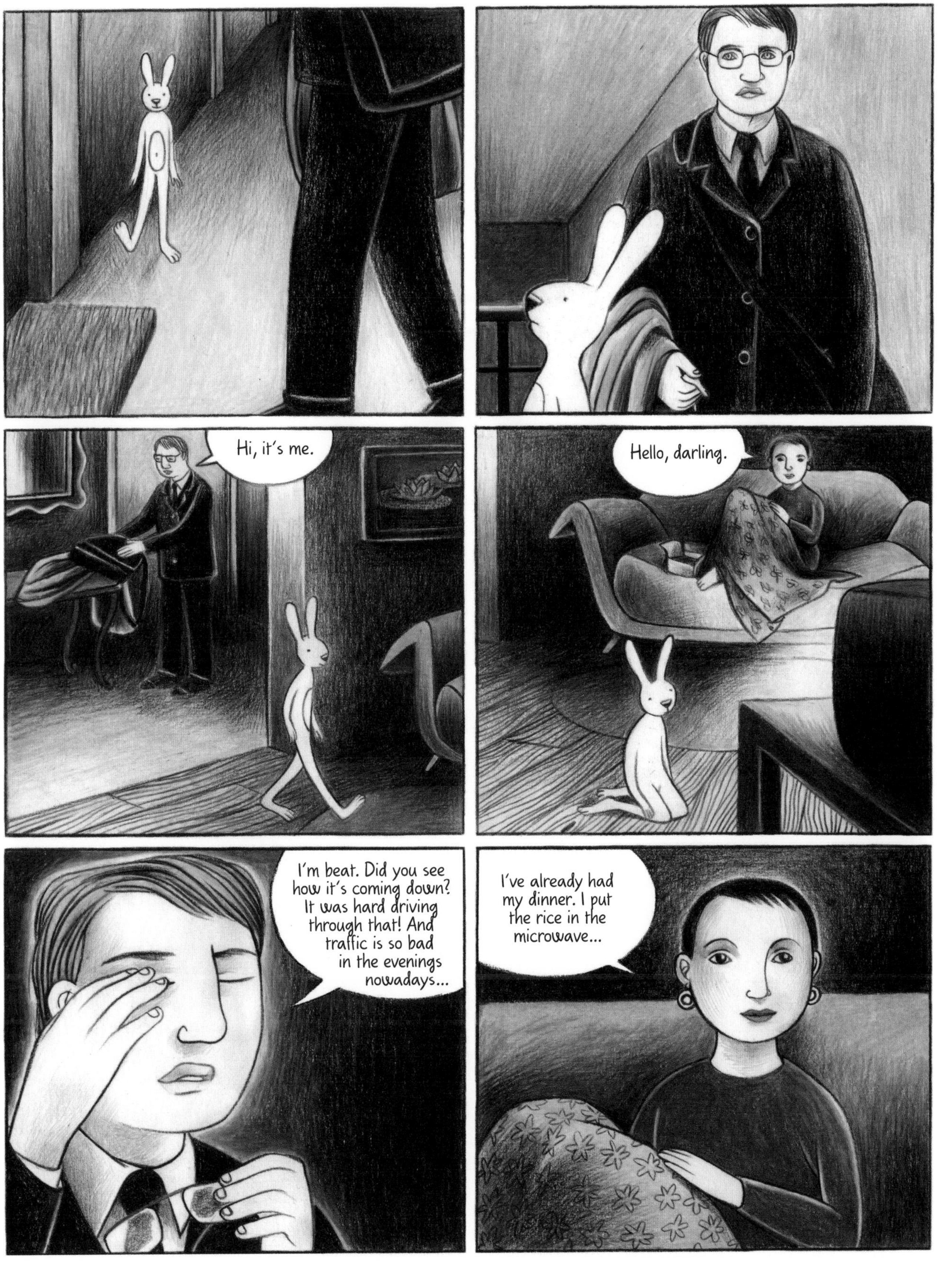
Hi, it's me.
Hello, darling.
I'm beat. Did you see how it's coming down? It was hard driving through that! And traffic is so bad in the evenings nowadays...
I've already had my dinner. I put the rice in the microwave...

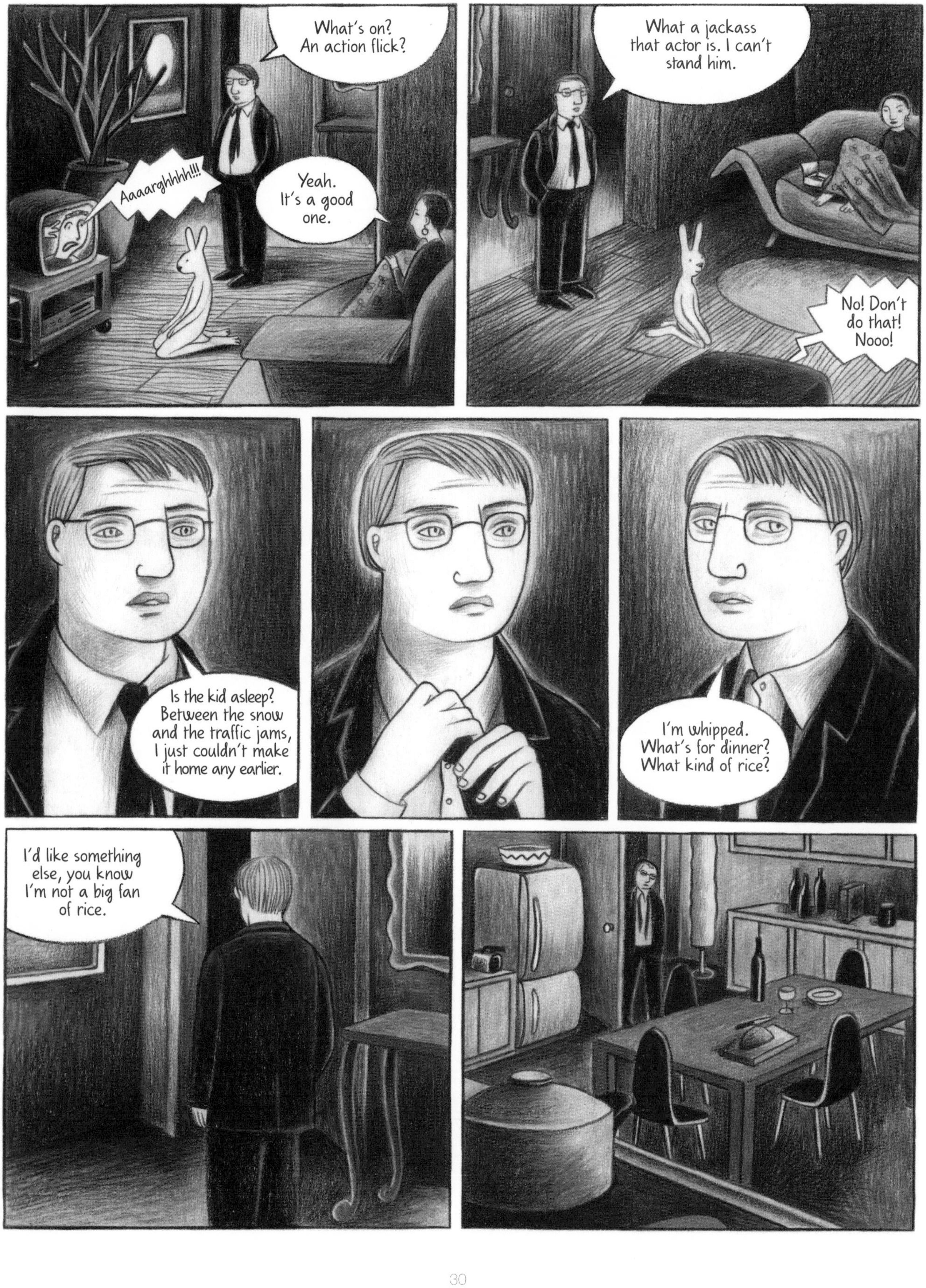
What's on?
An action flick?
Aaaarghhhh!!!
Yeah.
It's a good one.
What a jackass that actor is. I can't stand him.
No! Don't do that! Nooo!
Is the kid asleep? Between the snow and the traffic jams, I just couldn't make it home any earlier.
I'm whipped. What's for dinner? What kind of rice?
I'd like something else, you know I'm not a big fan of rice.

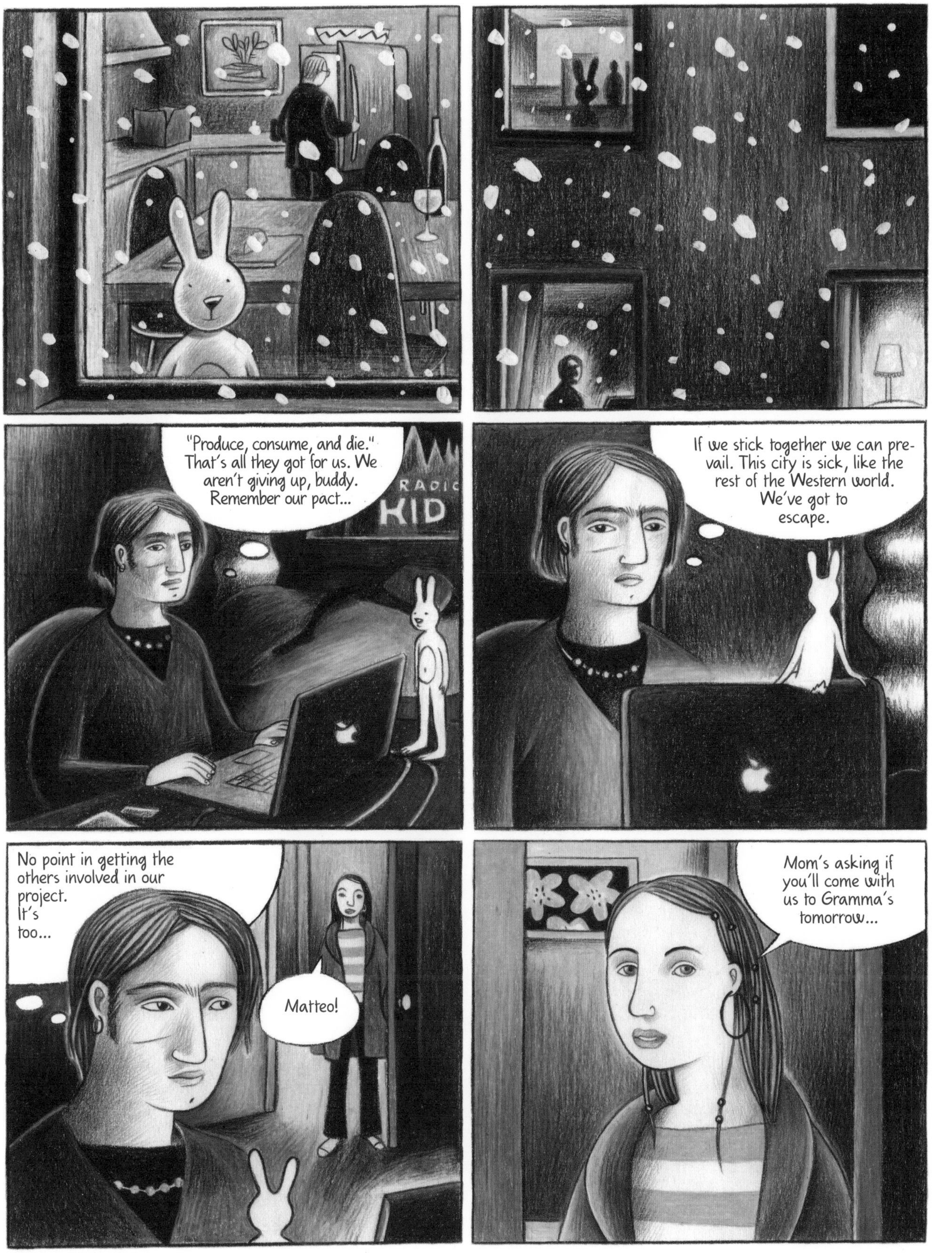
"Produce, consume, and die." That's all they got for us. We aren't giving up, buddy. Remember our pact...
RADIO KID
If we stick together we can prevail. This city is sick, like the rest of the Western world. We've got to escape.
No point in getting the others involved in our project. It's too...
Matteo!
Mom's asking if you'll come with us to Gramma's tomorrow...

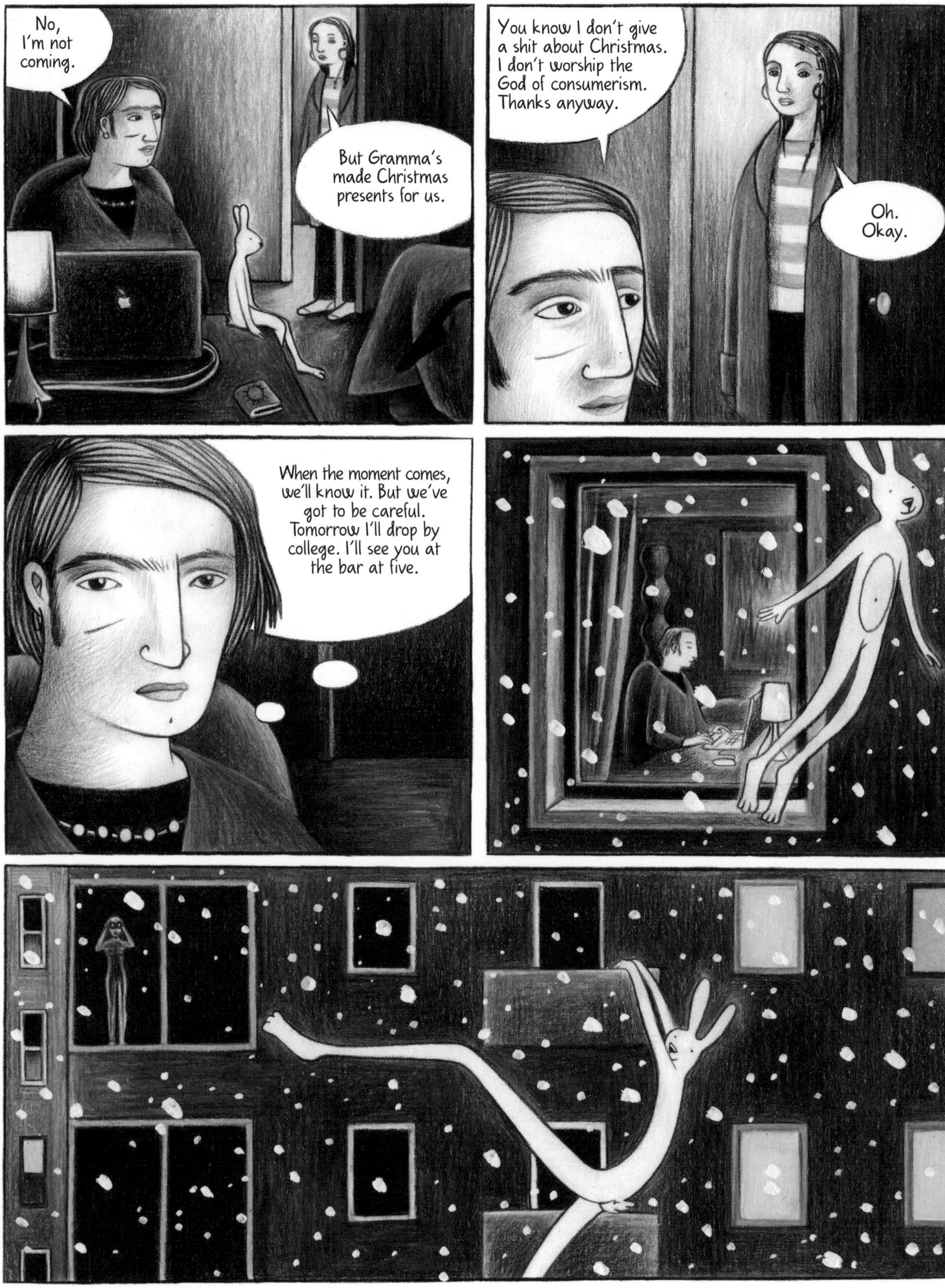
No, I'm not coming.
But Gramma's made Christmas presents for us.
You know I don't give a shit about Christmas. I don't worship the God of consumerism. Thanks anyway.
Oh. Okay.
When the moment comes, we'll know it. But we've got to be careful. Tomorrow I'll drop by college. I'll see you at the bar at five.

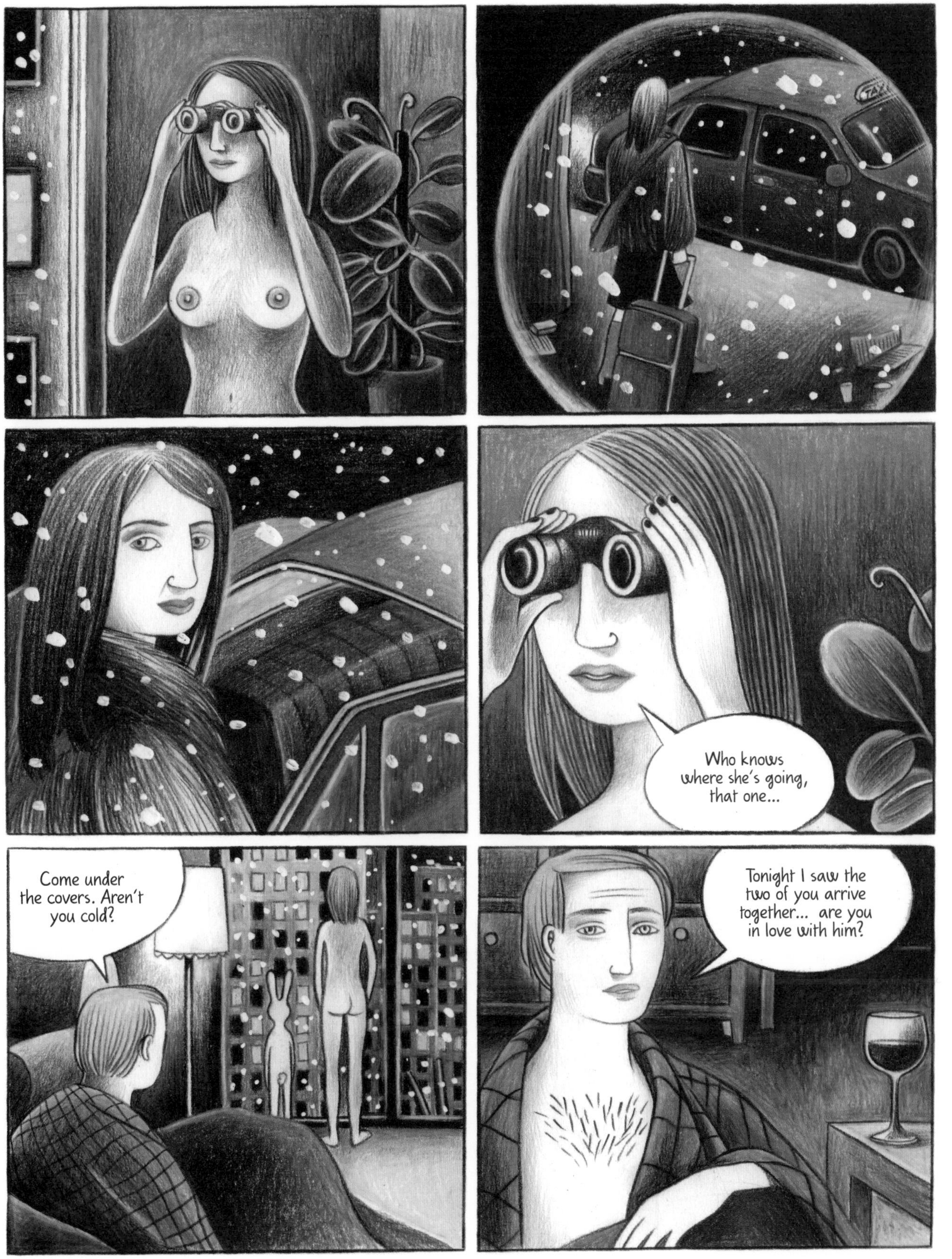
Who knows where she's going, that one...
Come under the covers. Aren't you cold?
Tonight I saw the two of you arrive together... are you in love with him?

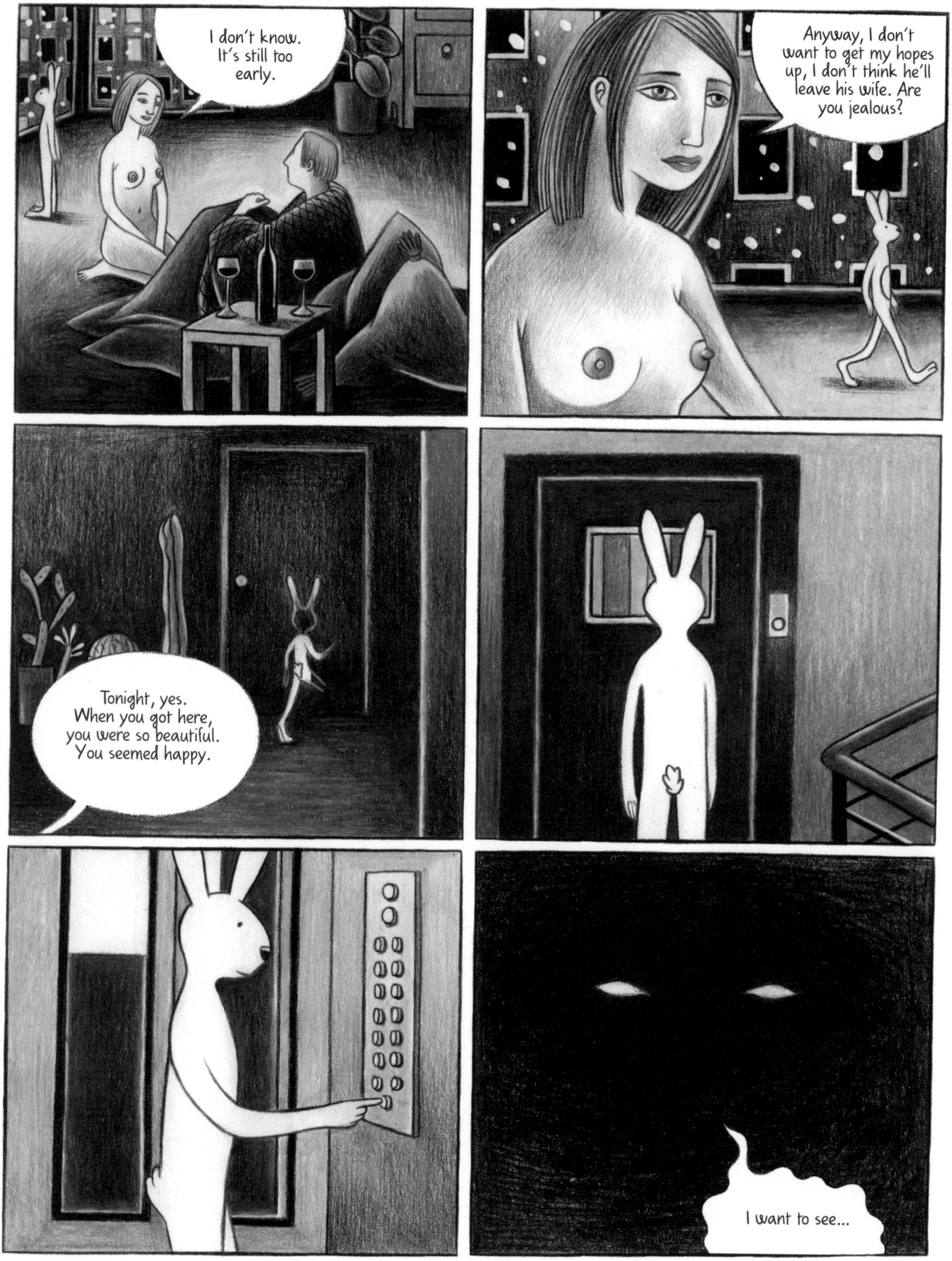

I don't know. It's still too early.
Anyway, I don't want to get my hopes up, I don't think he'll leave his wife. Are you jealous?
Tonight, yes. When you got here, you were so beautiful. You seemed happy.
I want to see...

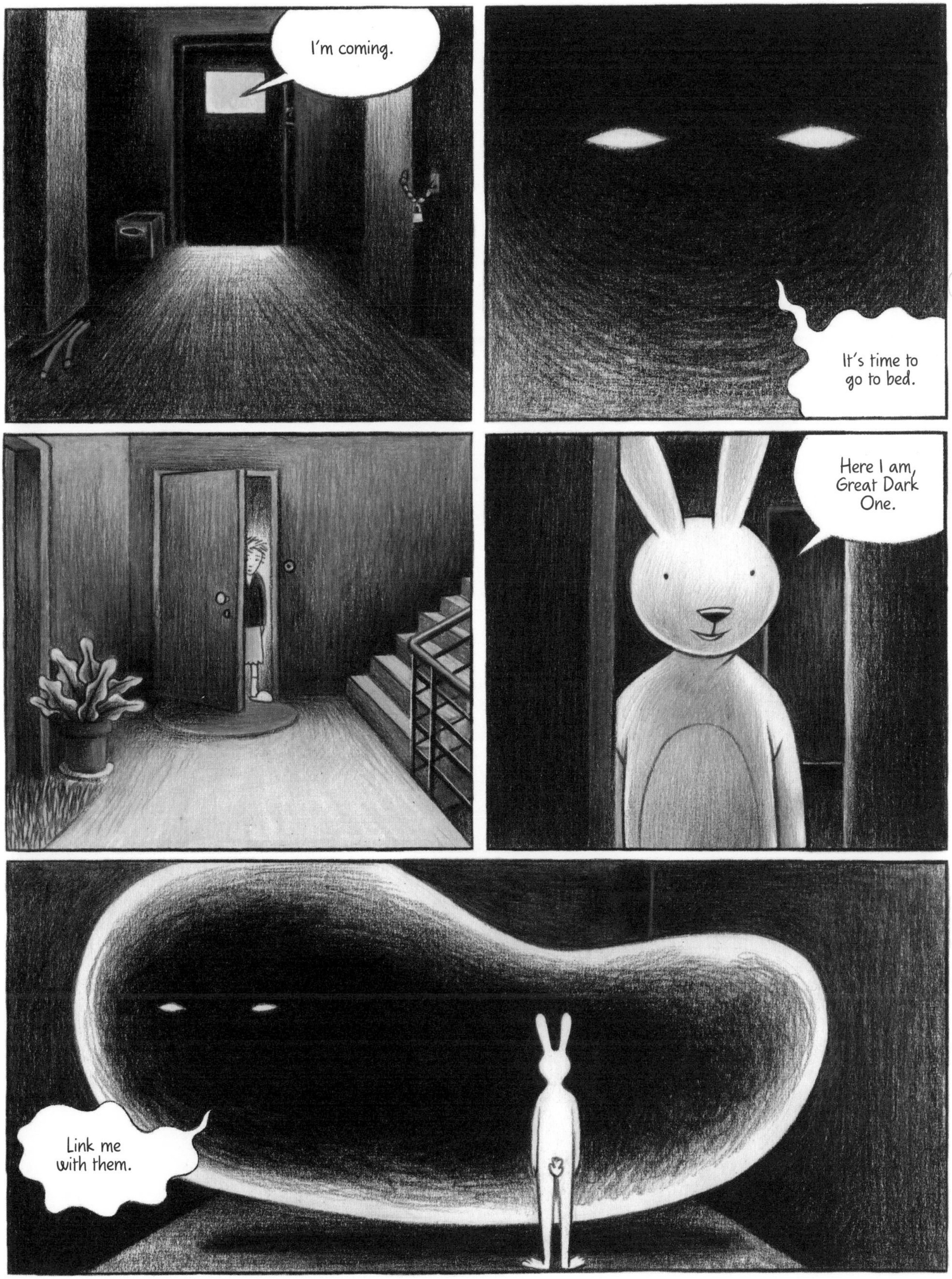
I'm coming.
It's time to go to bed.
Here I am, Great Dark One.
Link me with them.

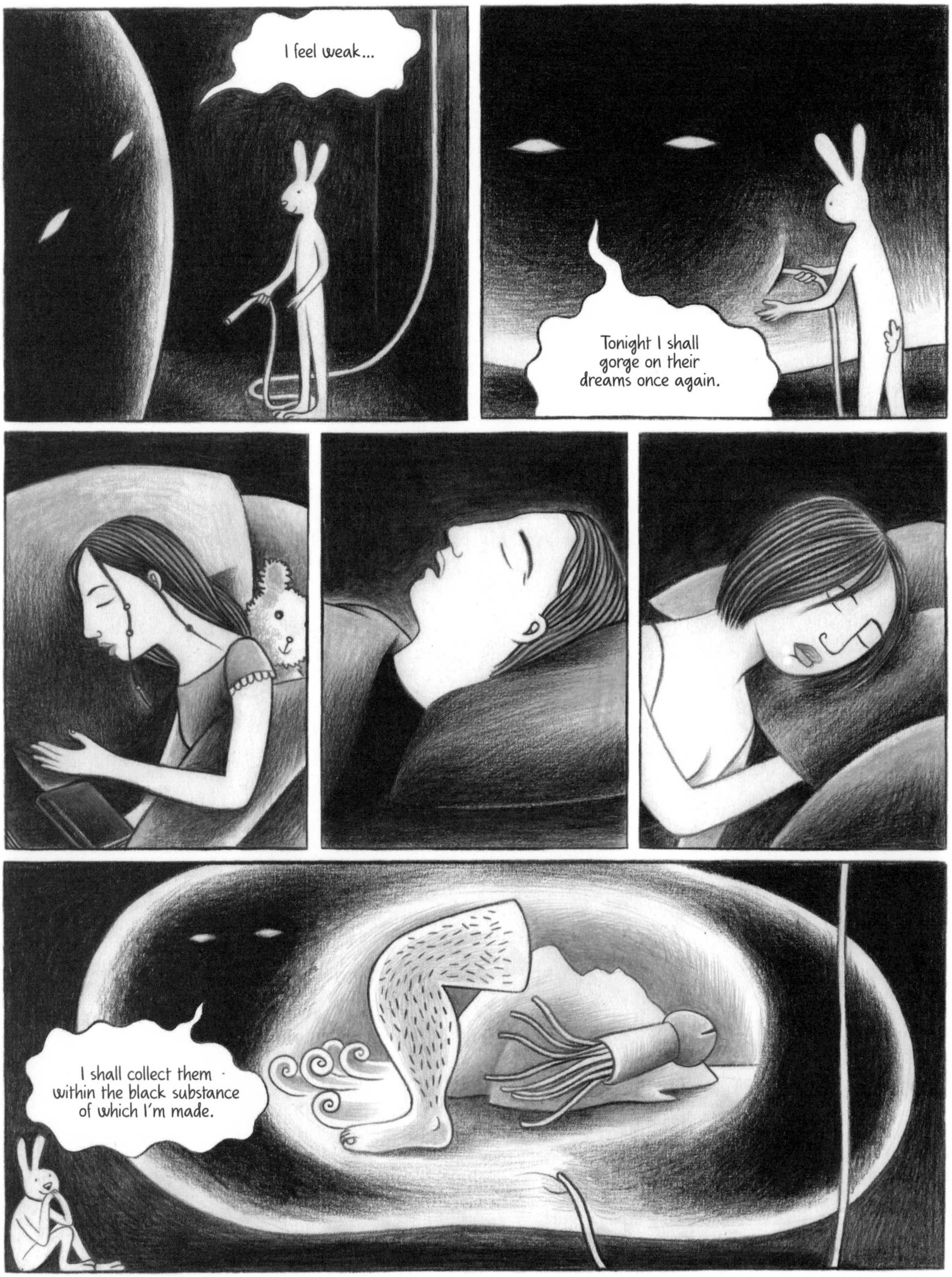

I feel weak...
Tonight I shall gorge on their dreams once again.
I shall collect them within the black substance of which I'm made.

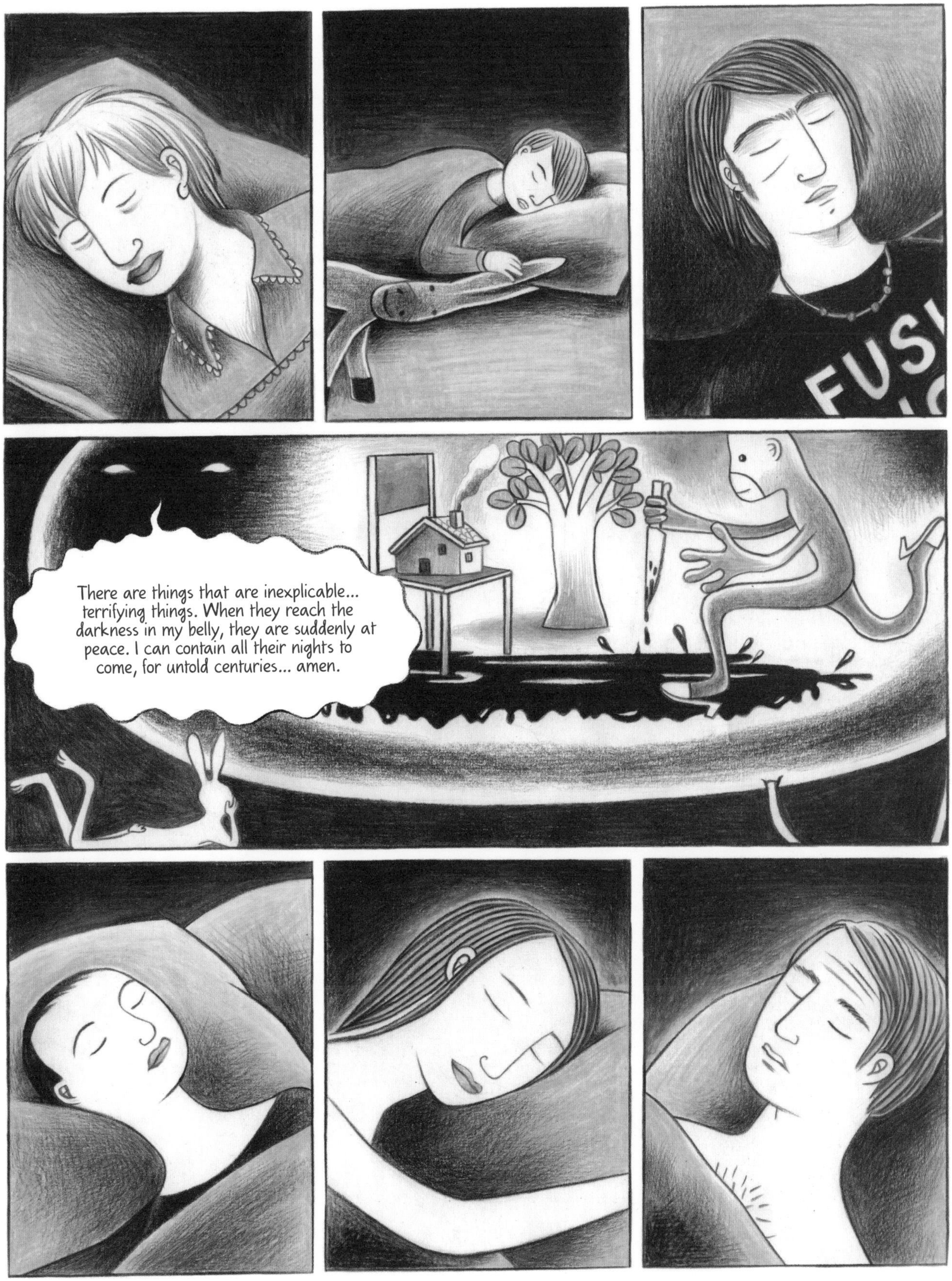
There are things that are inexplicable... terrifying things. When they reach the darkness in my belly, they are suddenly at peace. I can contain all their nights to come, for untold centuries... amen.

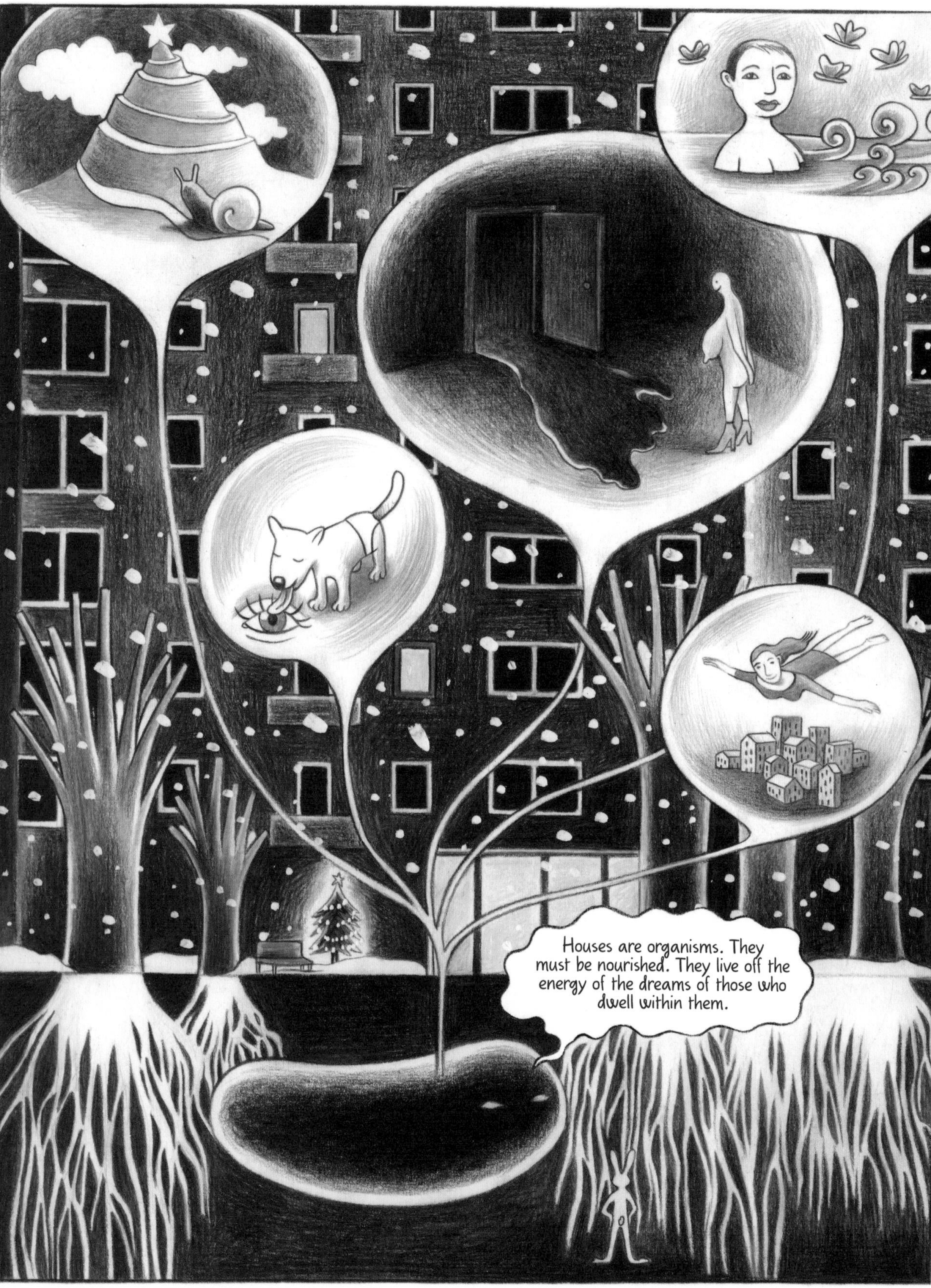
Houses are organisms. They must be nourished. They live off the energy of the dreams of those who dwell within them.

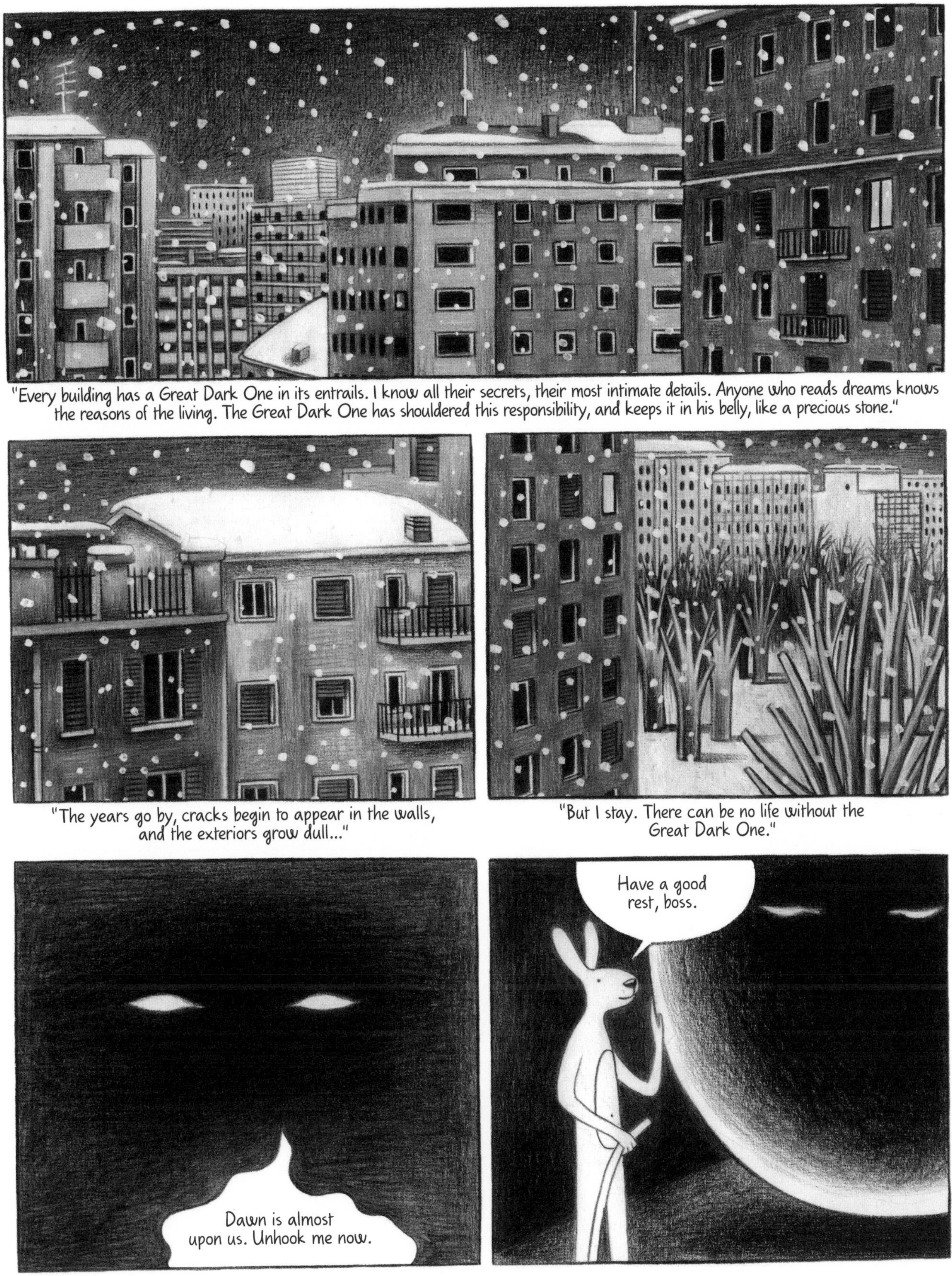
"Every building has a Great Dark One in its entrails. I know all their secrets, their most intimate details. Anyone who reads dreams knows the reasons of the living. The Great Dark One has shouldered this responsibility, and keeps it in his belly, like a precious stone."
"The years go by, cracks begin to appear in the walls, and the exteriors grow dull..."
"But I stay. There can be no life without the Great Dark One."
Dawn is almost upon us. Unhook me now.
Have a good rest, boss.

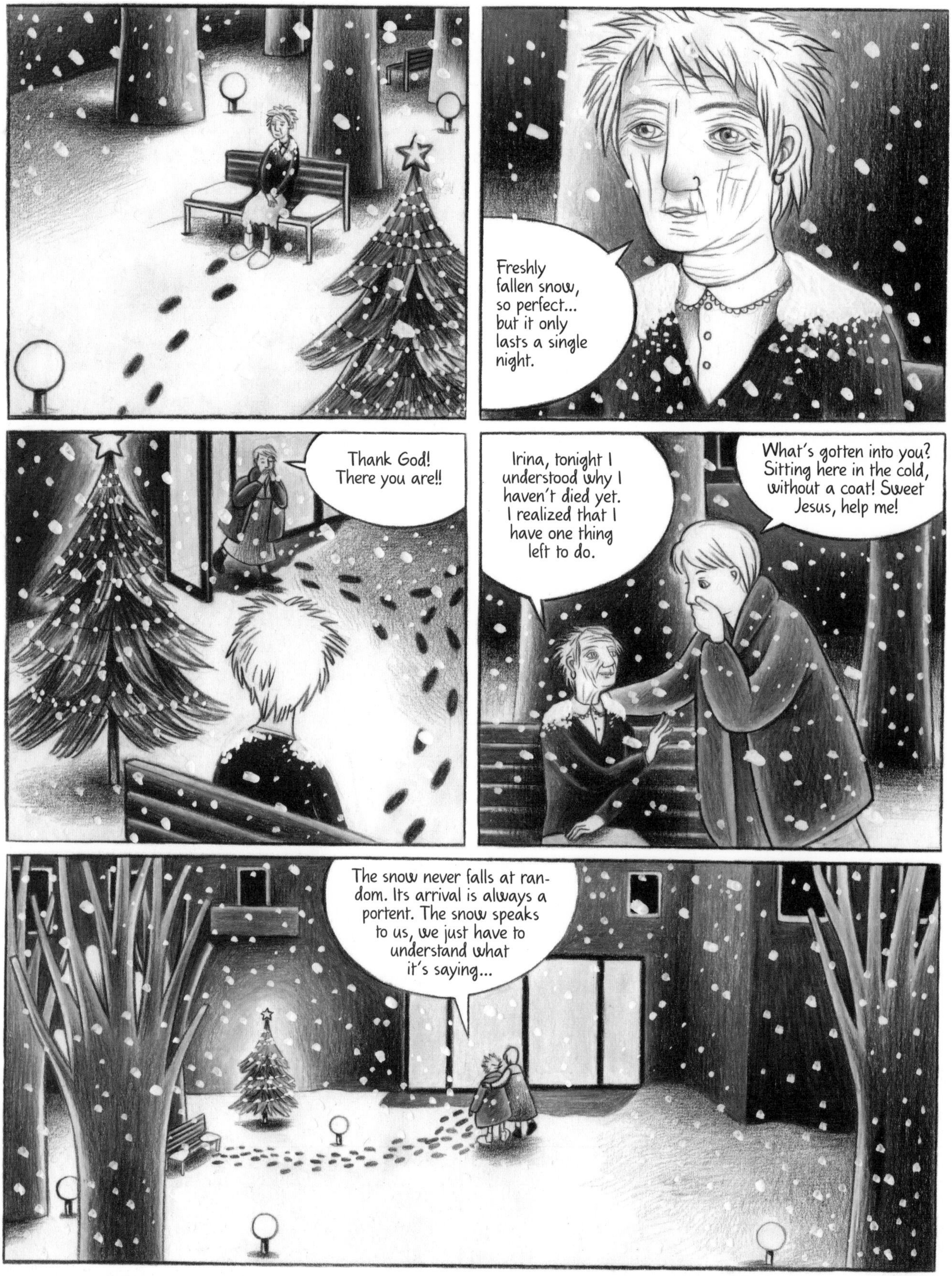
Freshly fallen snow, so perfect... but it only lasts a single night.
Thank God! There you are!!
Irina, tonight I understood why I haven't died yet. I realized that I have one thing left to do.
What's gotten into you? Sitting here in the cold, without a coat! Sweet Jesus, help me!
The snow never falls at random. Its arrival is always a portent. The snow speaks to us, we just have to understand what it's saying...

WEDNESDAY, DECEMBER 20

---

18 hours, 00 minutes, 37 seconds

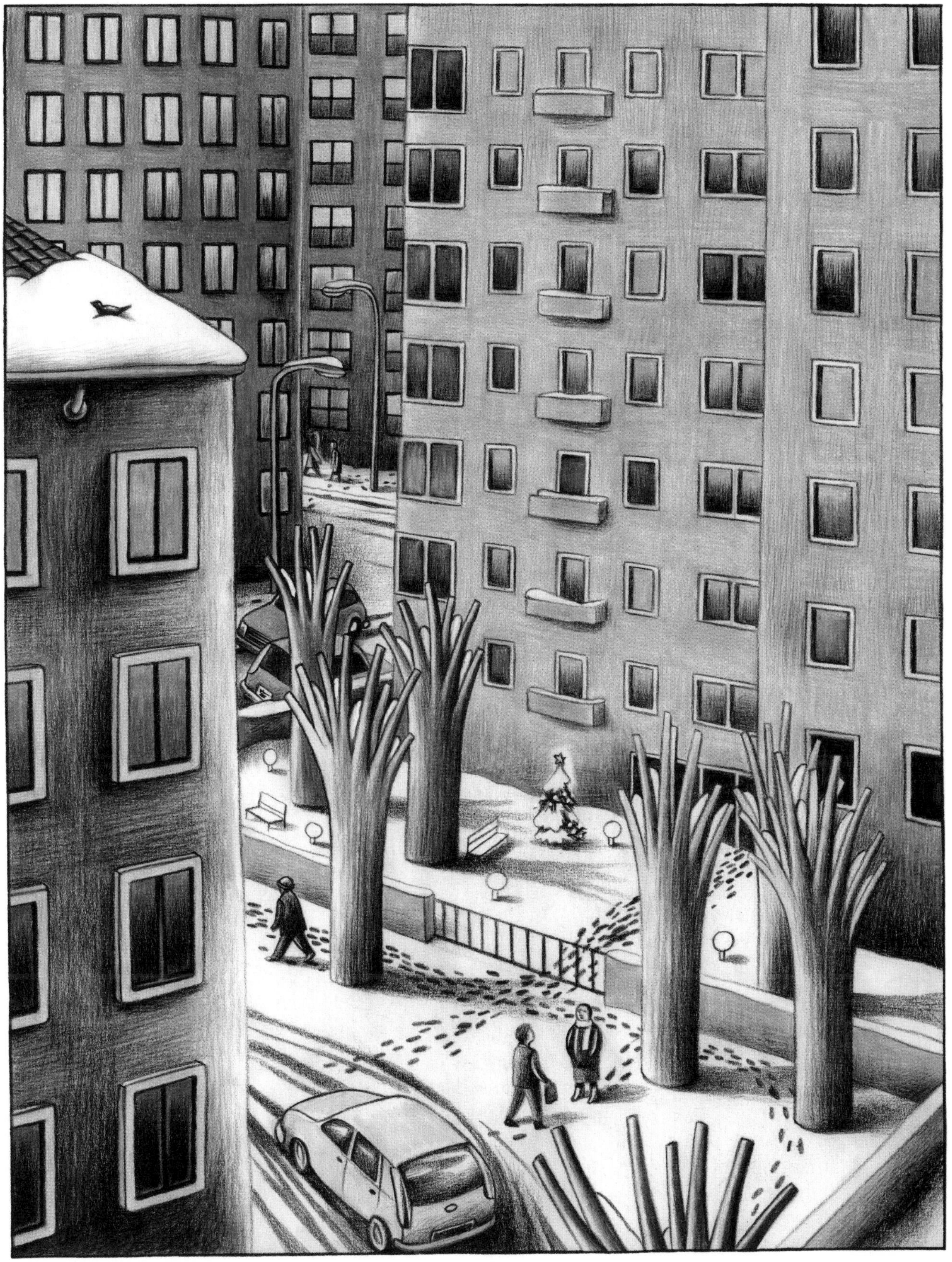

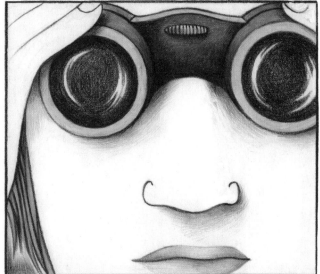

Off you go to work, like a good little girl.

I'm getting a little bit bored with you...

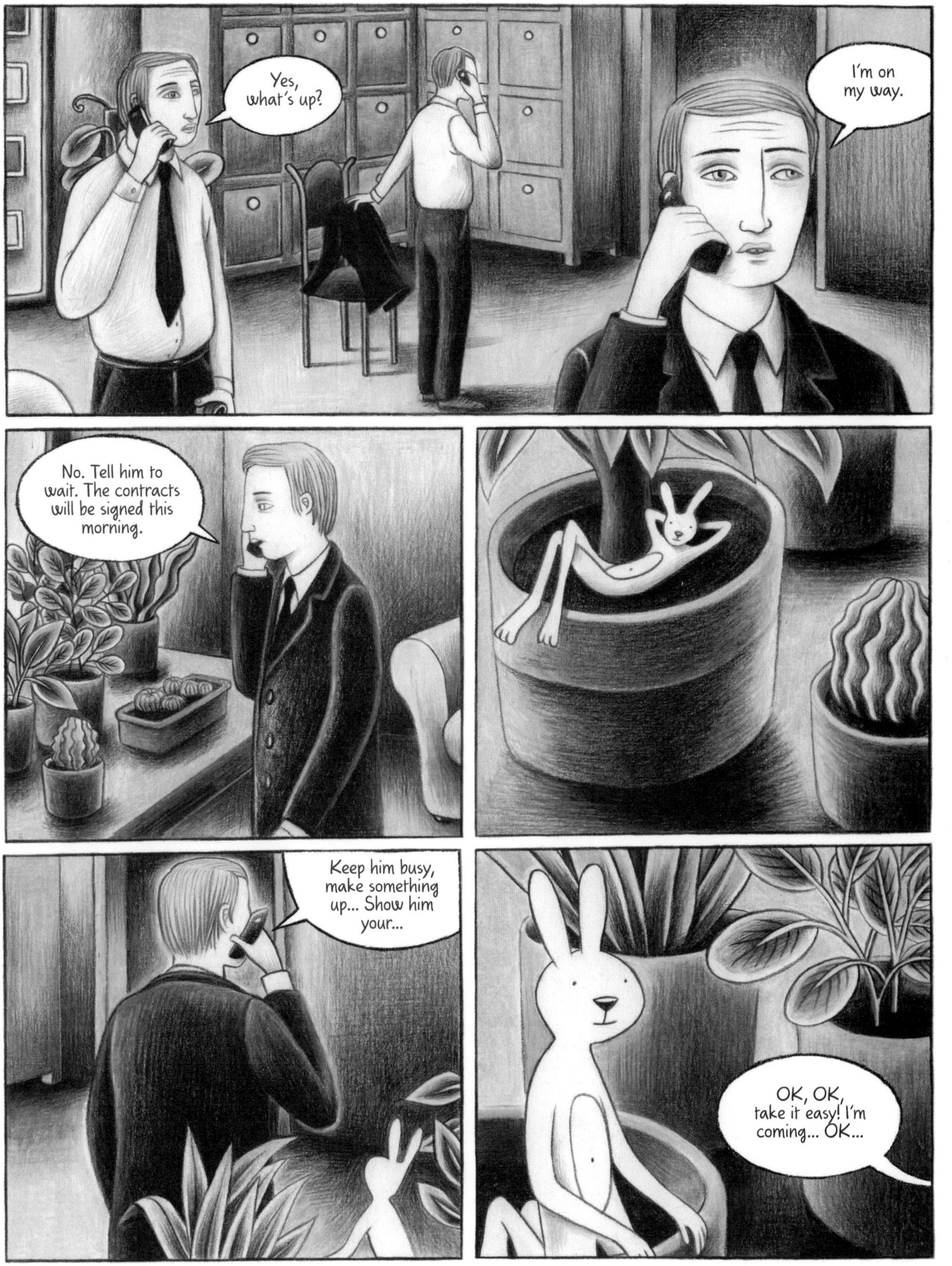
Yes, what's up?
I'm on my way.
No. Tell him to wait. The contracts will be signed this morning.
Keep him busy, make something up... Show him your...
OK, OK, take it easy! I'm coming... OK...

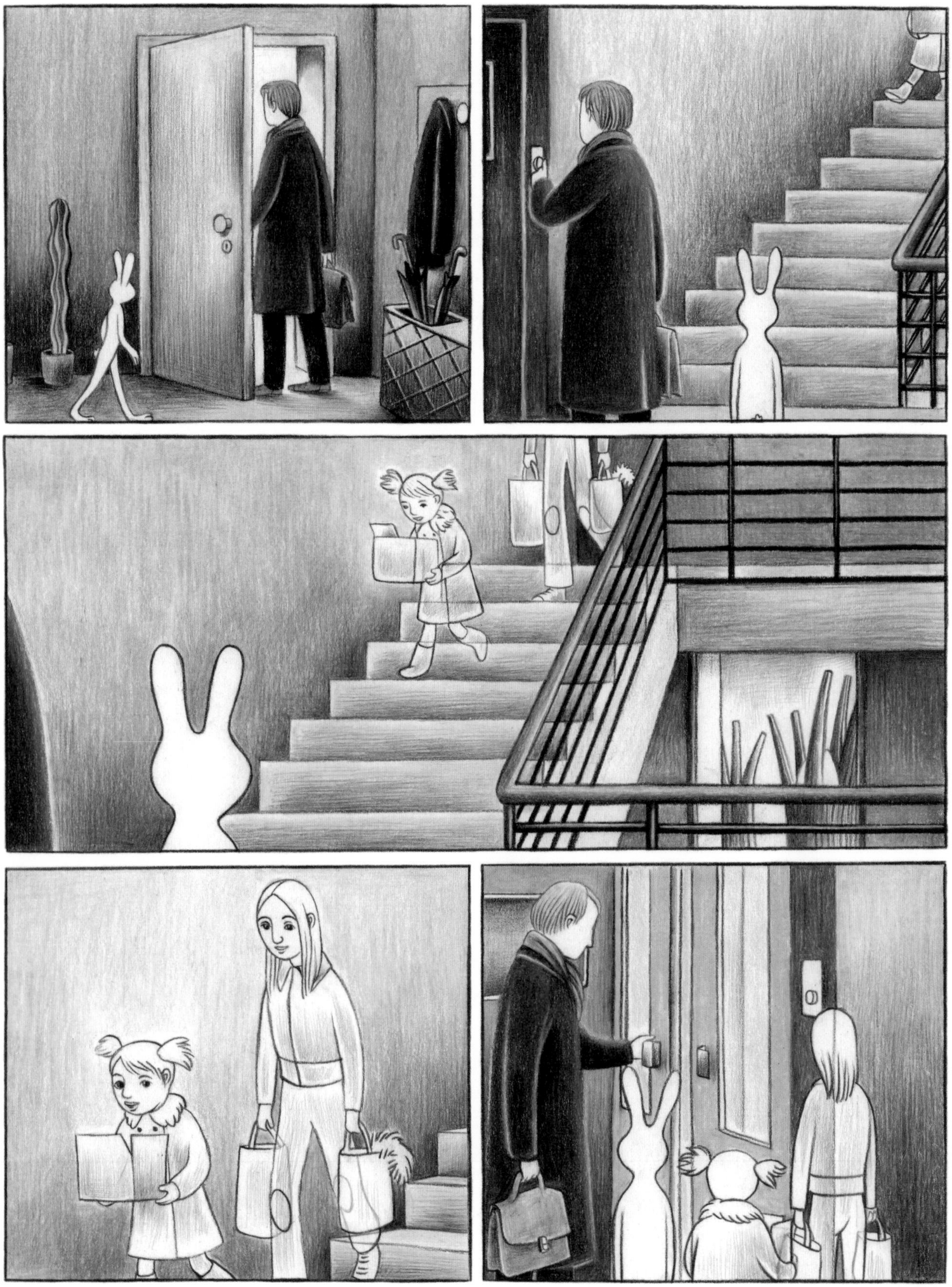

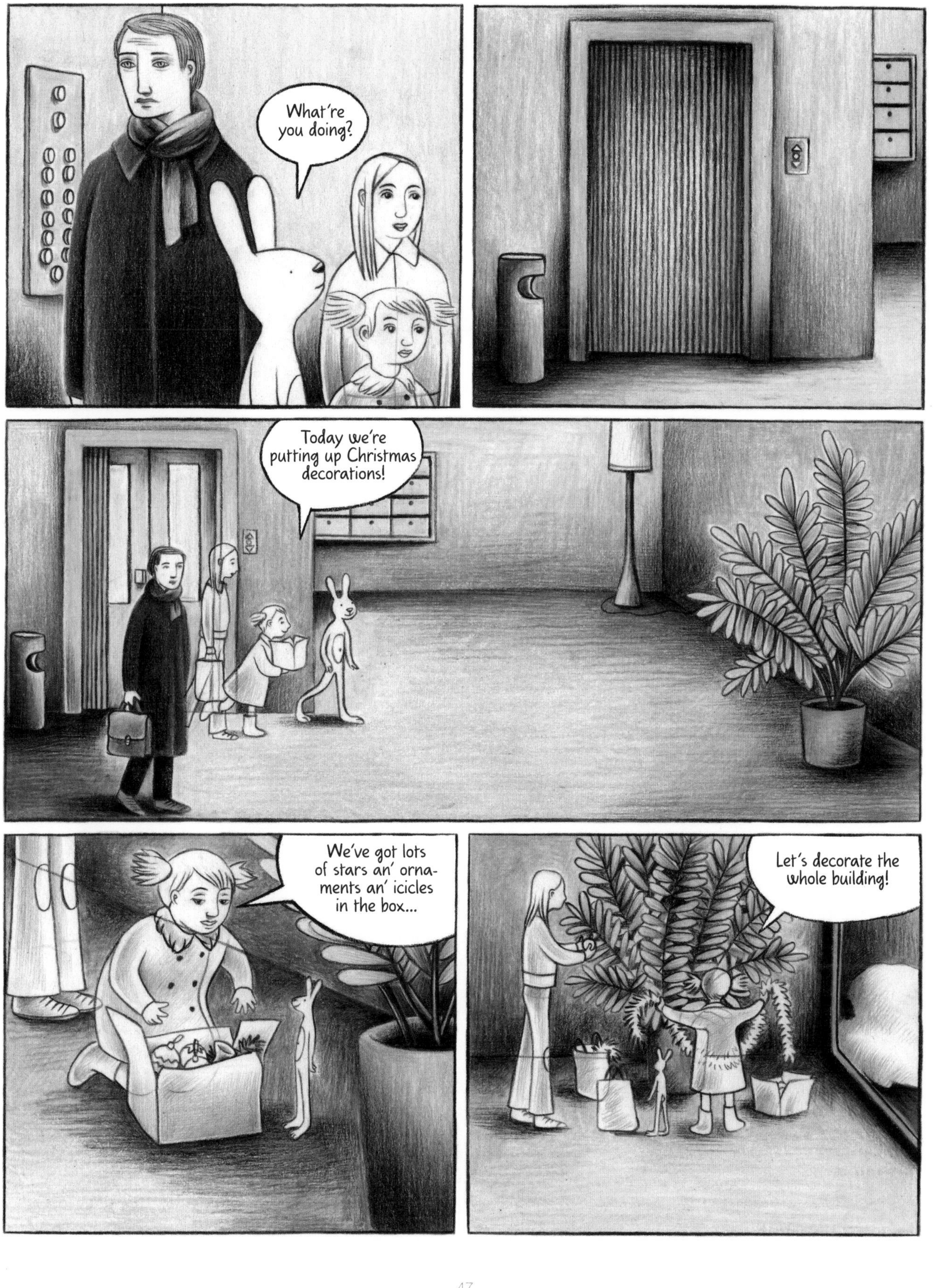
What're you doing?
Today we're putting up Christmas decorations!
We've got lots of stars an' ornaments an' icicles in the box...
Let's decorate the whole building!

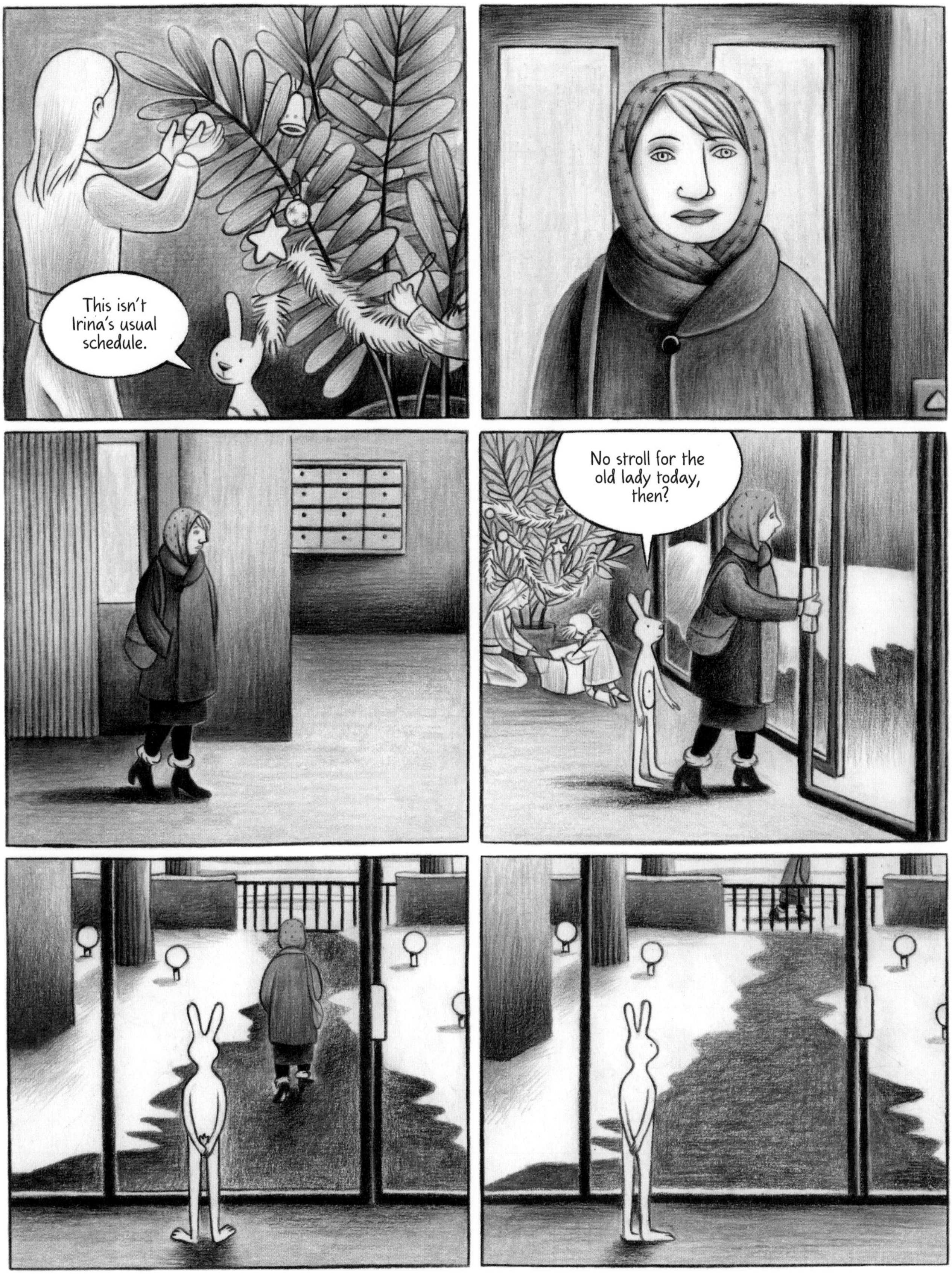
This isn't Irina's usual schedule.
No stroll for the old lady today, then?

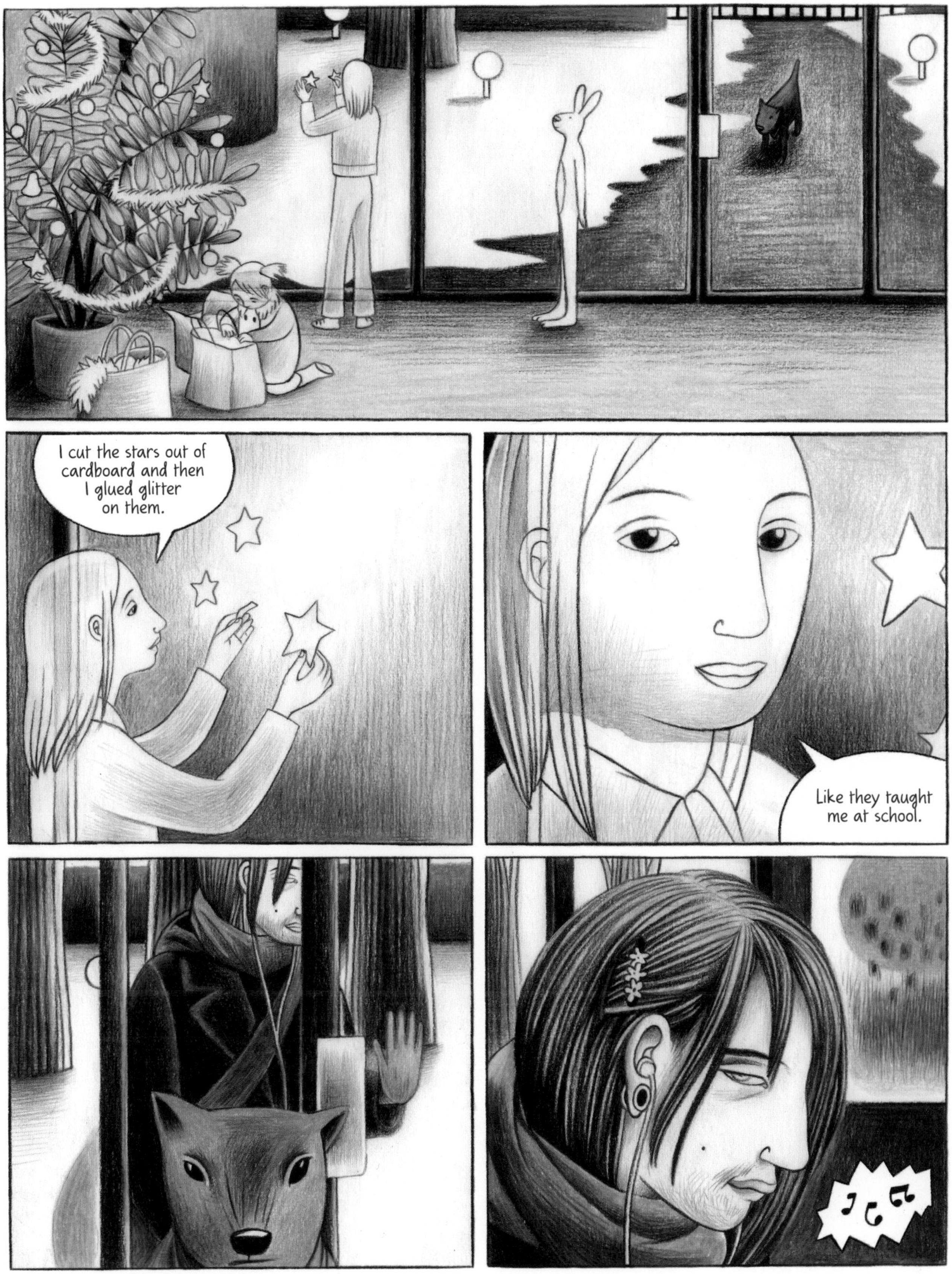
I cut the stars out of cardboard and then I glued glitter on them.
Like they taught me at school.

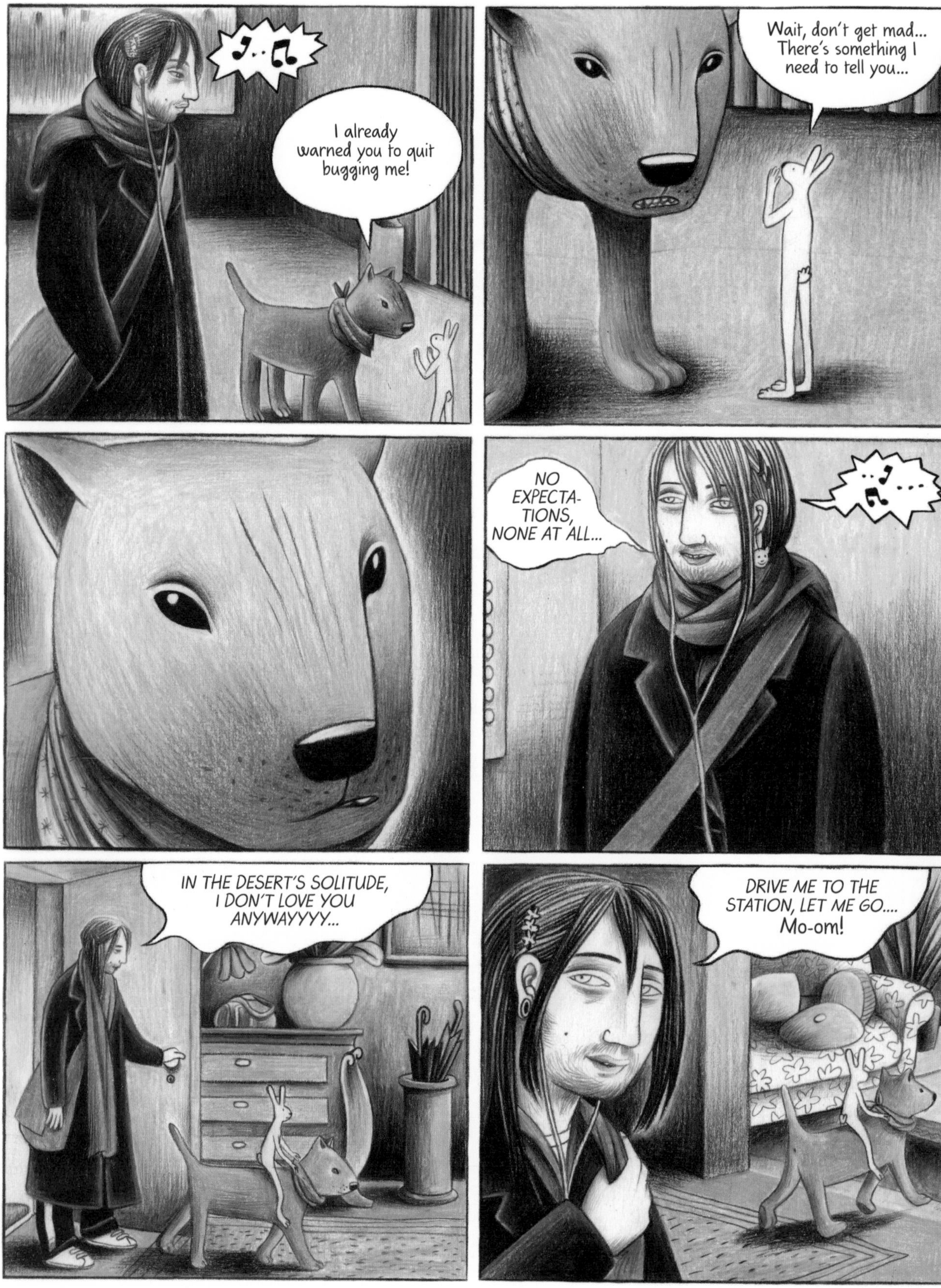
I already warned you to quit bugging me!
Wait, don't get mad... There's something I need to tell you...
NO EXPECTA-TIONS, NONE AT ALL...
IN THE DESERT'S SOLITUDE, I DON'T LOVE YOU ANYWAYYYY...
DRIVE ME TO THE STATION, LET ME GO.... Mo-om!

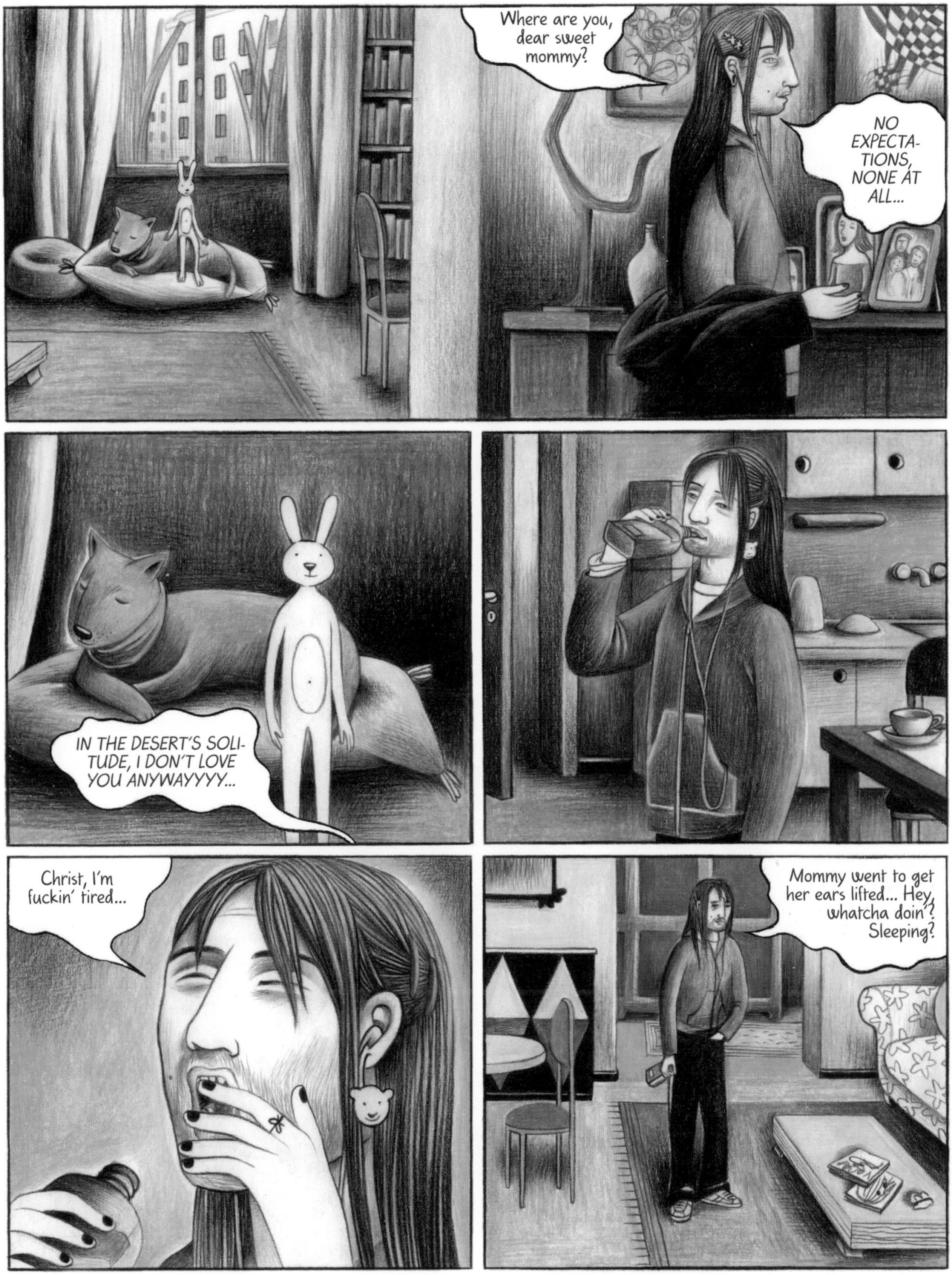
Where are you, dear sweet mommy?
NO EXPECTA-TIONS, NONE AT ALL...
IN THE DESERT'S SOLI-TUDE, I DON'T LOVE YOU ANYWAYYYY...
Christ, I'm fuckin' tired...
Mommy went to get her ears lifted... Hey, whatcha doin'? Sleeping?

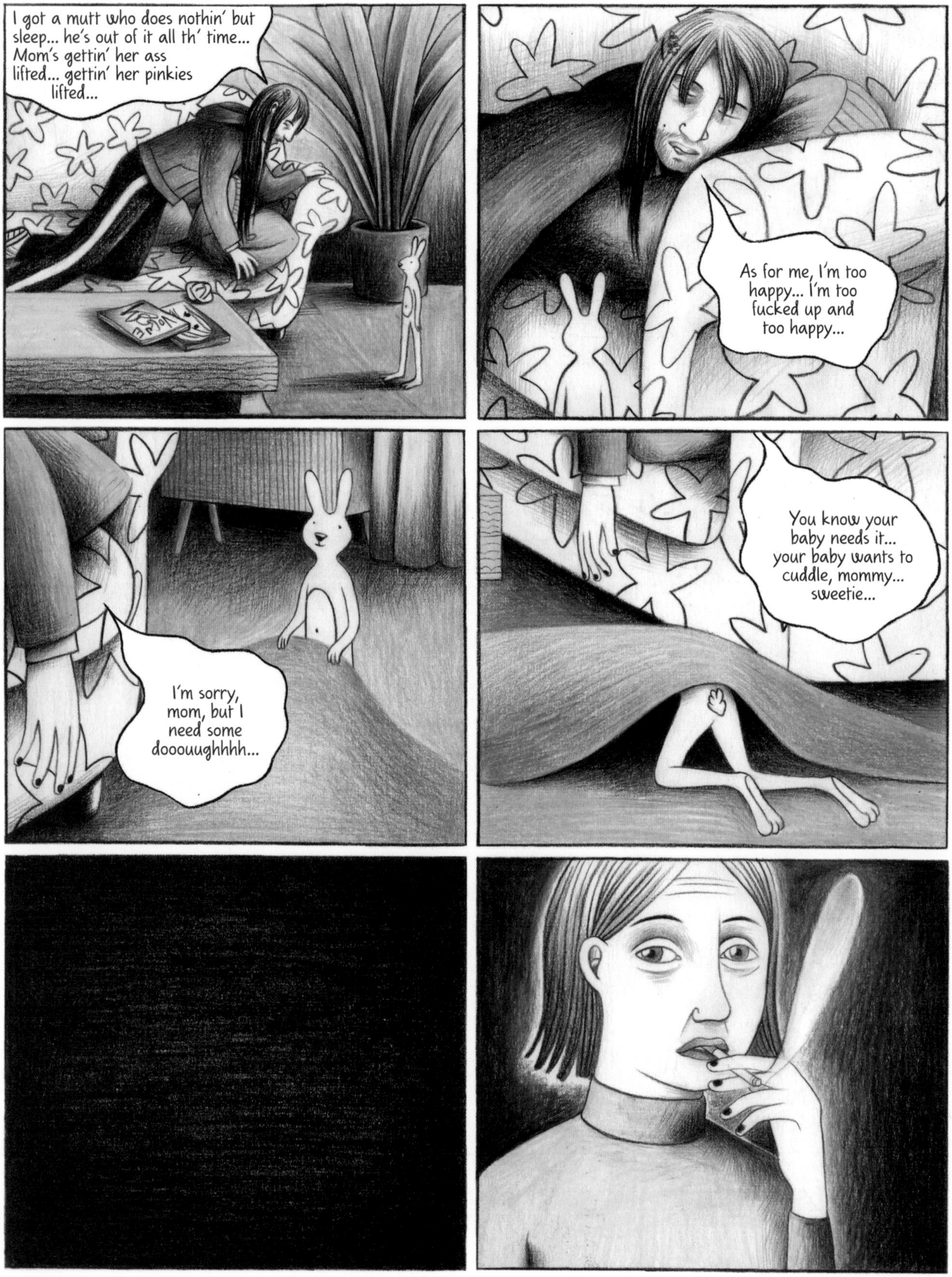
I got a mutt who does nothin' but sleep... he's out of it all th' time... Mom's gettin' her ass lifted... gettin' her pinkies lifted...
As for me, I'm too happy... I'm too fucked up and too happy...
I'm sorry, mom, but I need some dooouughhhh...
You know your baby needs it... your baby wants to cuddle, mommy... sweetie...

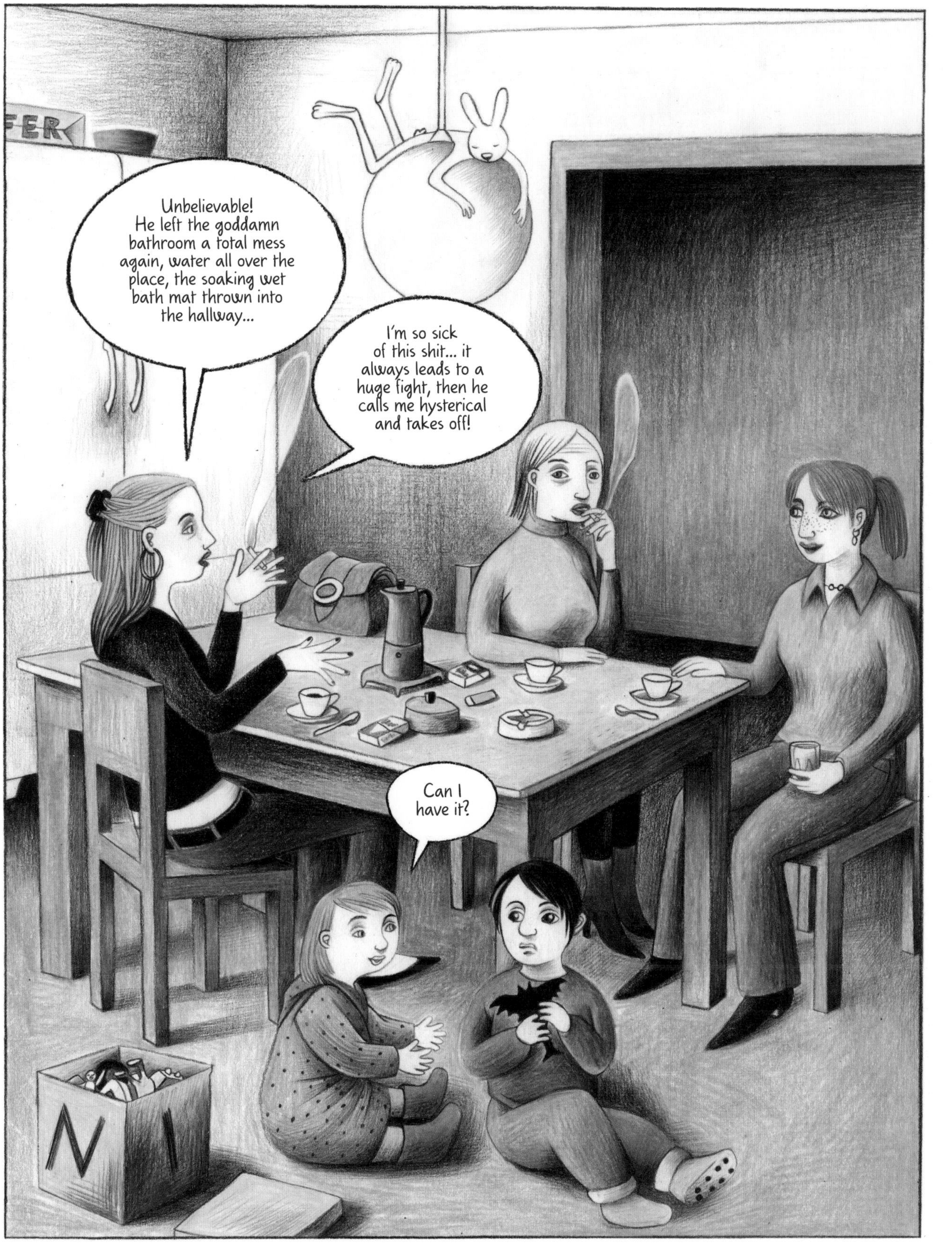
FER
Unbelievable! He left the goddamn bathroom a total mess again, water all over the place, the soaking wet bath mat thrown into the hallway...
I'm so sick of this shit... it always leads to a huge fight, then he calls me hysterical and takes off!
Can I have it?
N I

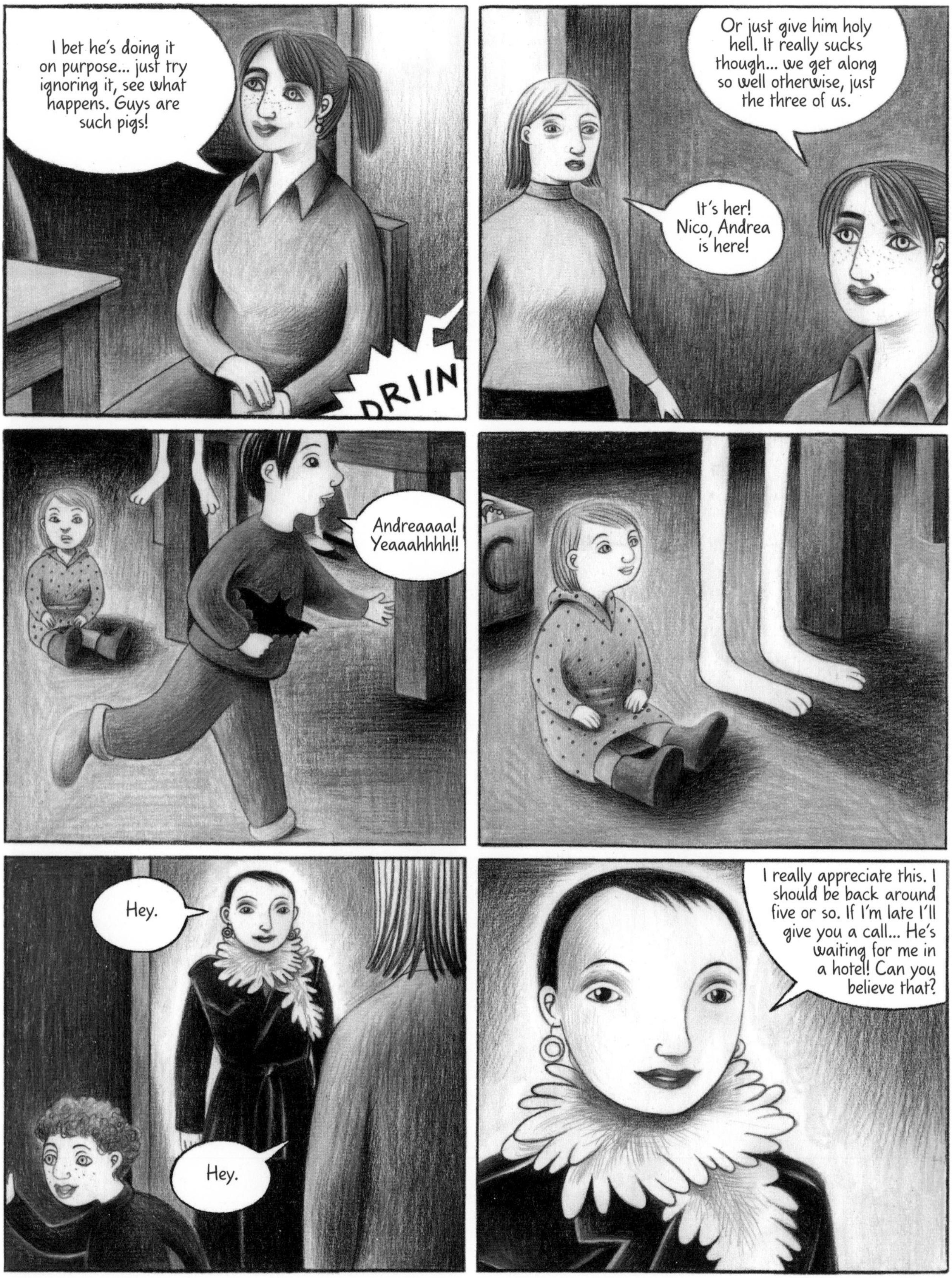
I bet he's doing it on purpose... just try ignoring it, see what happens. Guys are such pigs!
DRIIN
Or just give him holy hell. It really sucks though... we get along so well otherwise, just the three of us.
It's her! Nico, Andrea is here!
Andreaaaa! Yeaaahhhh!!
Hey.
Hey.
I really appreciate this. I should be back around five or so. If I'm late I'll give you a call... He's waiting for me in a hotel! Can you believe that?

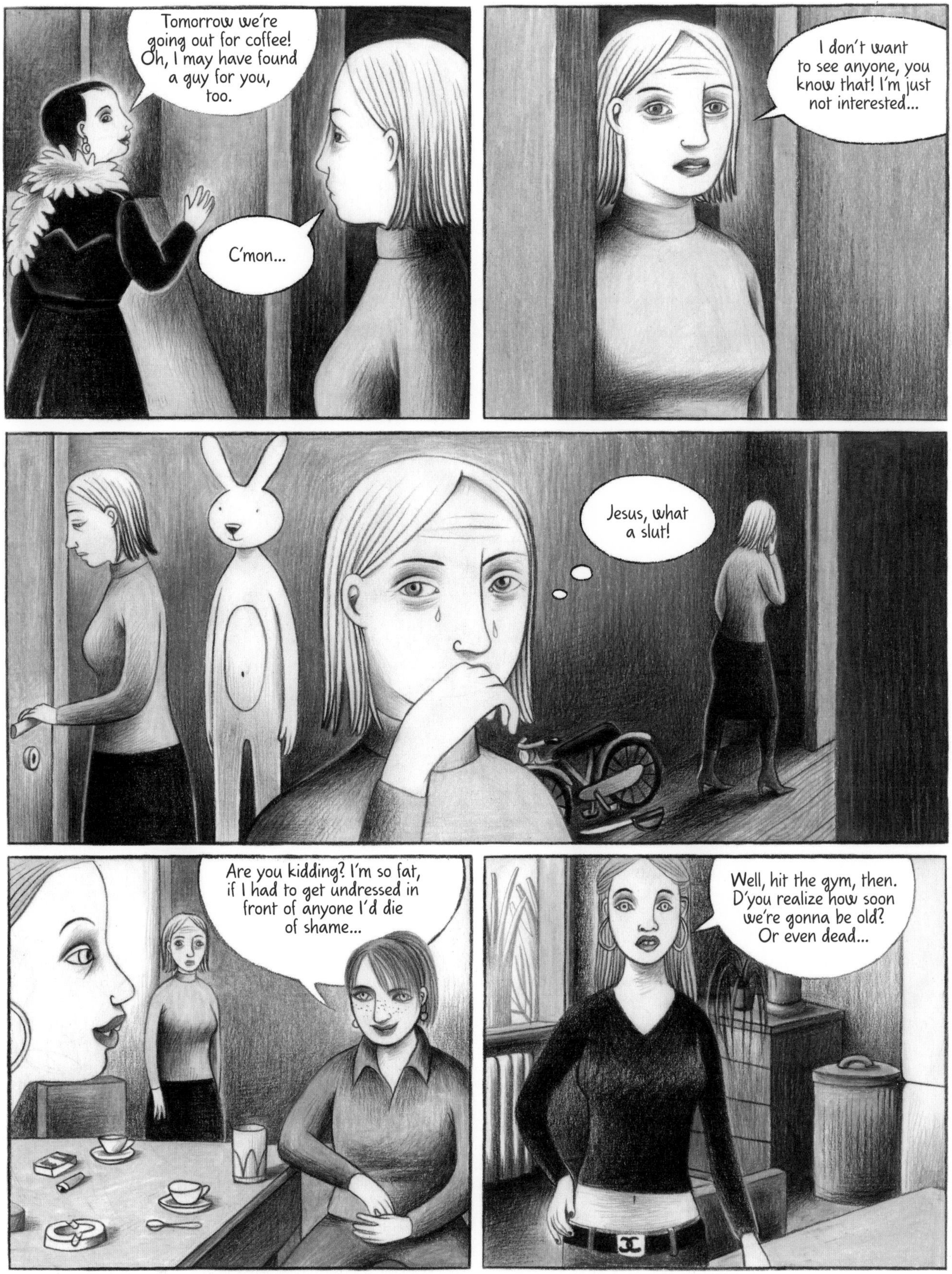

Tomorrow we're going out for coffee! Oh, I may have found a guy for you, too.
C'mon...
I don't want to see anyone, you know that! I'm just not interested...
Jesus, what a slut!
Are you kidding? I'm so fat, if I had to get undressed in front of anyone I'd die of shame...
Well, hit the gym, then. D'you realize how soon we're gonna be old? Or even dead...

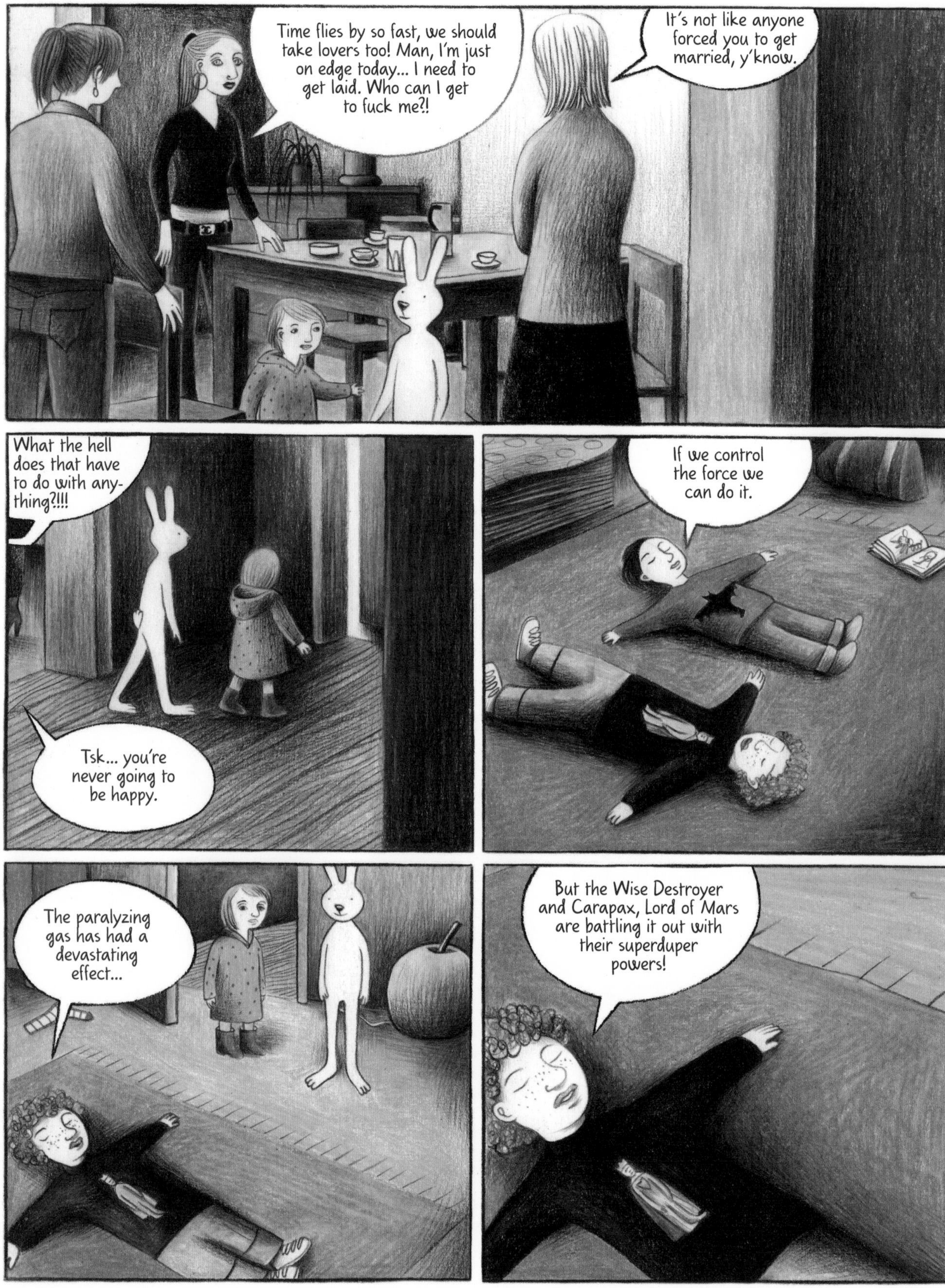
Time flies by so fast, we should take lovers too! Man, I'm just on edge today... I need to get laid. Who can I get to fuck me?!
It's not like anyone forced you to get married, y'know.
What the hell does that have to do with anything?!!!
Tsk... you're never going to be happy.
If we control the force we can do it.
The paralyzing gas has had a devastating effect...
But the Wise Destroyer and Carapax, Lord of Mars are battling it out with their superduper powers!

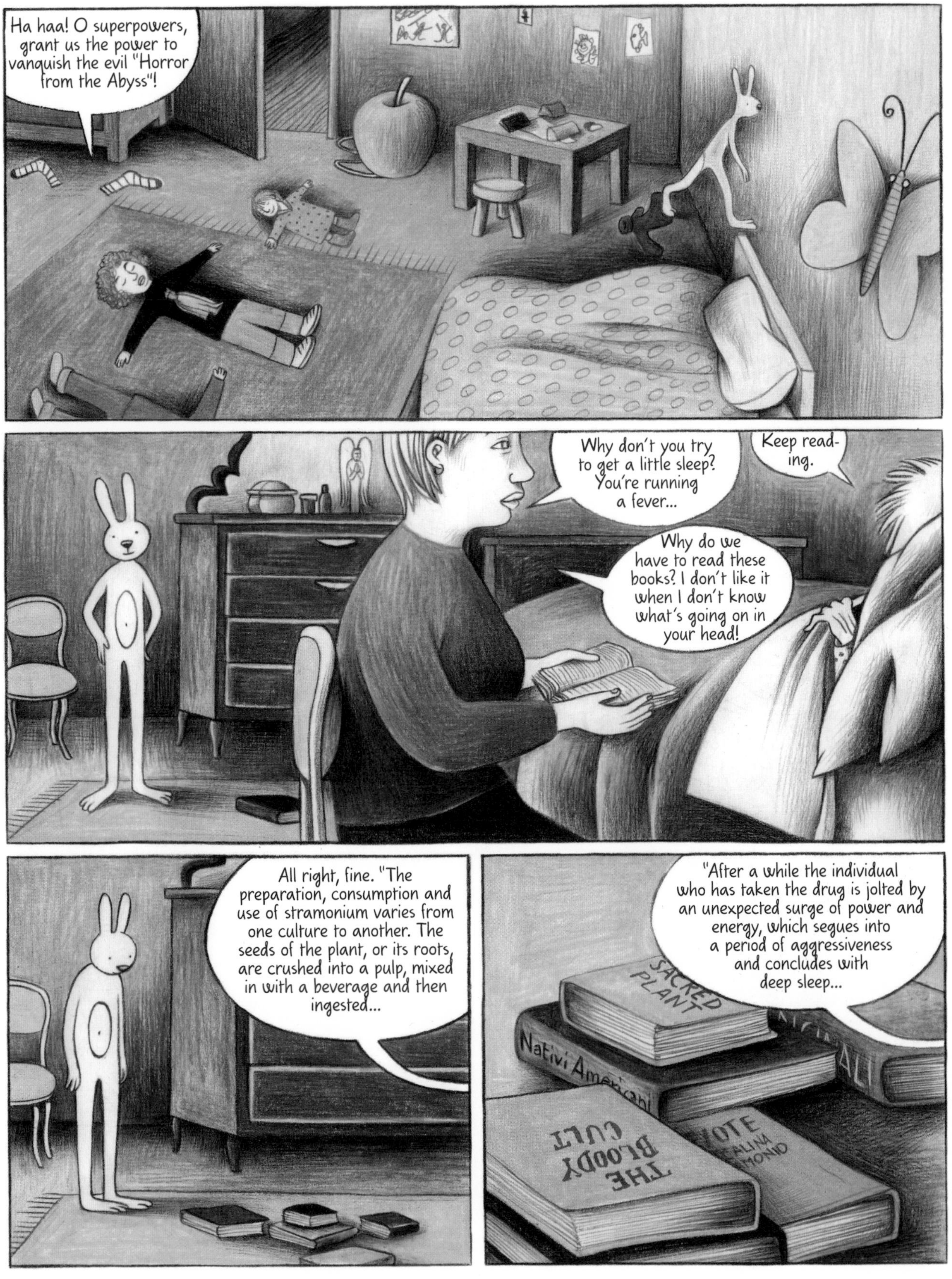

Ha haa! O superpowers, grant us the power to vanquish the evil "Horror from the Abyss"!
Why don't you try to get a little sleep? You're running a fever...
Keep reading.
Why do we have to read these books? I don't like it when I don't know what's going on in your head!
All right, fine. "The preparation, consumption and use of stramonium varies from one culture to another. The seeds of the plant, or its roots, are crushed into a pulp, mixed in with a beverage and then ingested...
"After a while the individual who has taken the drug is jolted by an unexpected surge of power and energy, which segues into a period of aggressiveness and concludes with deep sleep...
SACRED PLANT
Nativi Americani
THE BLOODY CULT

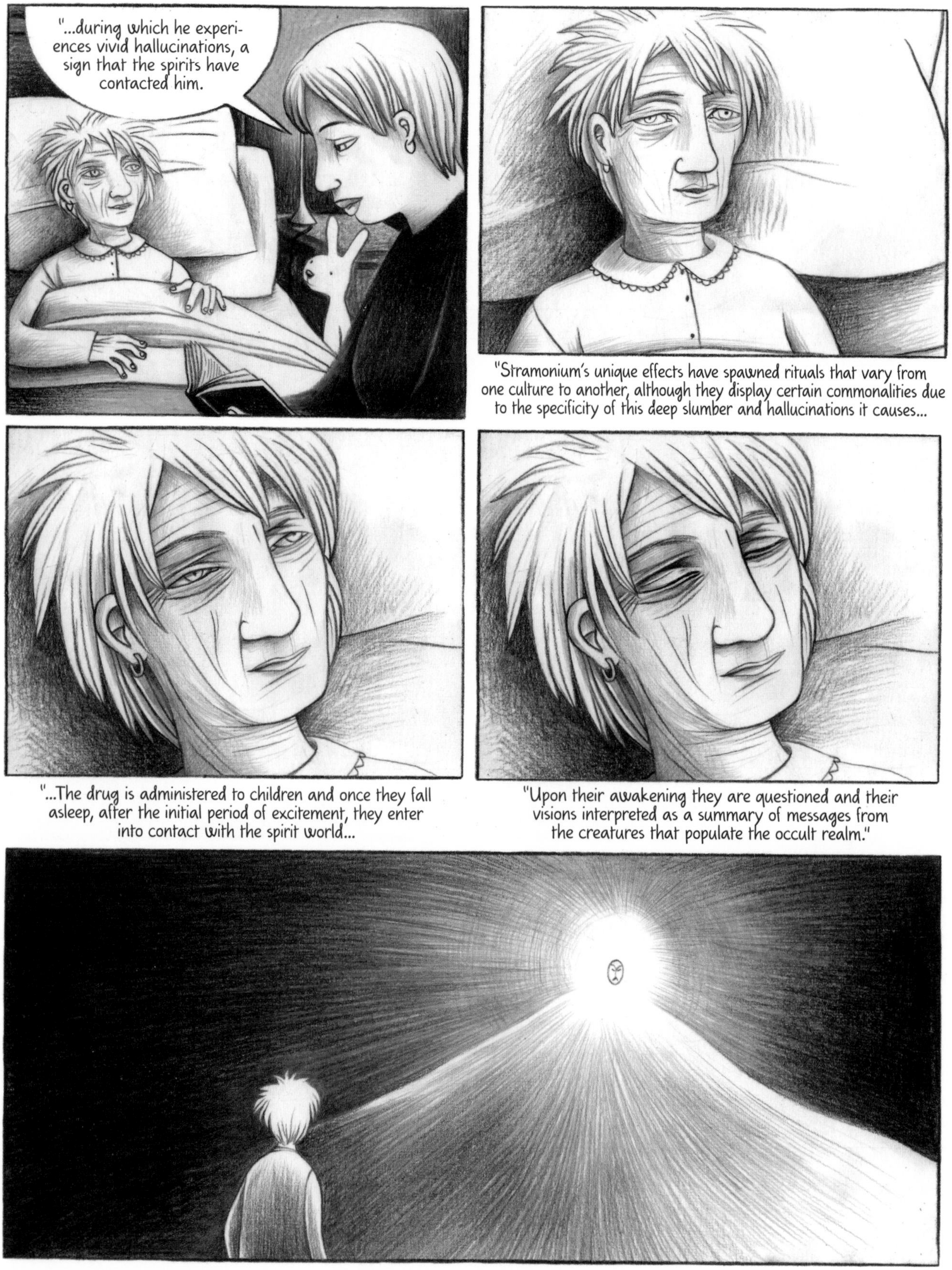
"...during which he experiences vivid hallucinations, a sign that the spirits have contacted him.
"Stramonium's unique effects have spawned rituals that vary from one culture to another, although they display certain commonalities due to the specificity of this deep slumber and hallucinations it causes...
"...The drug is administered to children and once they fall asleep, after the initial period of excitement, they enter into contact with the spirit world...
"Upon their awakening they are questioned and their visions interpreted as a summary of messages from the creatures that populate the occult realm."

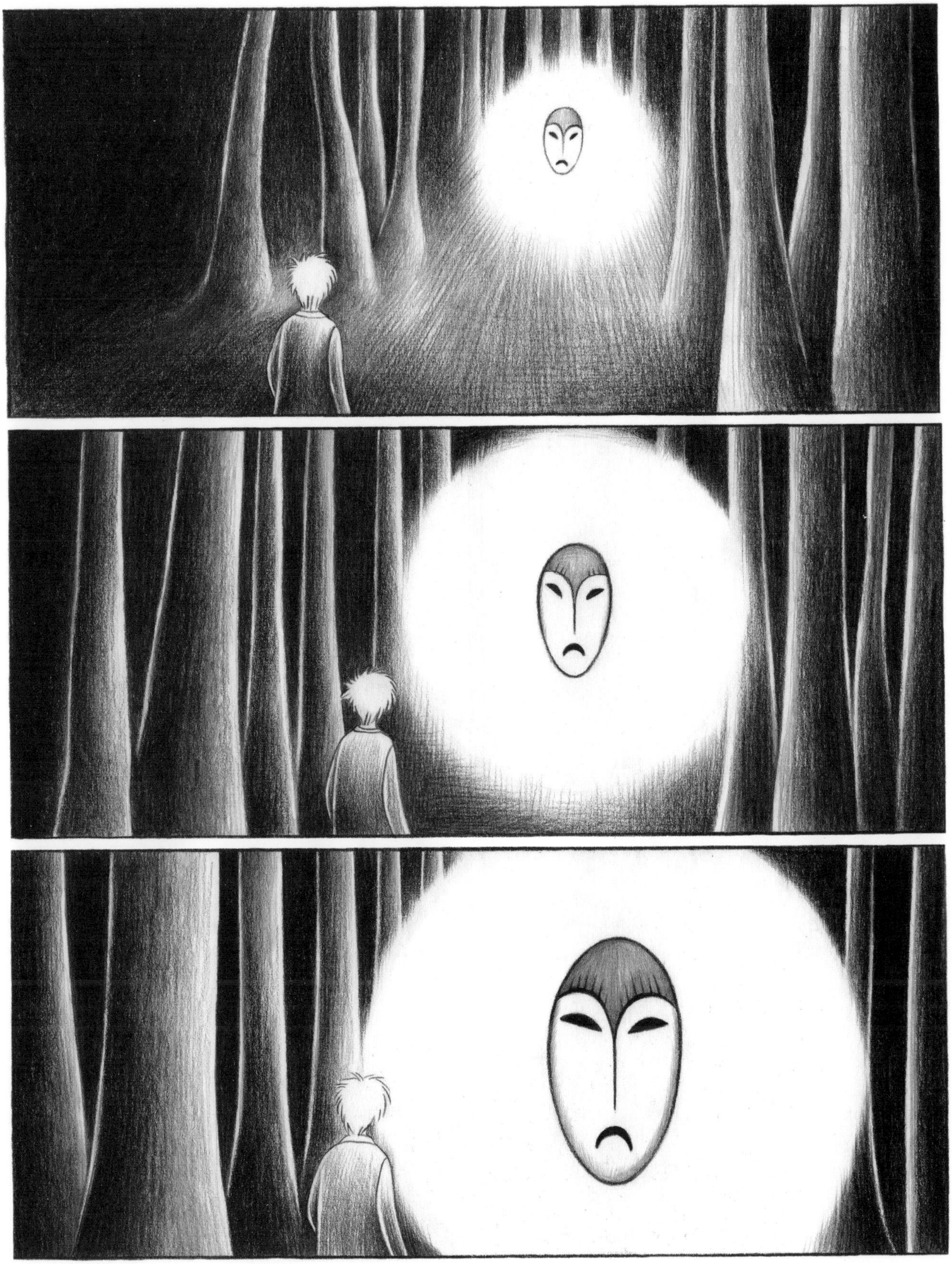

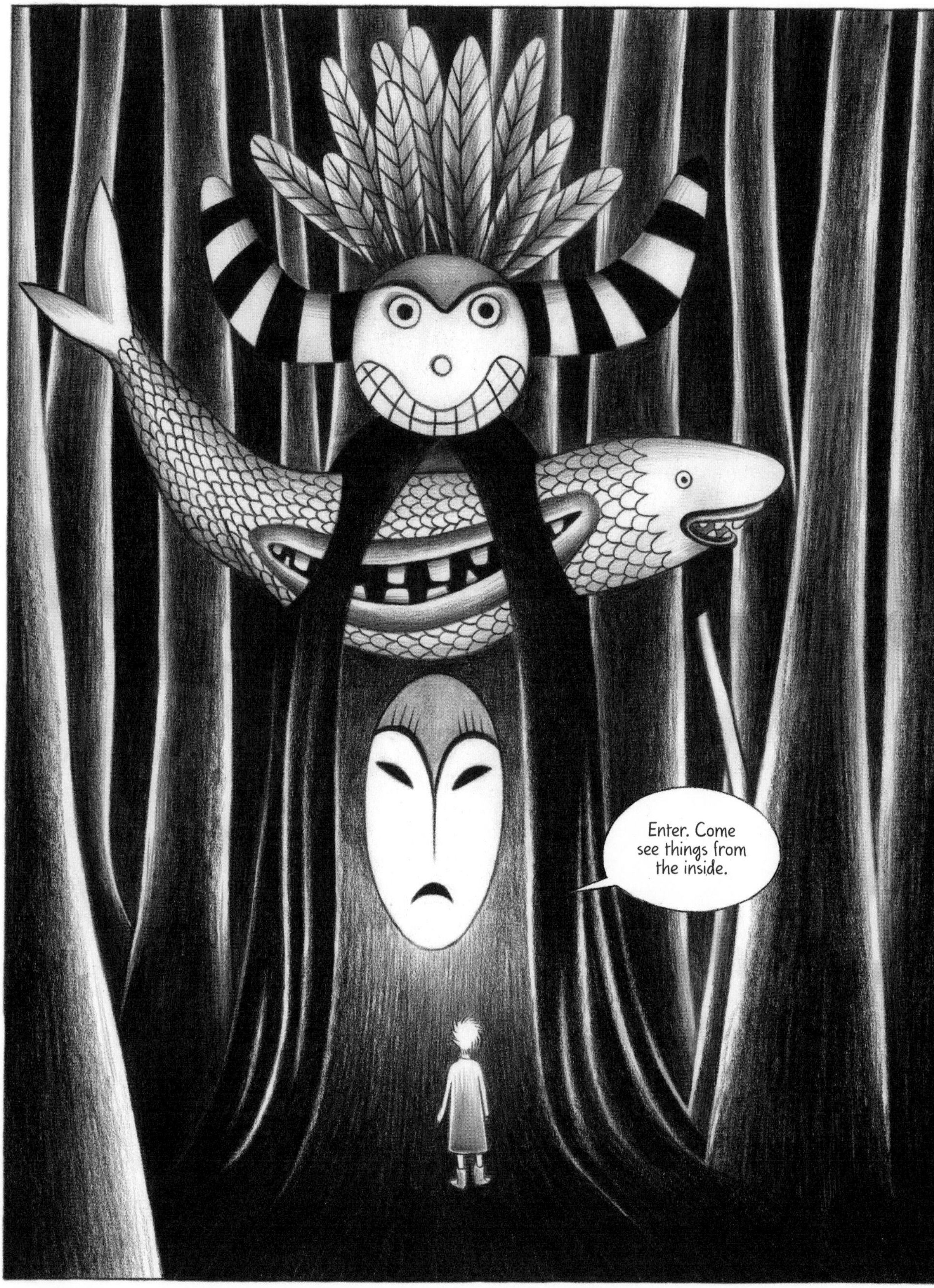
Enter. Come see things from the inside.

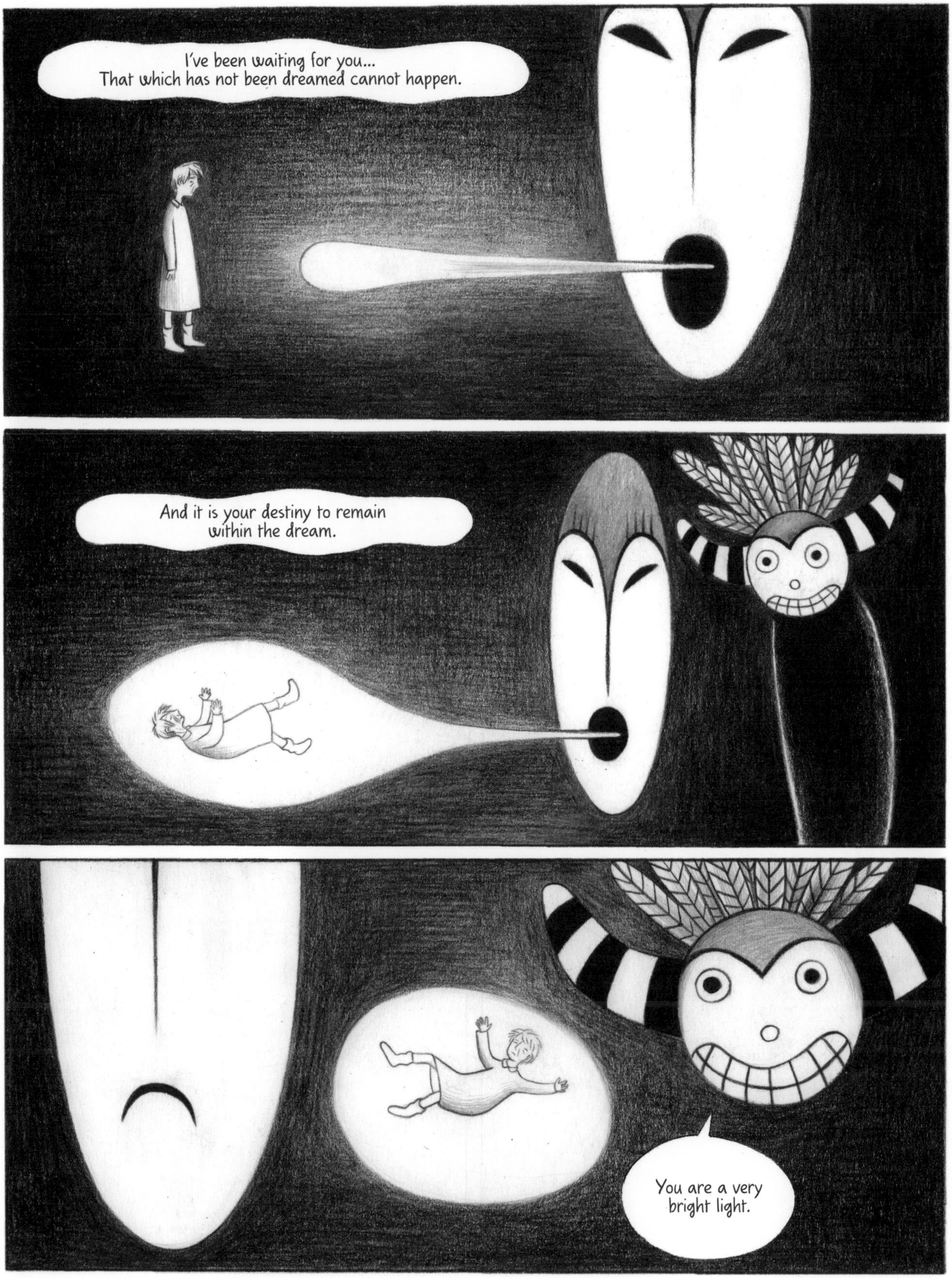
I've been waiting for you...
That which has not been dreamed cannot happen.
And it is your destiny to remain within the dream.
You are a very bright light.

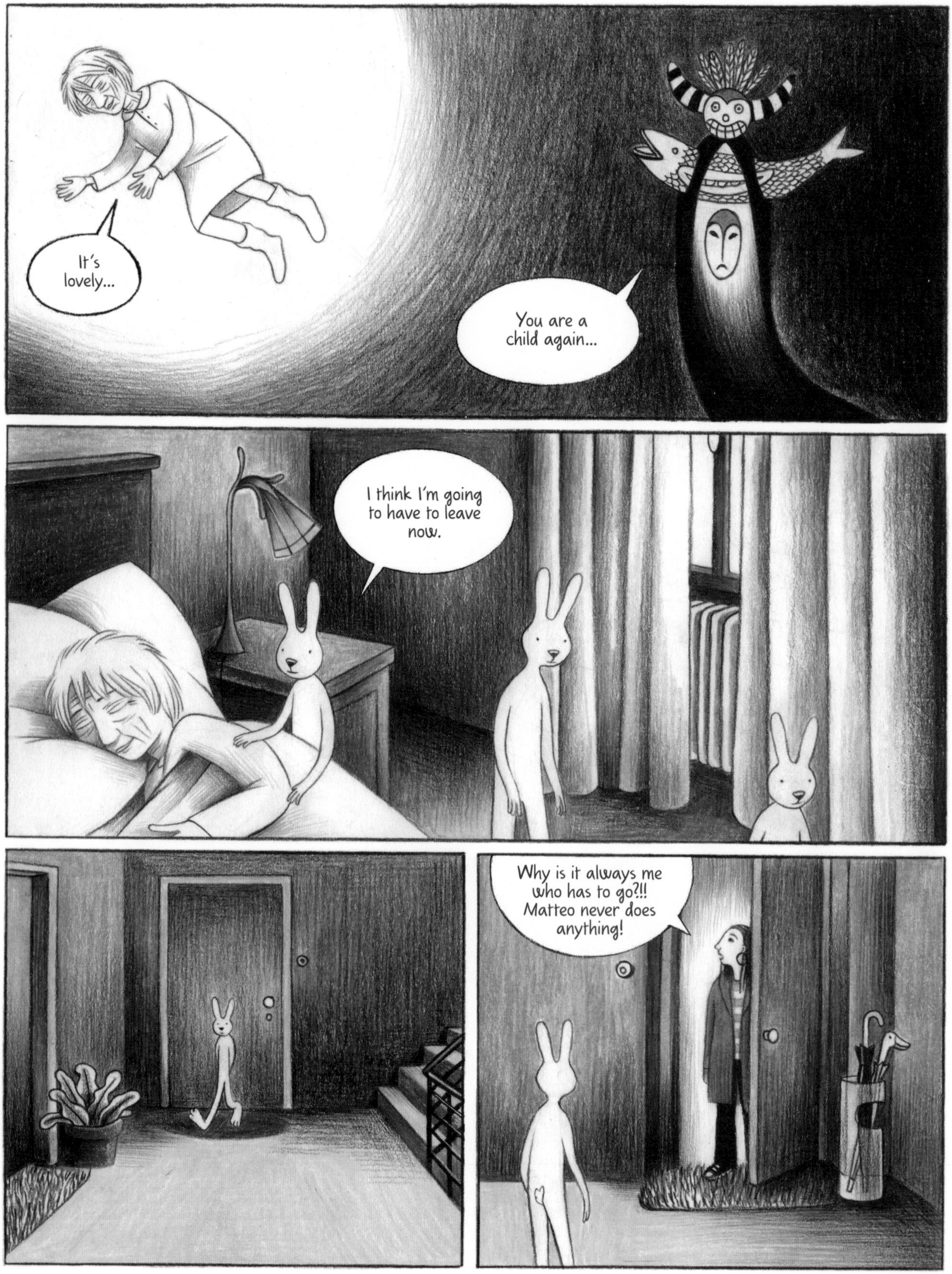
It's lovely...
You are a child again...
I think I'm going to have to leave now.
Why is it always me who has to go?!! Matteo never does anything!

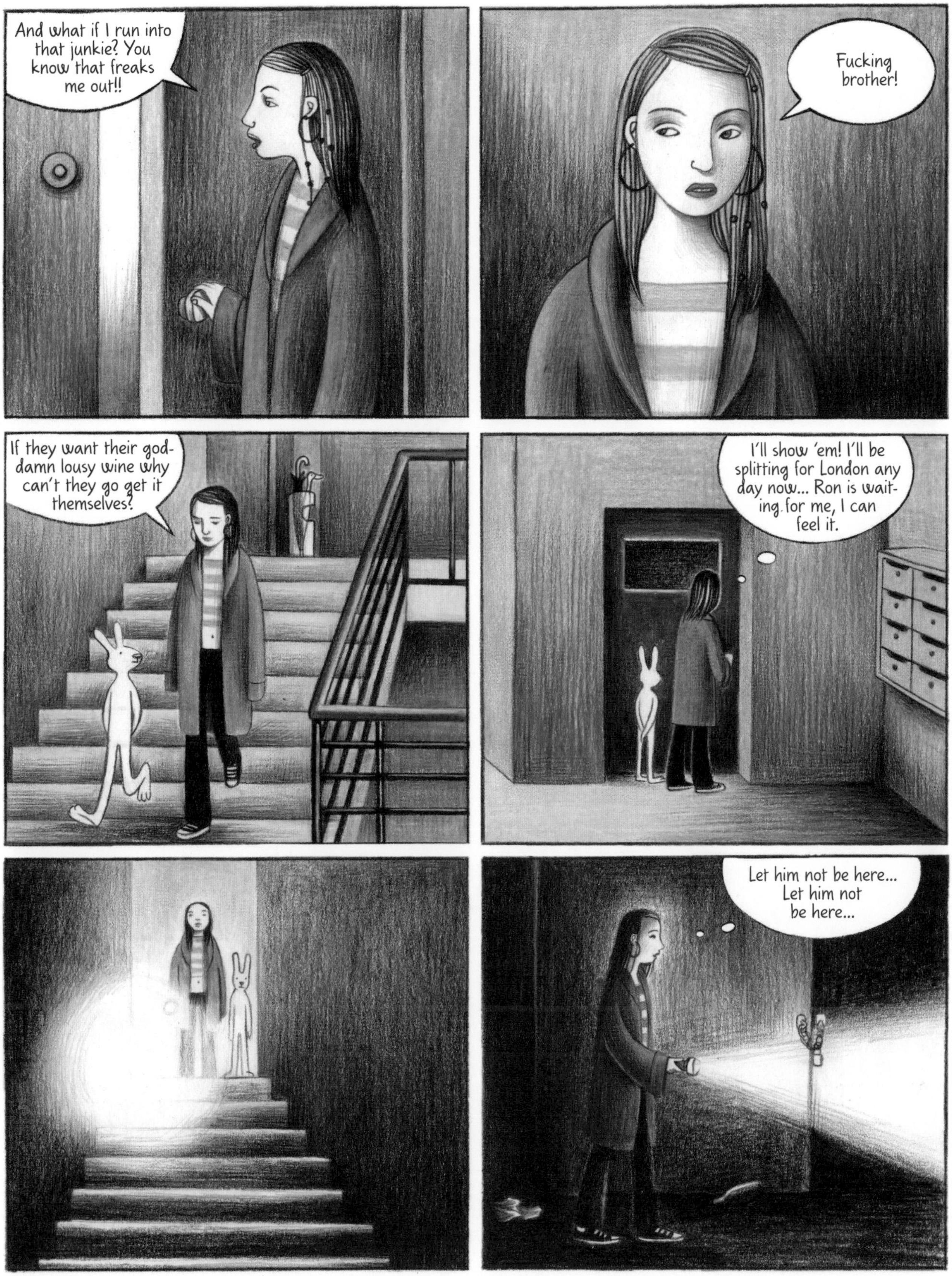
And what if I run into that junkie? You know that freaks me out!!
Fucking brother!
If they want their god-damn lousy wine why can't they go get it themselves?
I'll show 'em! I'll be splitting for London any day now... Ron is wait-ing for me, I can feel it.
Let him not be here... Let him not be here...

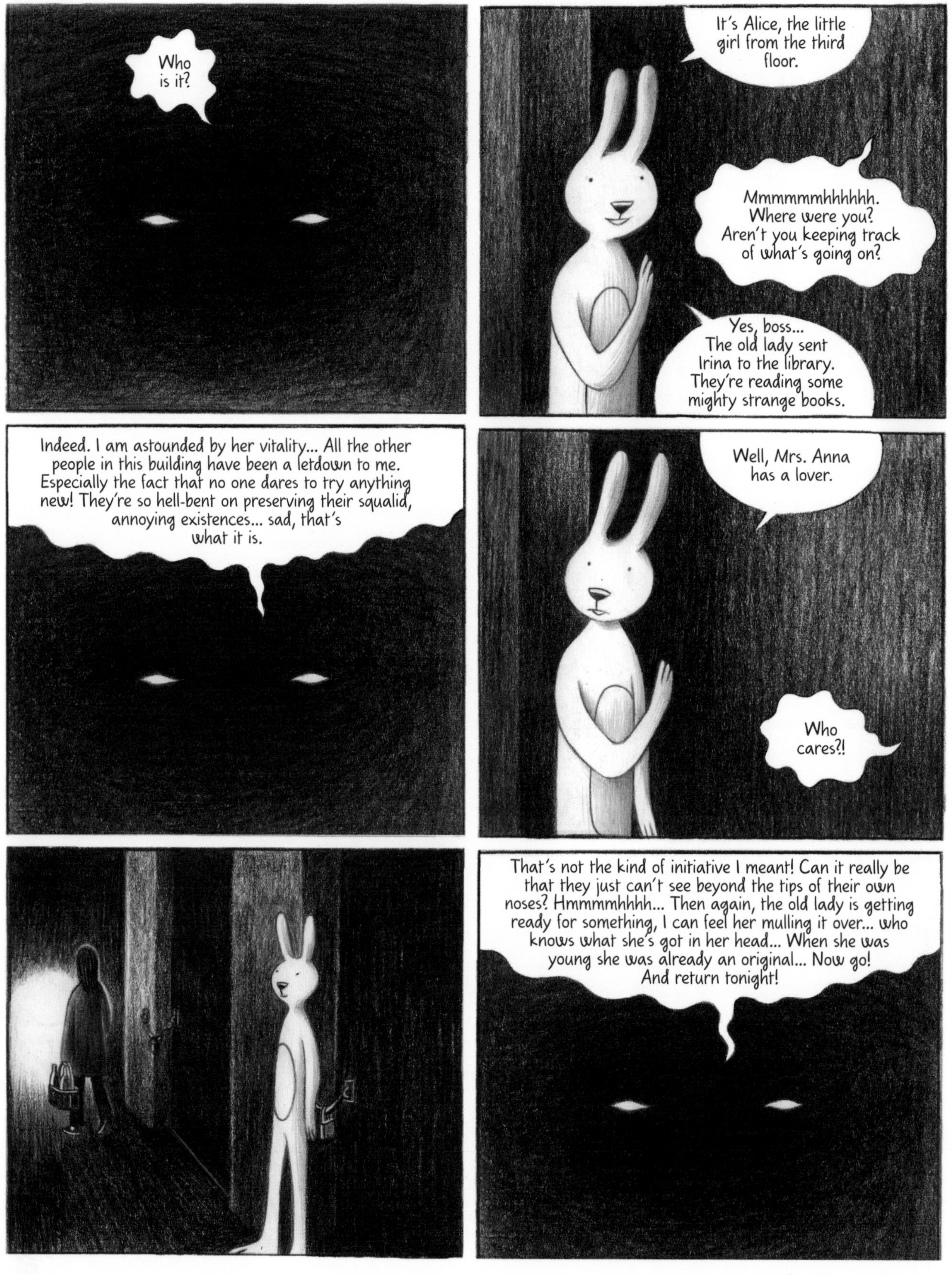
Who is it?
It's Alice, the little girl from the third floor.
Mmmmmmhhhhhh. Where were you? Aren't you keeping track of what's going on?
Yes, boss... The old lady sent Irina to the library. They're reading some mighty strange books.
Indeed. I am astounded by her vitality... All the other people in this building have been a letdown to me. Especially the fact that no one dares to try anything new! They're so hell-bent on preserving their squalid, annoying existences... sad, that's what it is.
Well, Mrs. Anna has a lover.
Who cares?!
That's not the kind of initiative I meant! Can it really be that they just can't see beyond the tips of their own noses? Hmmmmhhhh... Then again, the old lady is getting ready for something, I can feel her mulling it over... who knows what she's got in her head... When she was young she was already an original... Now go! And return tonight!

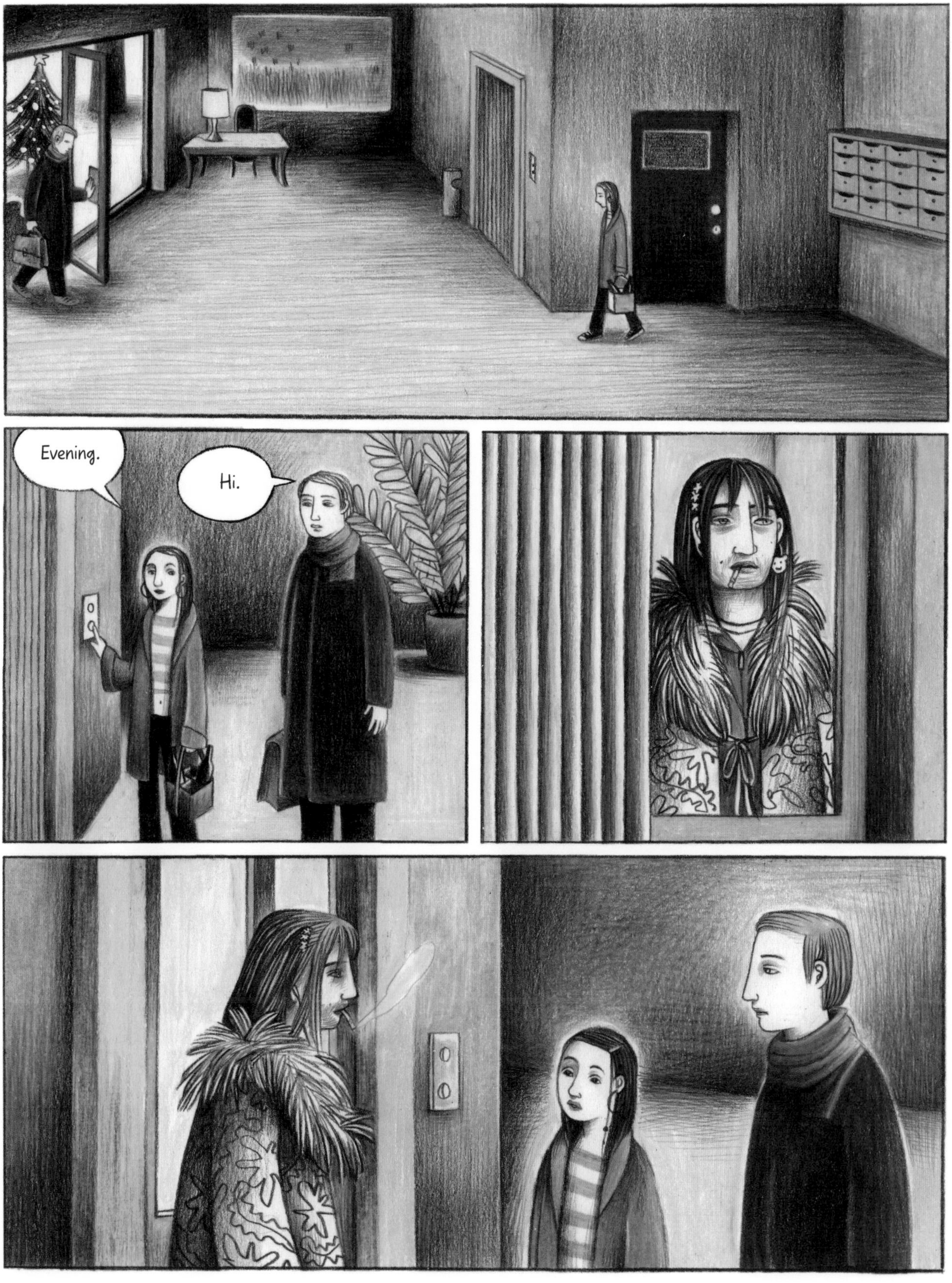
Evening.
Hi.

He's always
hanging out in the
basement.

I hate
that dog
of his.

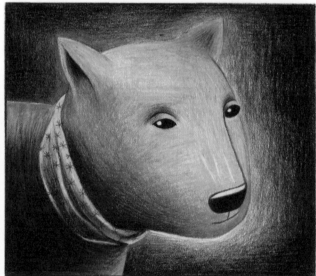

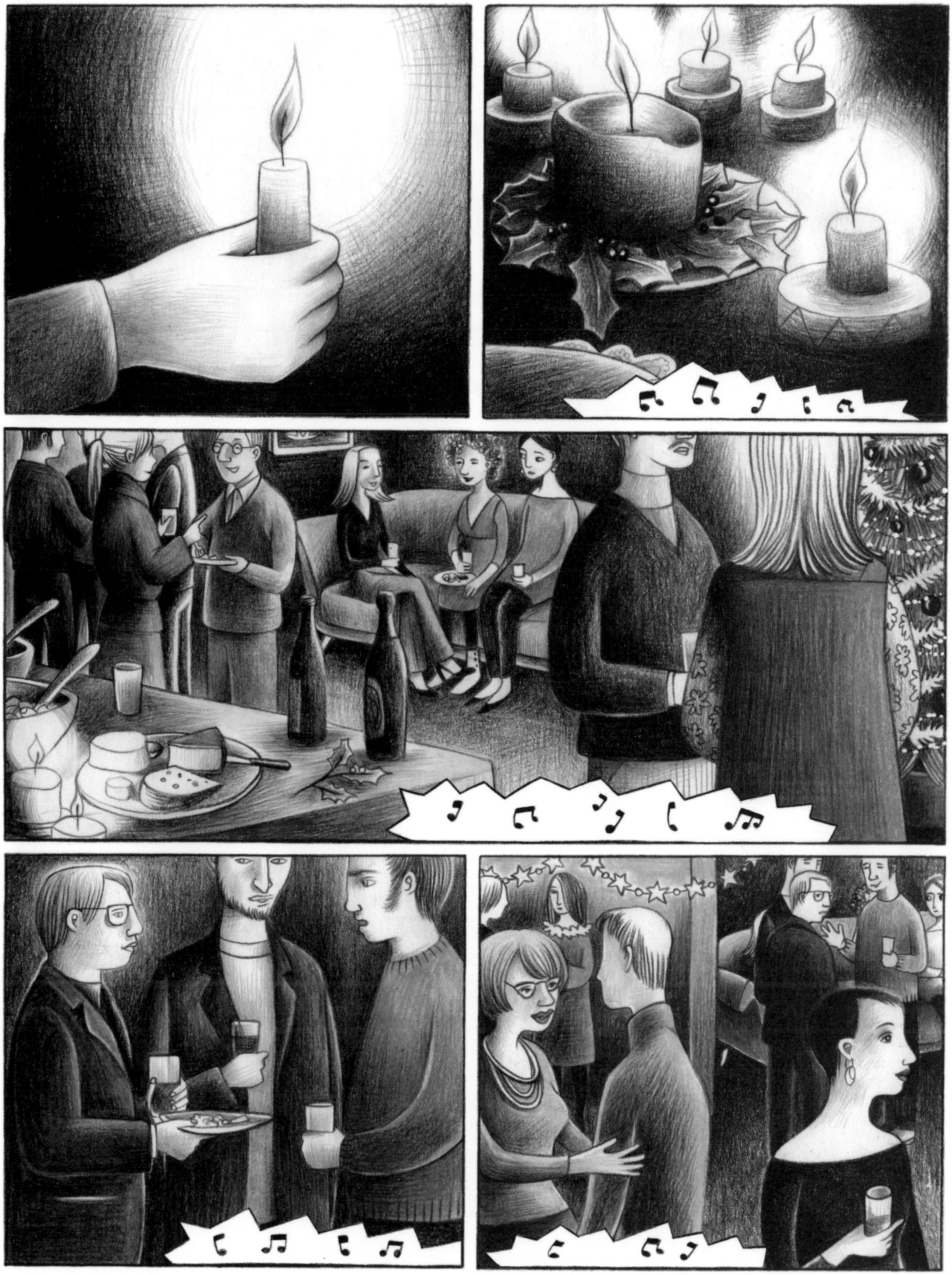

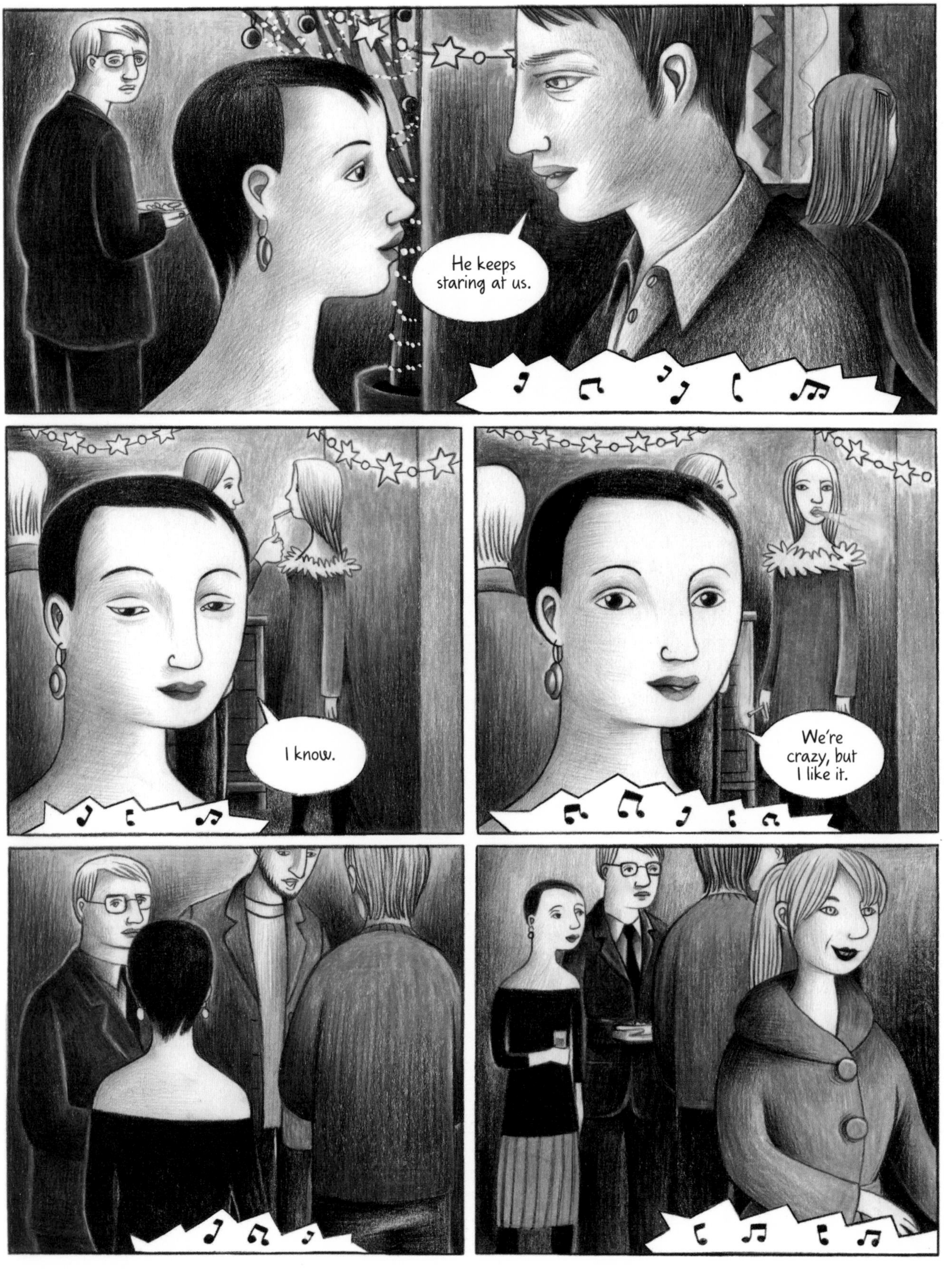
He keeps staring at us.
I know.
We're crazy, but I like it.

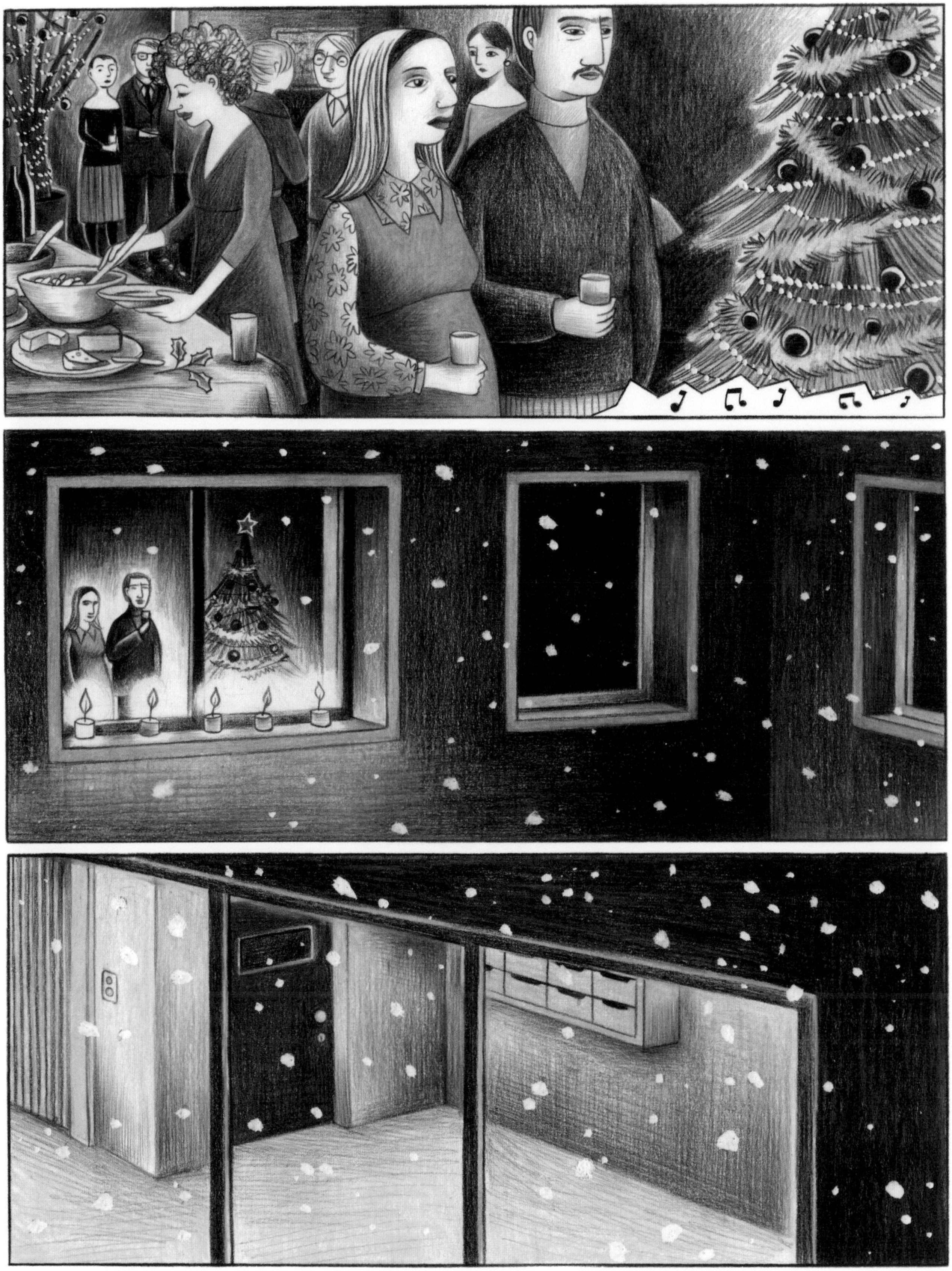

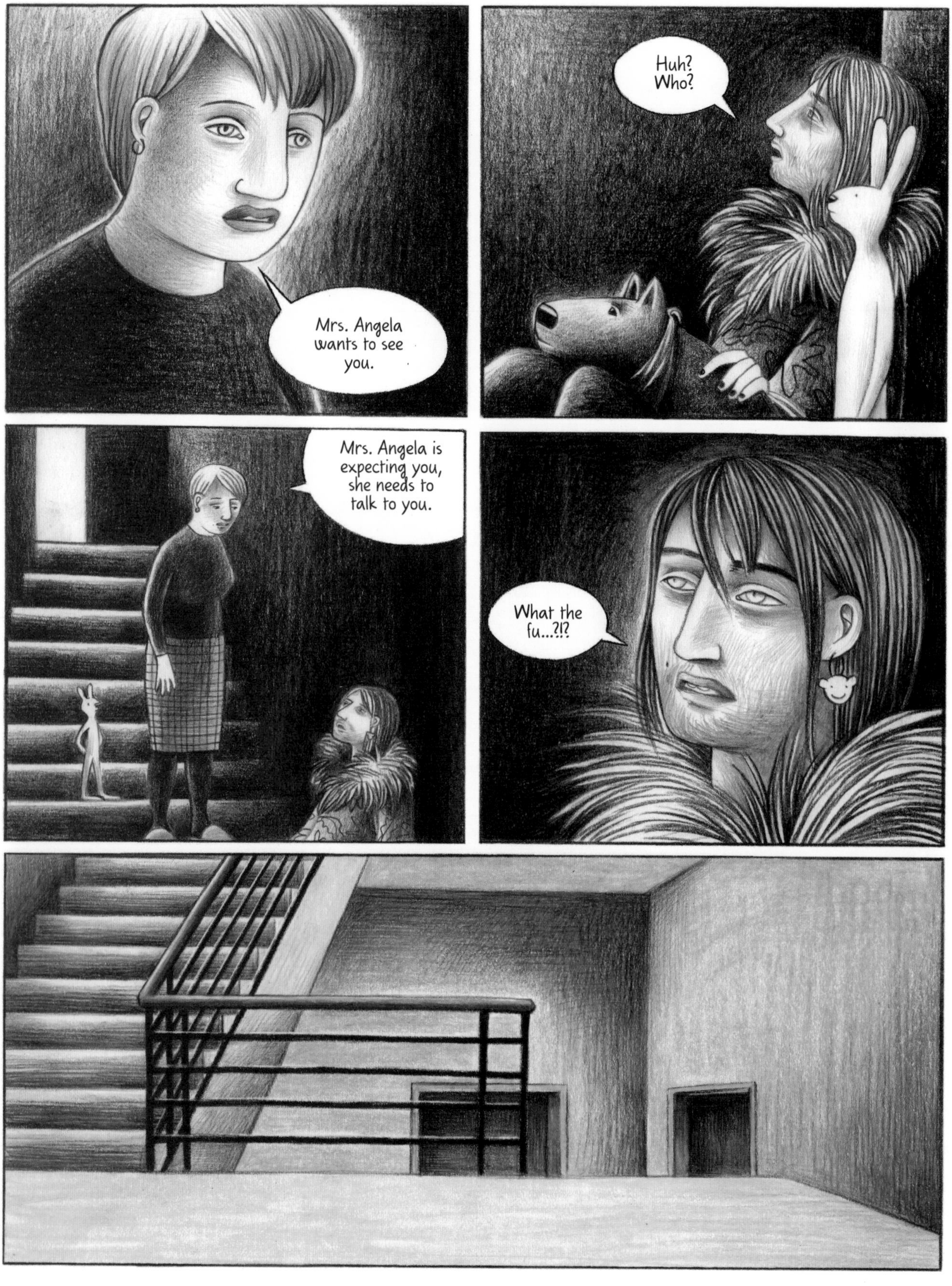
Mrs. Angela wants to see you.
Huh? Who?
Mrs. Angela is expecting you, she needs to talk to you.
What the fu...?!?

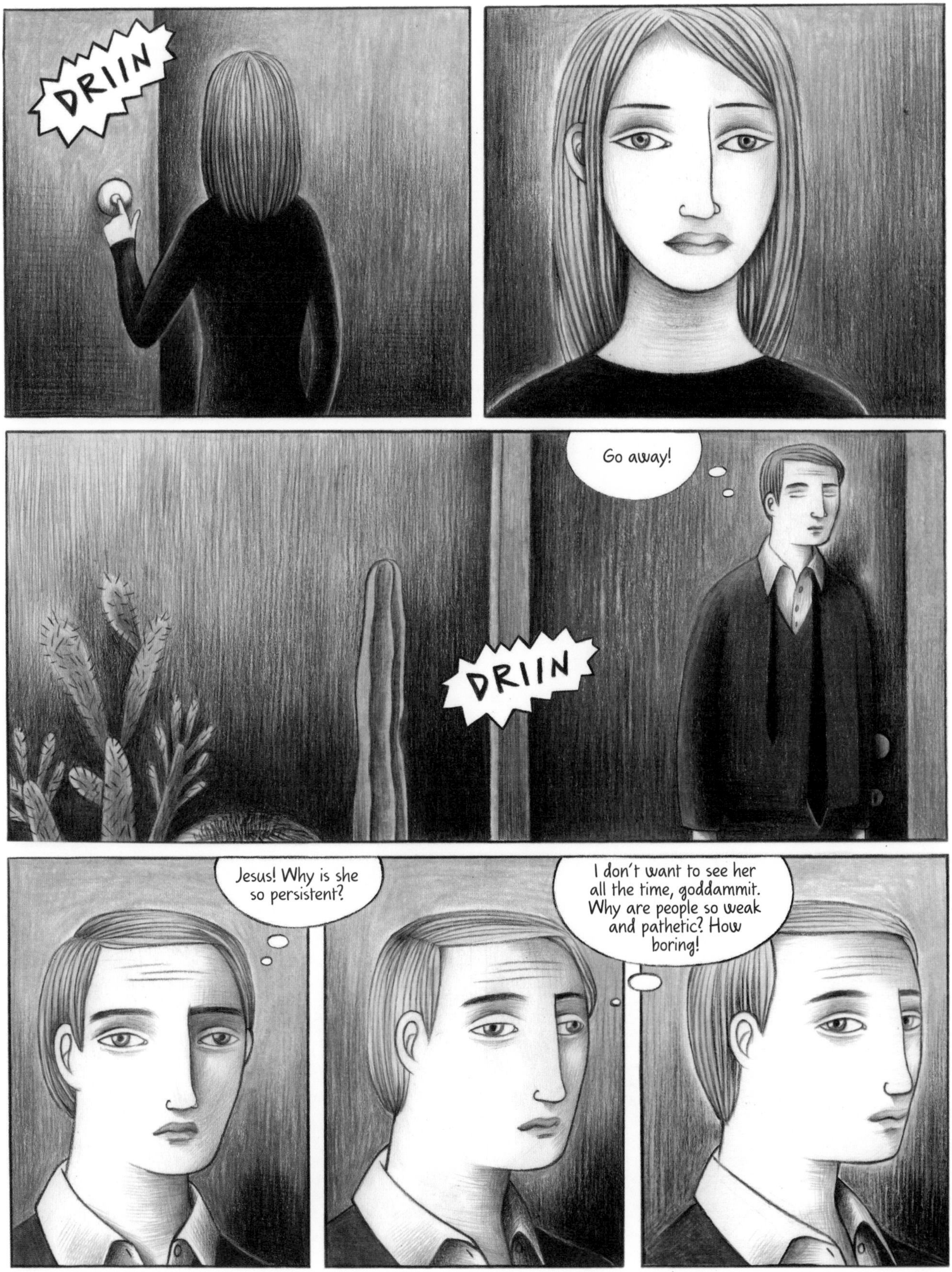
DRIIN
Go away!
DRIIN
Jesus! Why is she so persistent?
I don't want to see her all the time, goddammit. Why are people so weak and pathetic? How boring!

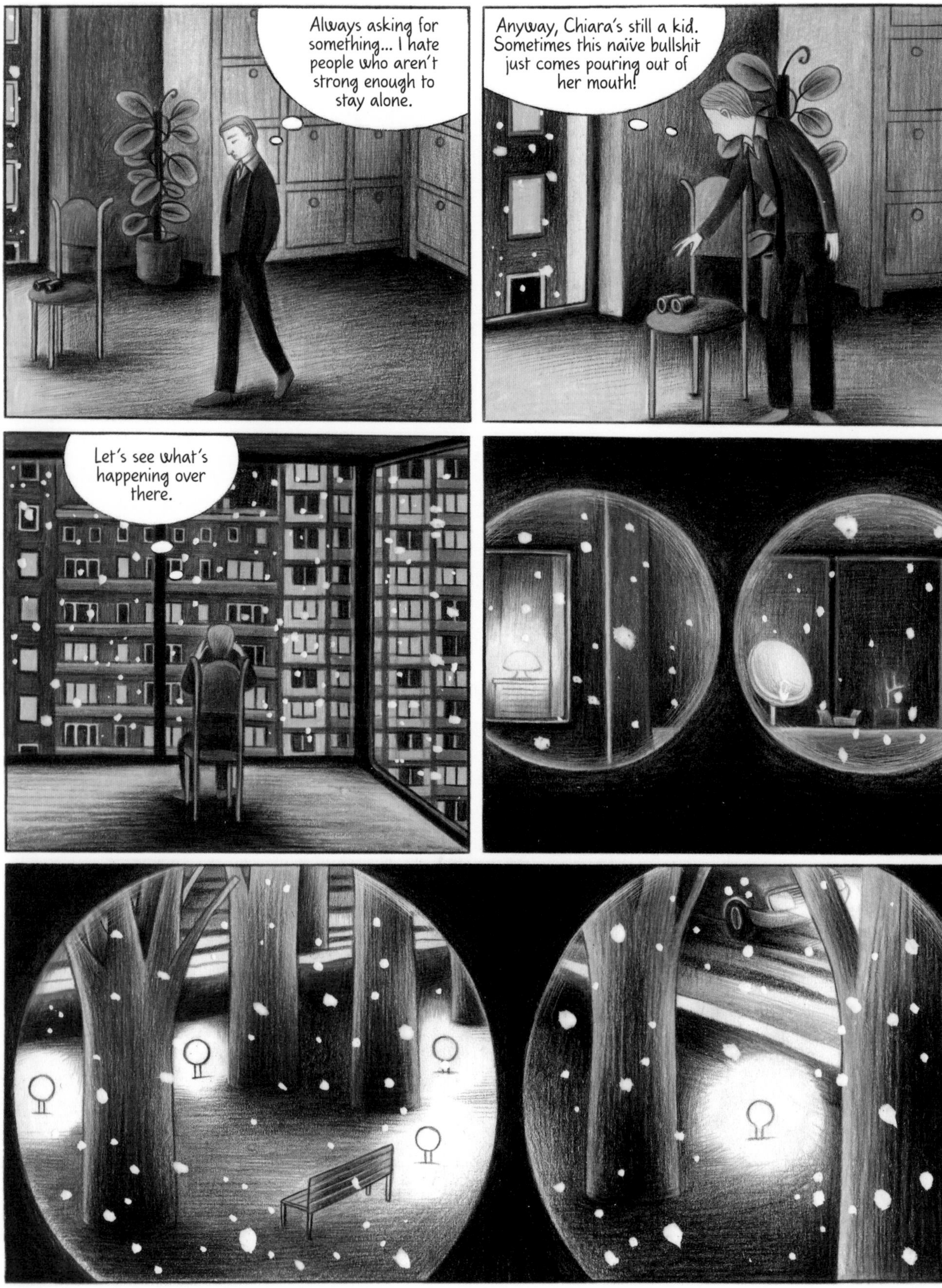
Always asking for something... I hate people who aren't strong enough to stay alone.
Anyway, Chiara's still a kid. Sometimes this naïve bullshit just comes pouring out of her mouth!
Let's see what's happening over there.

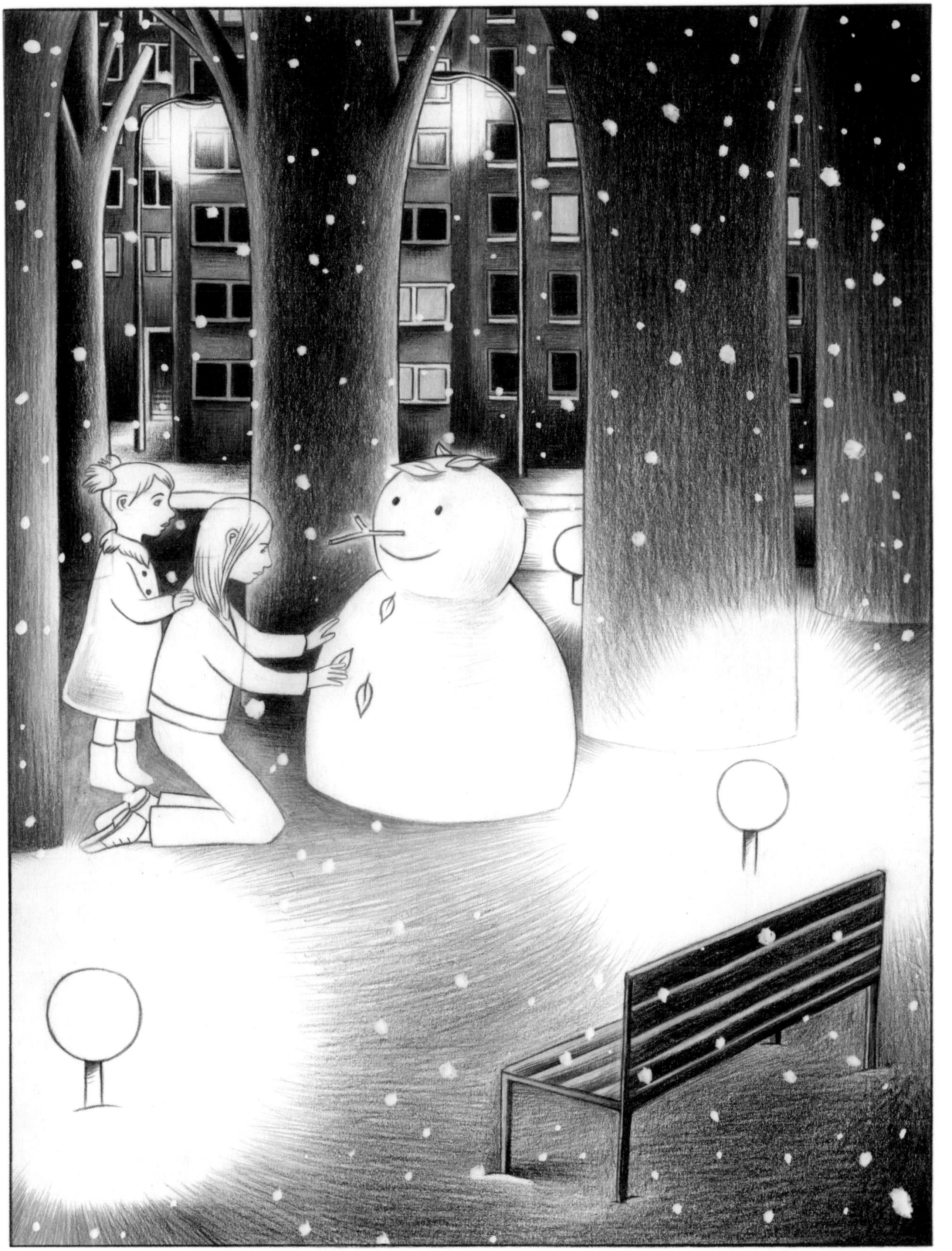

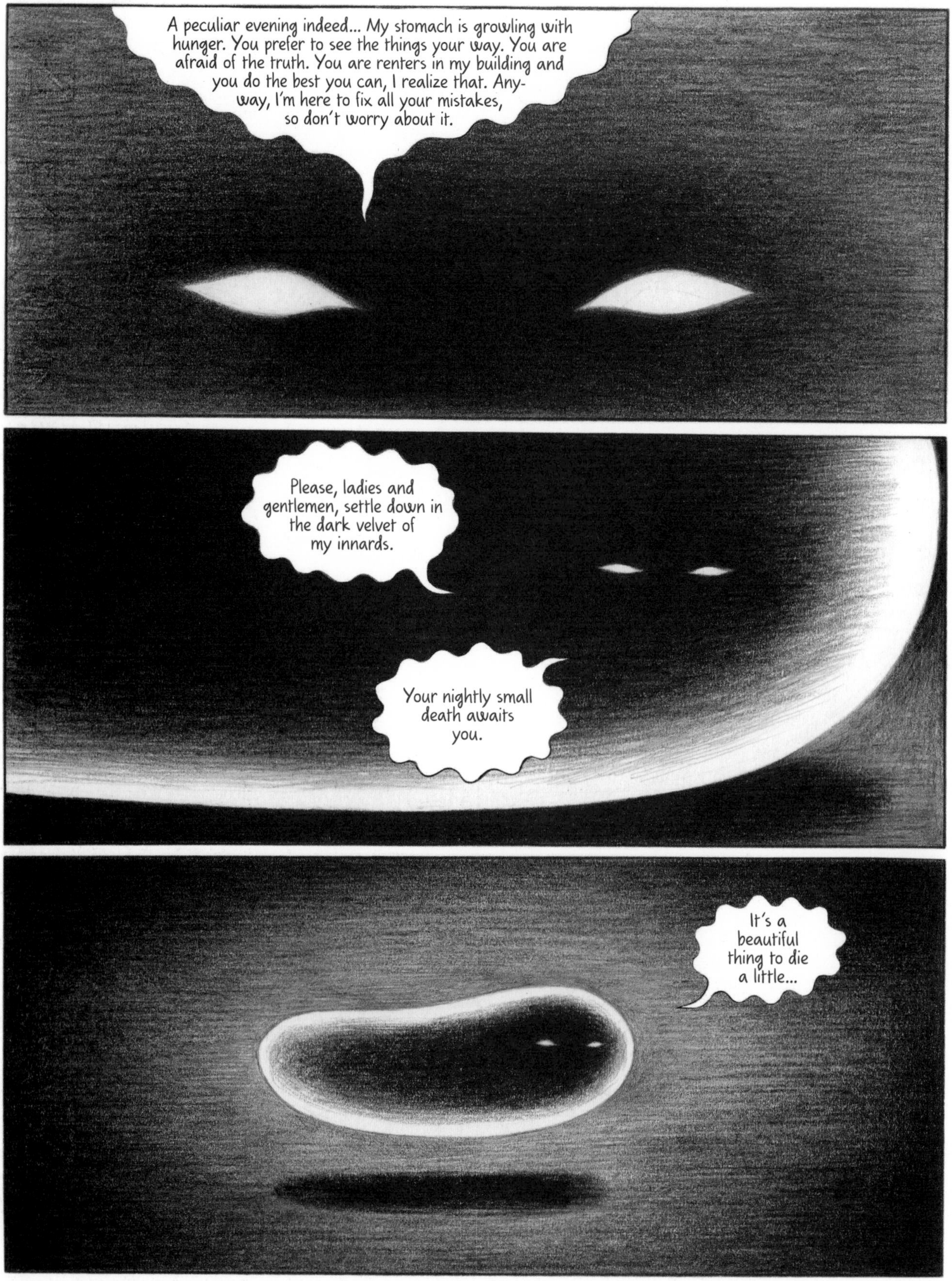
A peculiar evening indeed... My stomach is growling with hunger. You prefer to see the things your way. You are afraid of the truth. You are renters in my building and you do the best you can, I realize that. Anyway, I'm here to fix all your mistakes, so don't worry about it.
Please, ladies and gentlemen, settle down in the dark velvet of my innards.
Your nightly small death awaits you.
It's a beautiful thing to die a little...

WEDNESDAY, DECEMBER 20

---

04 hours, 15 minutes, 33 seconds

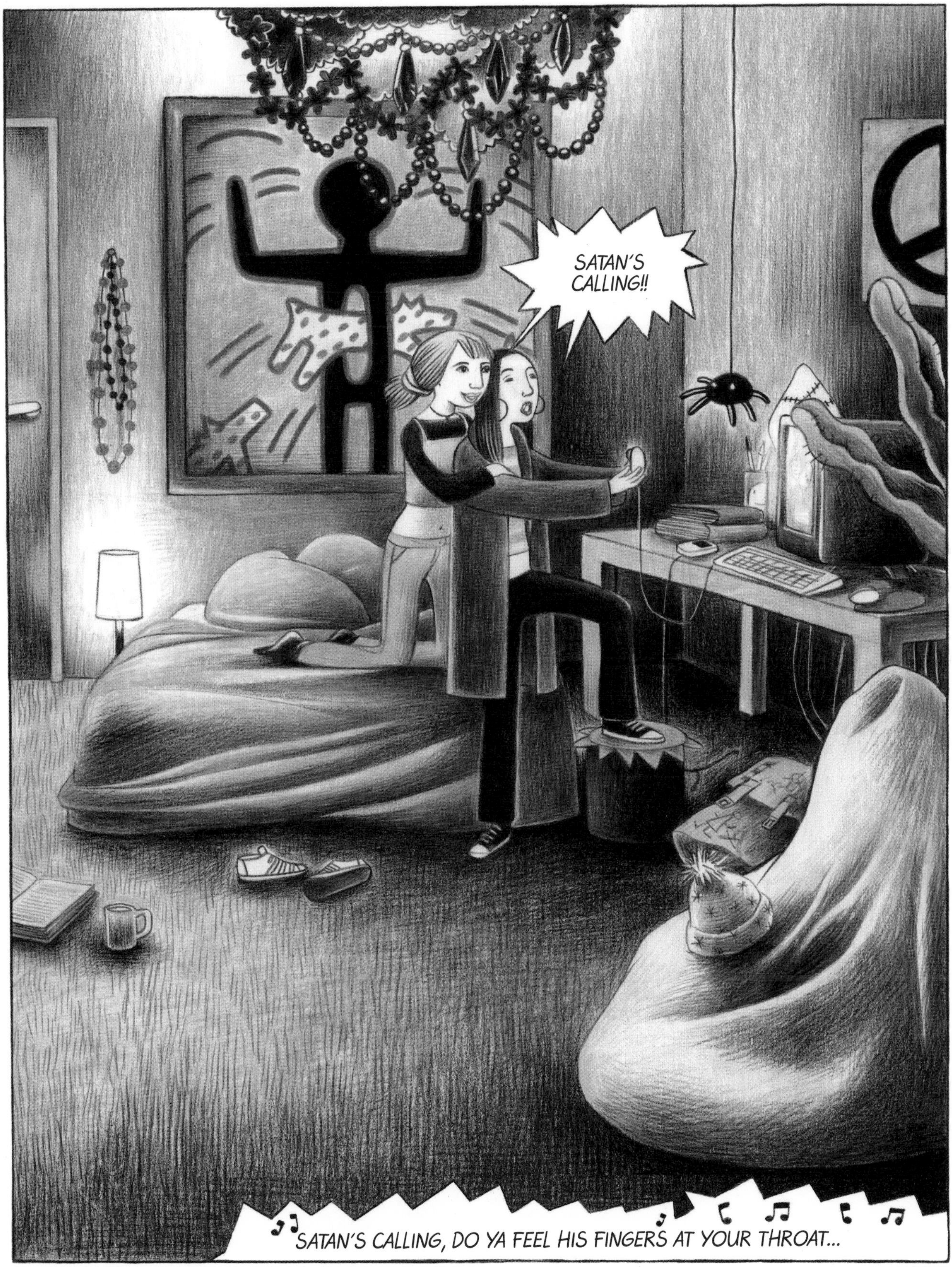
SATAN'S CALLING!!
SATAN'S CALLING, DO YA FEEL HIS FINGERS AT YOUR THROAT...

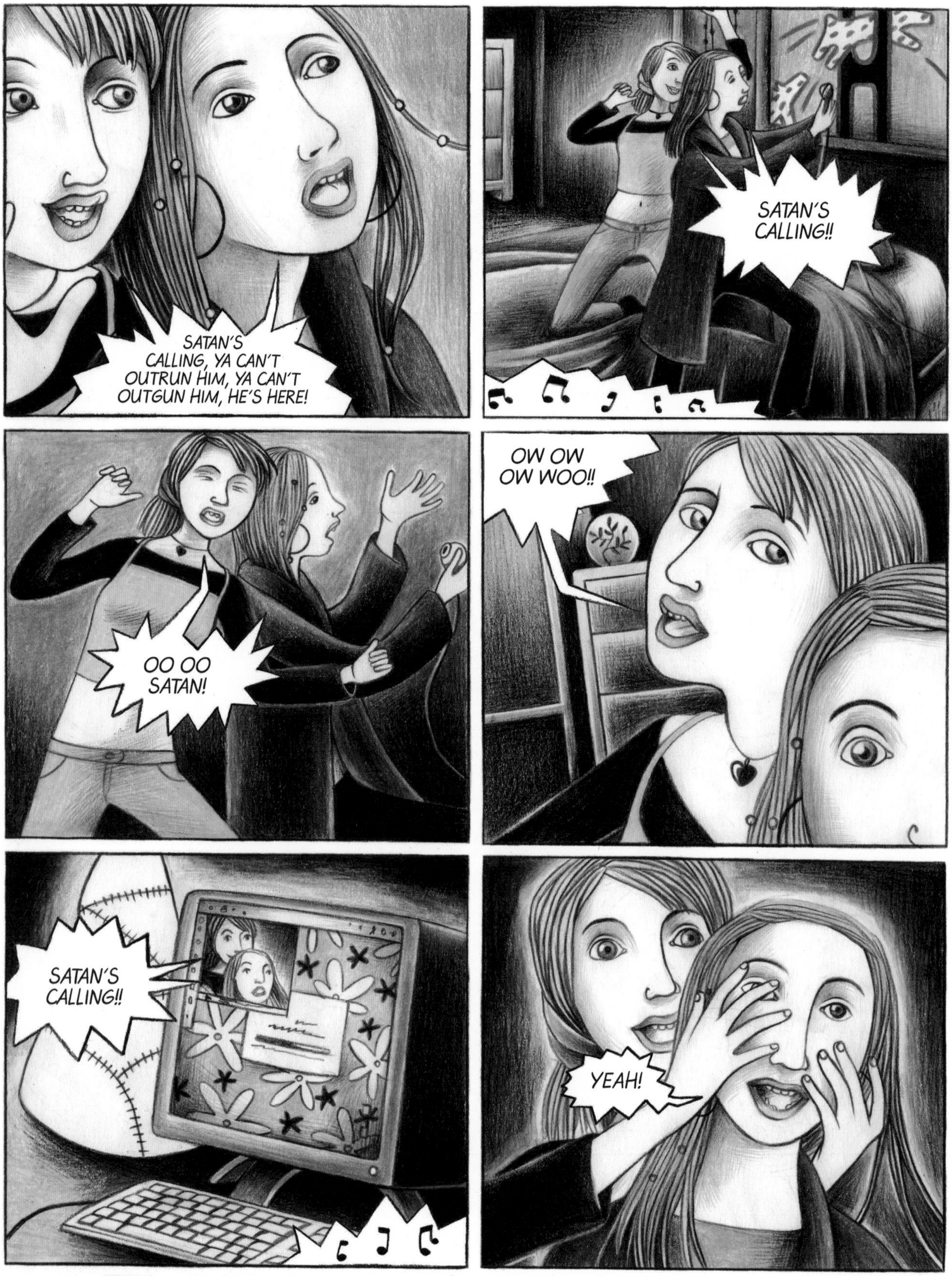
SATAN'S CALLING, YA CAN'T OUTRUN HIM, YA CAN'T OUTGUN HIM, HE'S HERE!
SATAN'S CALLING!!
OO OO SATAN!
OW OW OW WOO!!
SATAN'S CALLING!!
YEAH!

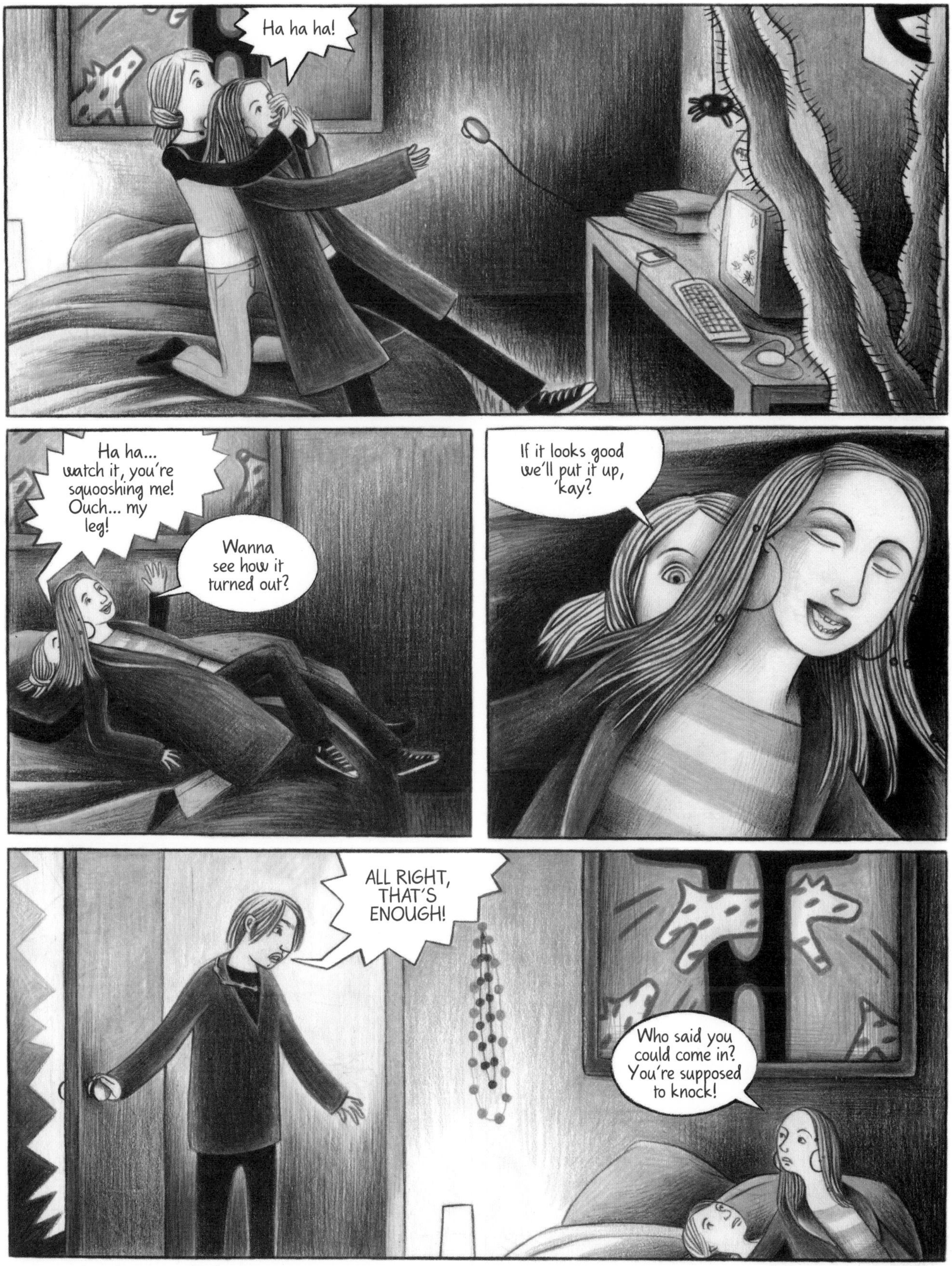
Ha ha ha!
Ha ha... watch it, you're squooshing me! Ouch... my leg!
Wanna see how it turned out?
If it looks good we'll put it up, 'kay?
ALL RIGHT, THAT'S ENOUGH!
Who said you could come in? You're supposed to knock!

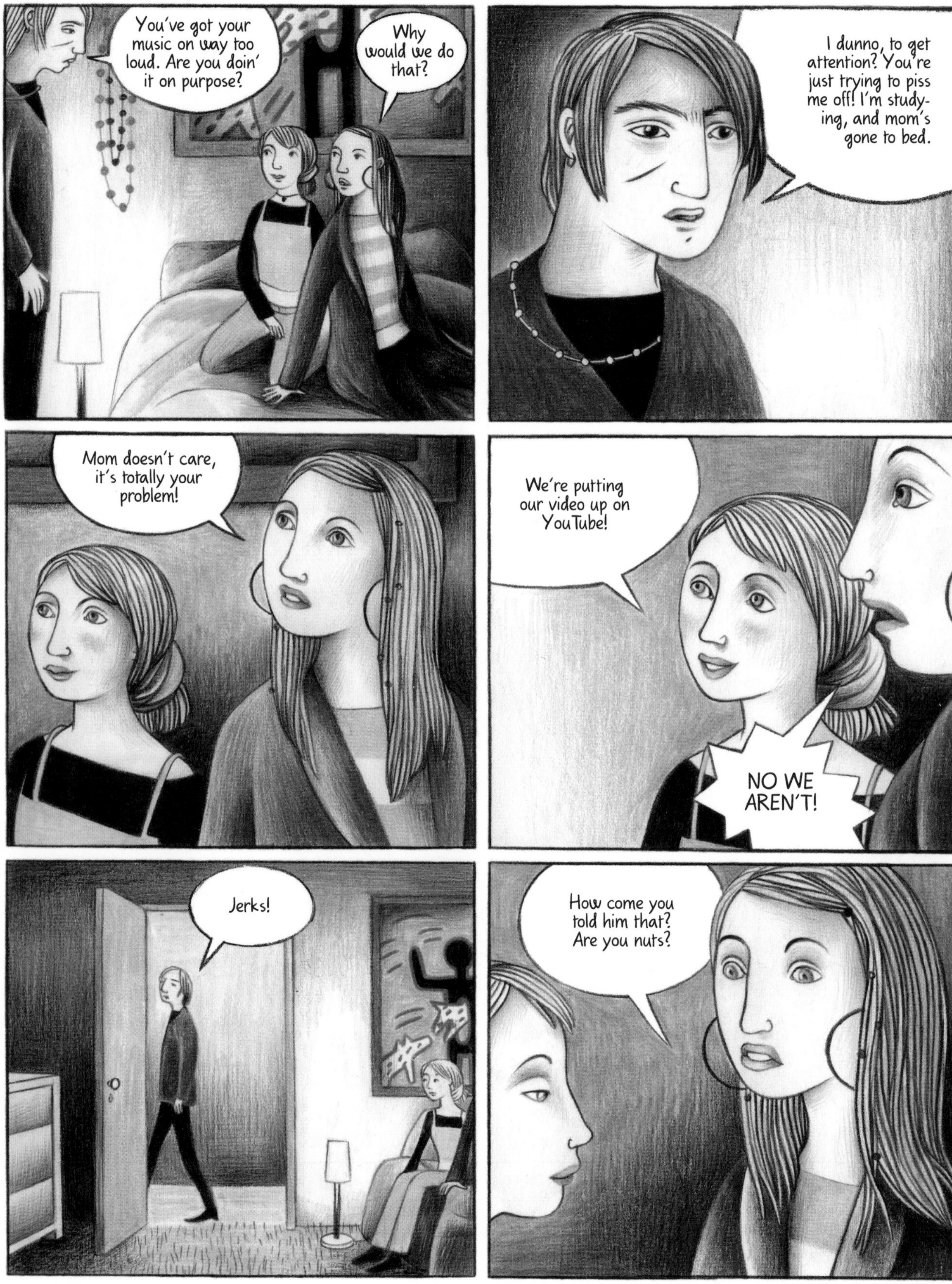

You've got your music on way too loud. Are you doin' it on purpose?
Why would we do that?
I dunno, to get attention? You're just trying to piss me off! I'm studying, and mom's gone to bed.
Mom doesn't care, it's totally your problem!
We're putting our video up on YouTube!
NO WE AREN'T!
Jerks!
How come you told him that? Are you nuts?

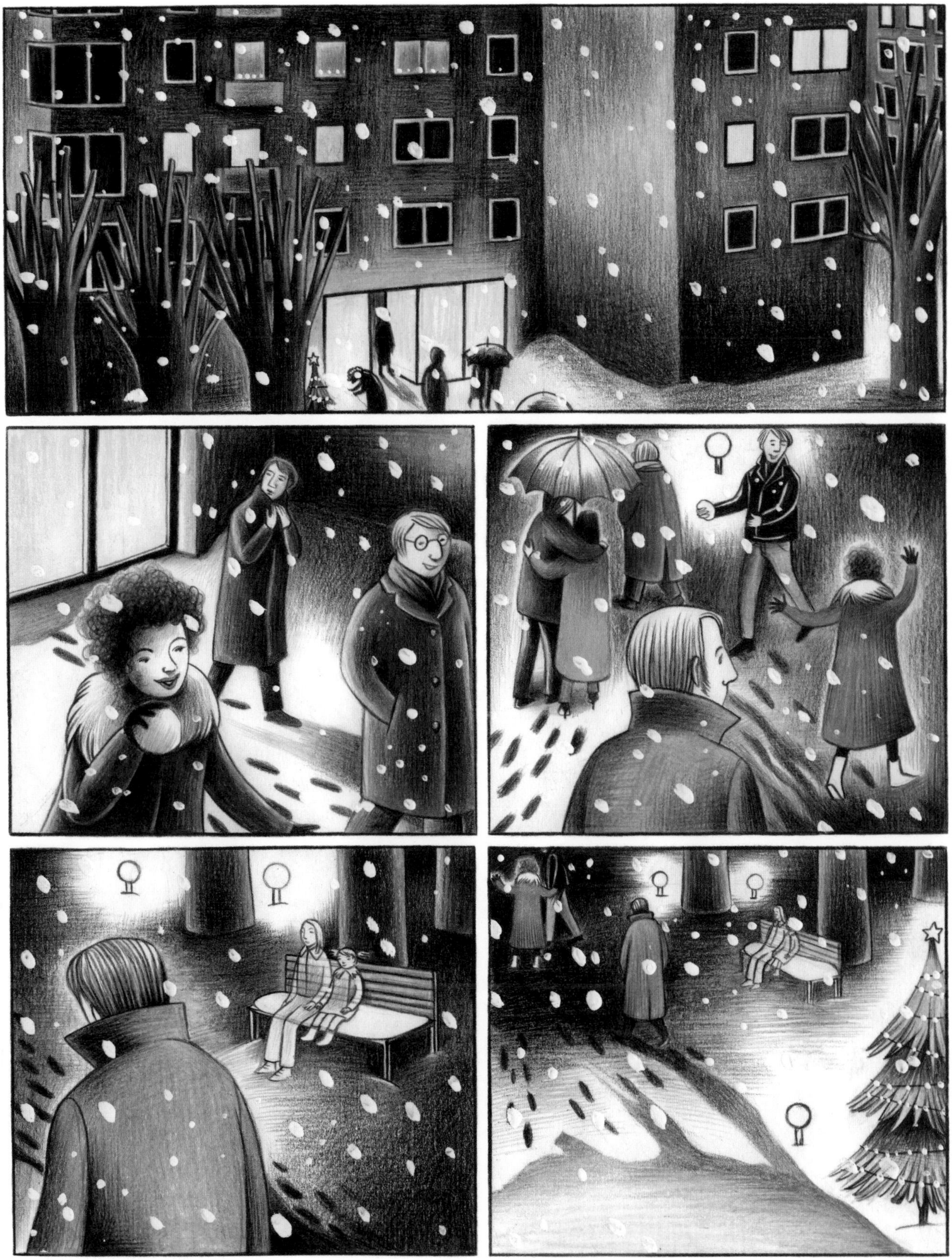

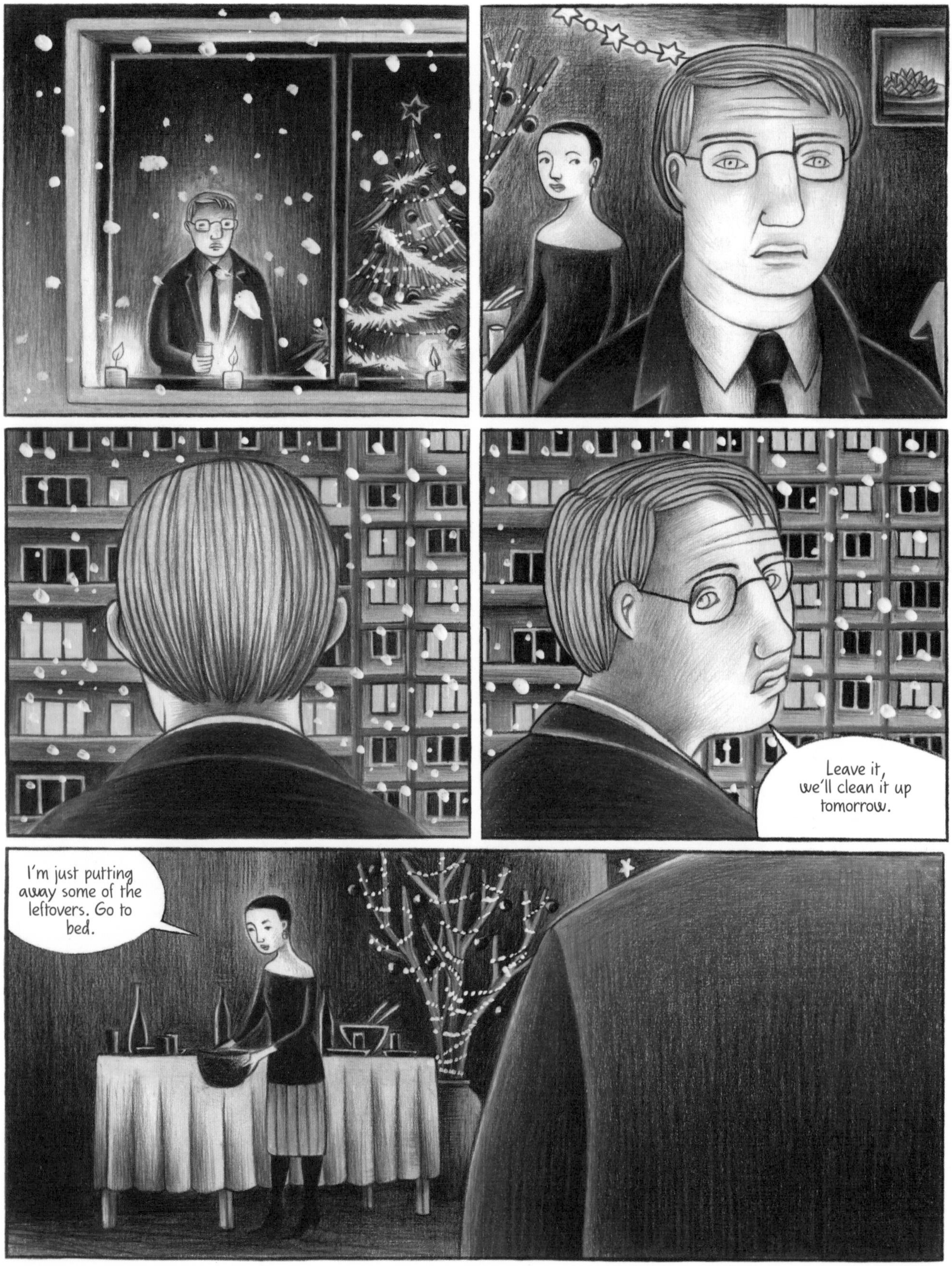
Leave it, we'll clean it up tomorrow.
I'm just putting away some of the leftovers. Go to bed.

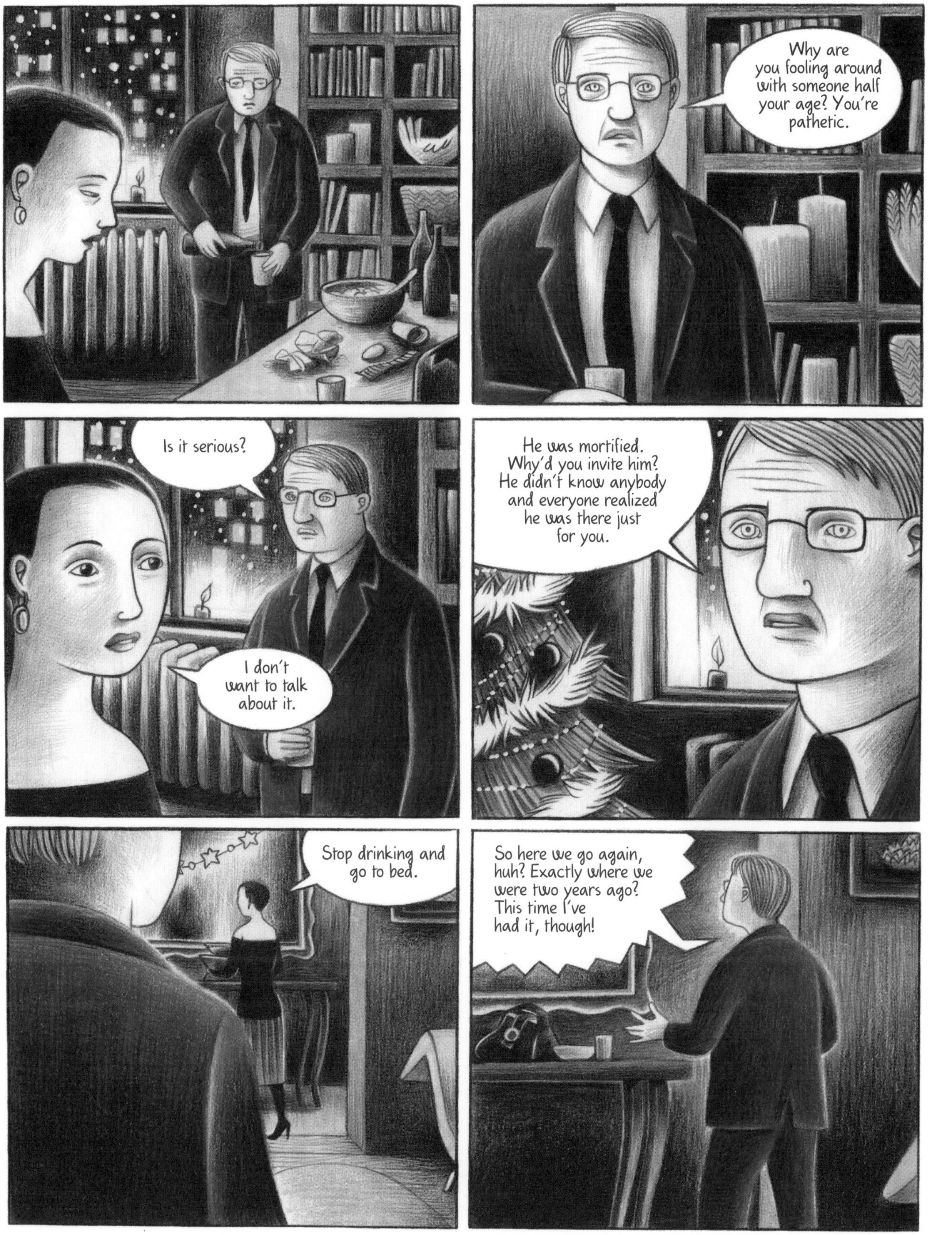

Why are you fooling around with someone half your age? You're pathetic.
Is it serious?
I don't want to talk about it.
He was mortified. Why'd you invite him? He didn't know anybody and everyone realized he was there just for you.
Stop drinking and go to bed.
So here we go again, huh? Exactly where we were two years ago? This time I've had it, though!

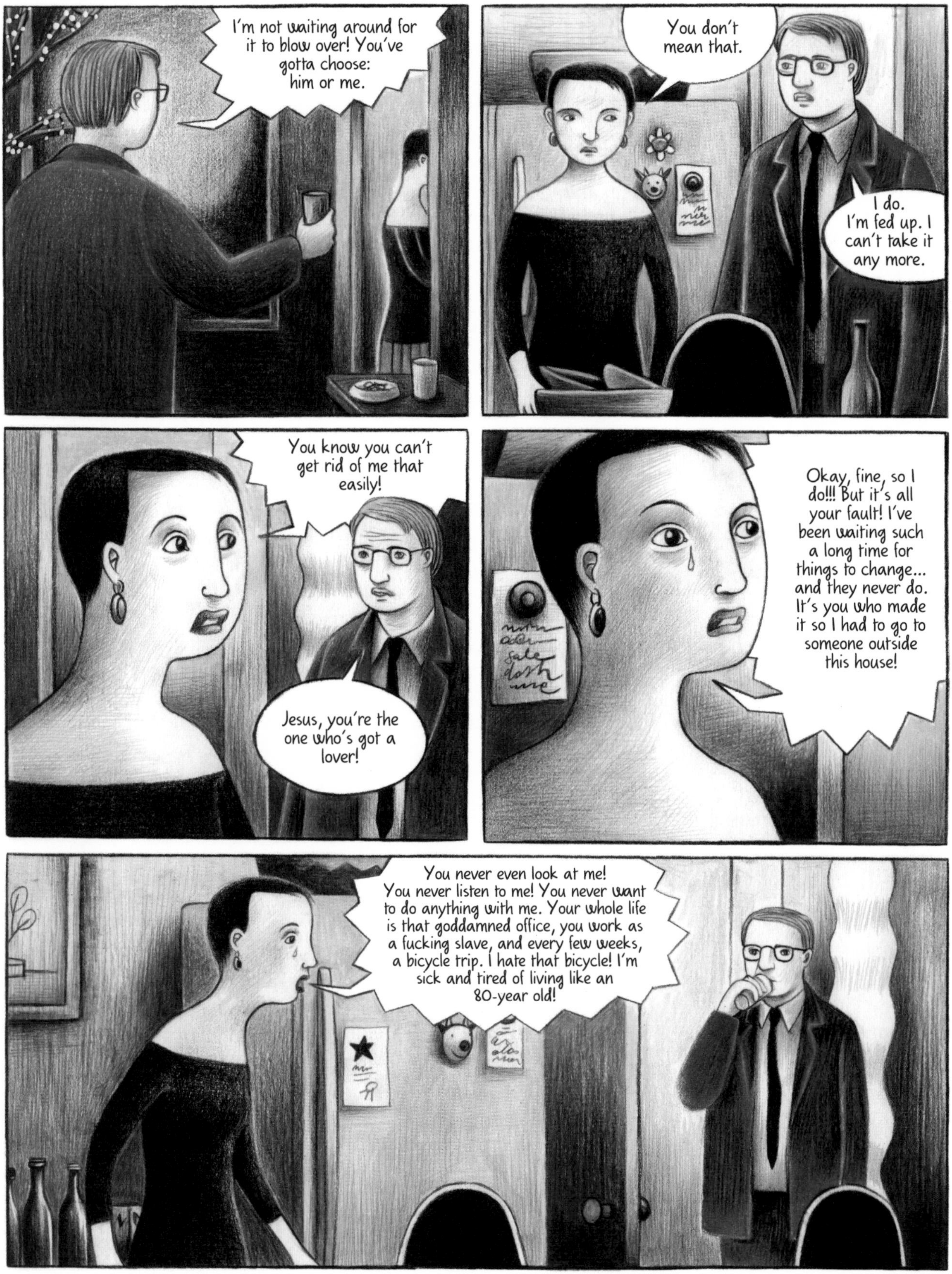
I'm not waiting around for it to blow over! You've gotta choose: him or me.
You don't mean that.
I do. I'm fed up. I can't take it any more.
You know you can't get rid of me that easily!
Jesus, you're the one who's got a lover!
Okay, fine, so I do!!! But it's all your fault! I've been waiting such a long time for things to change... and they never do. It's you who made it so I had to go to someone outside this house!
You never even look at me! You never listen to me! You never want to do anything with me. Your whole life is that goddamned office, you work as a fucking slave, and every few weeks, a bicycle trip. I hate that bicycle! I'm sick and tired of living like an 80-year old!

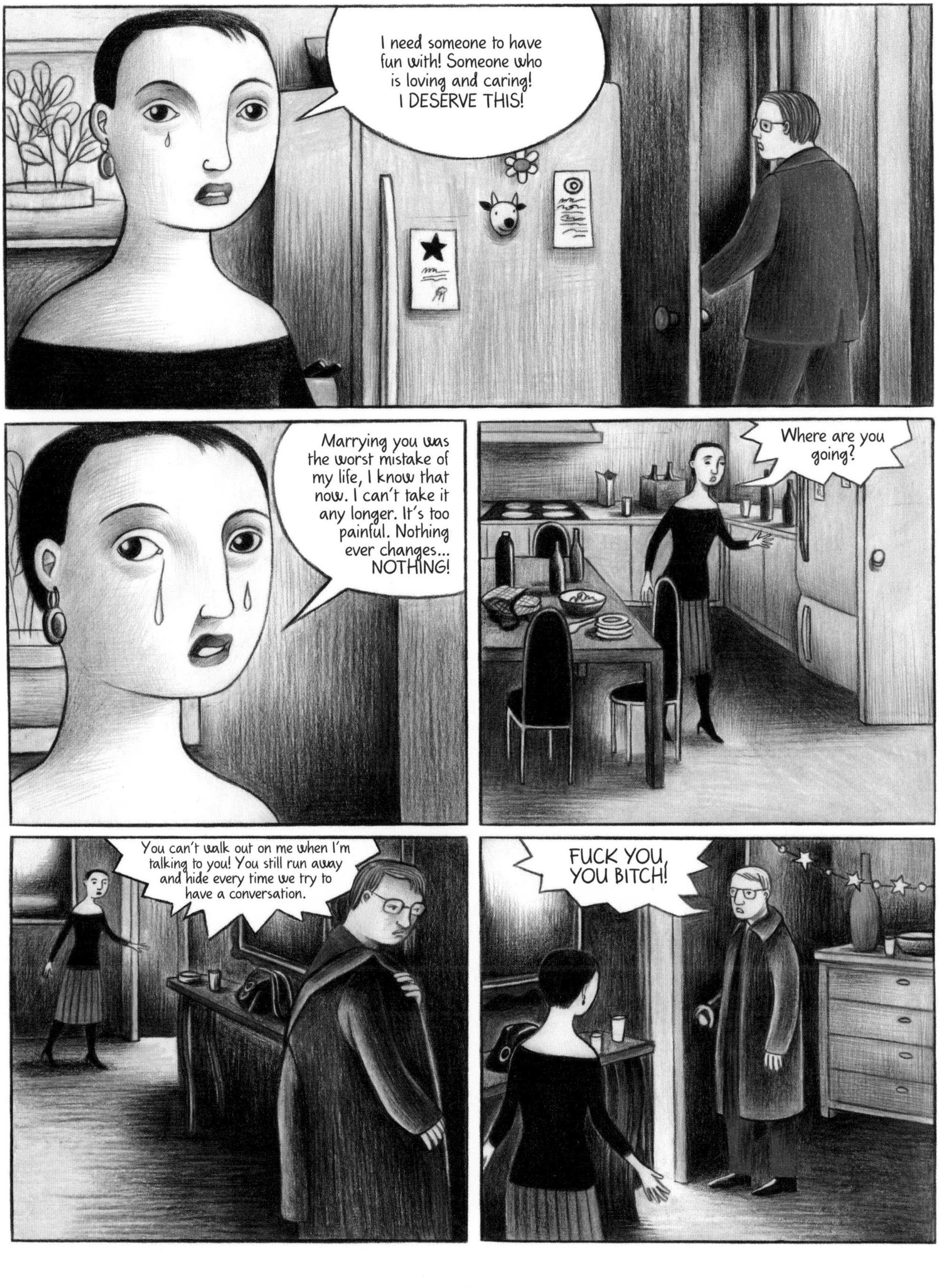
I need someone to have fun with! Someone who is loving and caring! I DESERVE THIS!
Marrying you was the worst mistake of my life, I know that now. I can't take it any longer. It's too painful. Nothing ever changes... NOTHING!
Where are you going?
You can't walk out on me when I'm talking to you! You still run away and hide every time we try to have a conversation.
FUCK YOU, YOU BITCH!

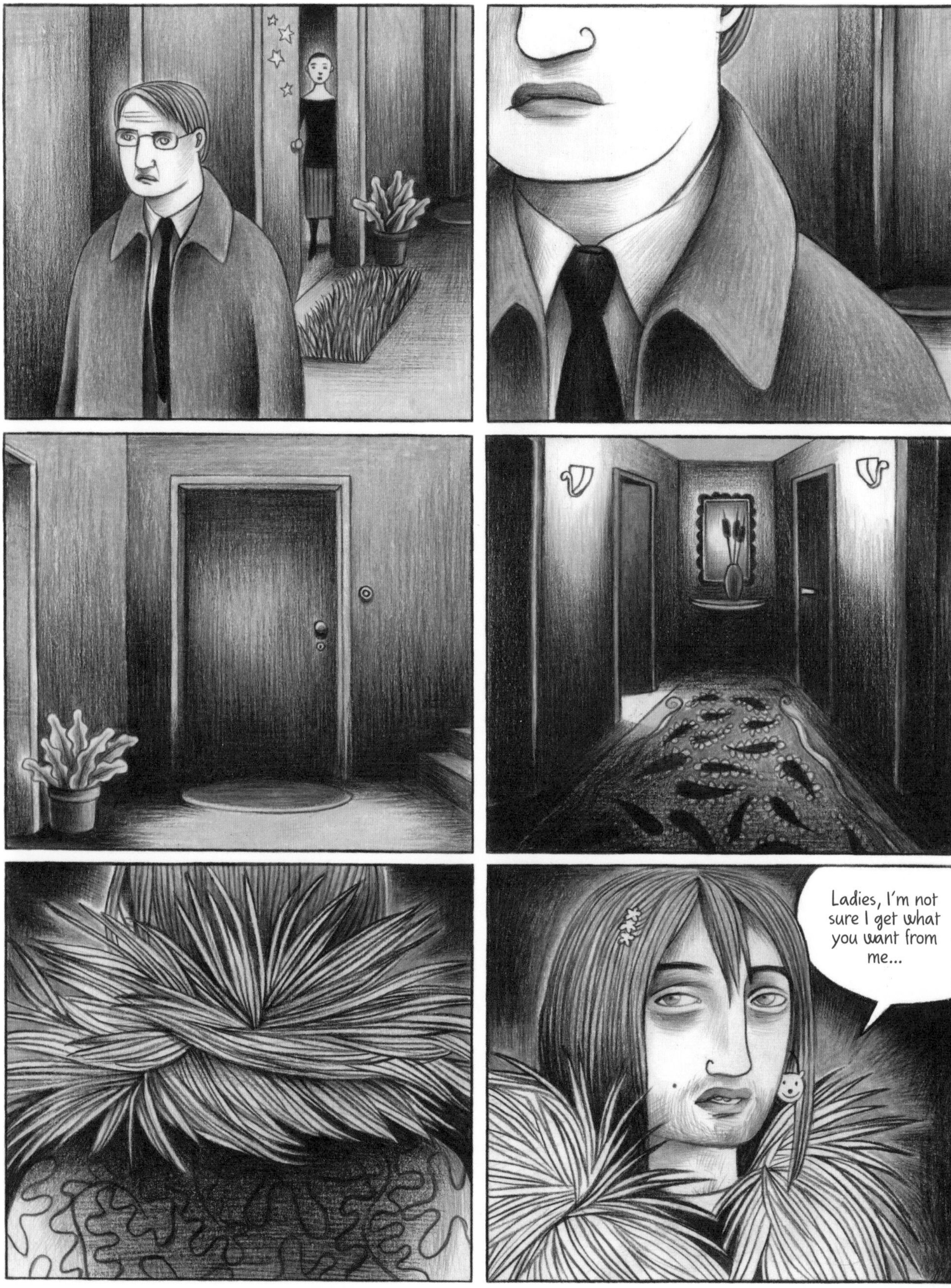
Ladies, I'm not sure I get what you want from me...

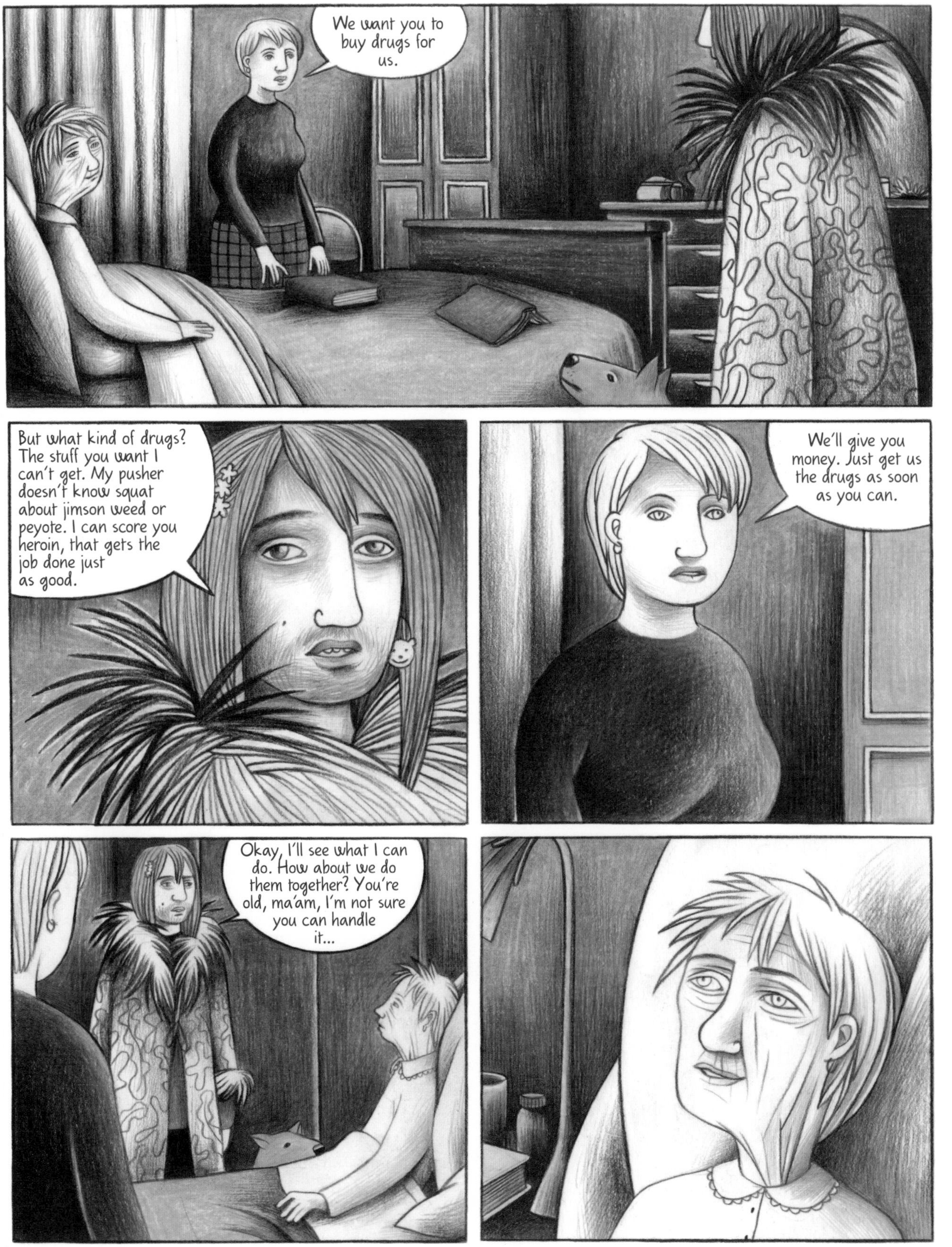

We want you to buy drugs for us.
But what kind of drugs? The stuff you want I can't get. My pusher doesn't know squat about jimson weed or peyote. I can score you heroin, that gets the job done just as good.
We'll give you money. Just get us the drugs as soon as you can.
Okay, I'll see what I can do. How about we do them together? You're old, ma'am, I'm not sure you can handle it...

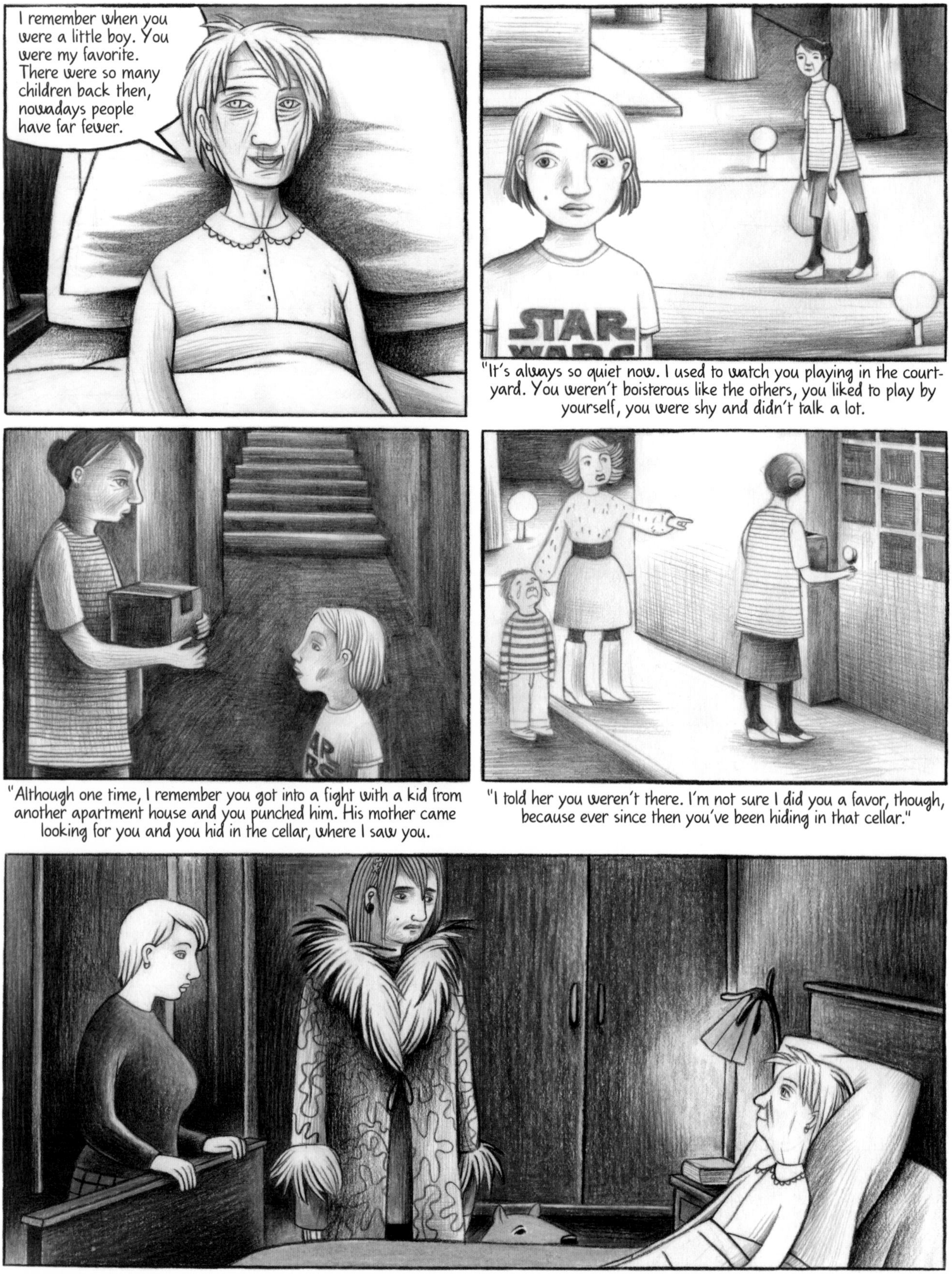
I remember when you were a little boy. You were my favorite. There were so many children back then, nowadays people have far fewer.
STAR WARS
"It's always so quiet now. I used to watch you playing in the courtyard. You weren't boisterous like the others, you liked to play by yourself, you were shy and didn't talk a lot.
"Although one time, I remember you got into a fight with a kid from another apartment house and you punched him. His mother came looking for you and you hid in the cellar, where I saw you.
"I told her you weren't there. I'm not sure I did you a favor, though, because ever since then you've been hiding in that cellar."

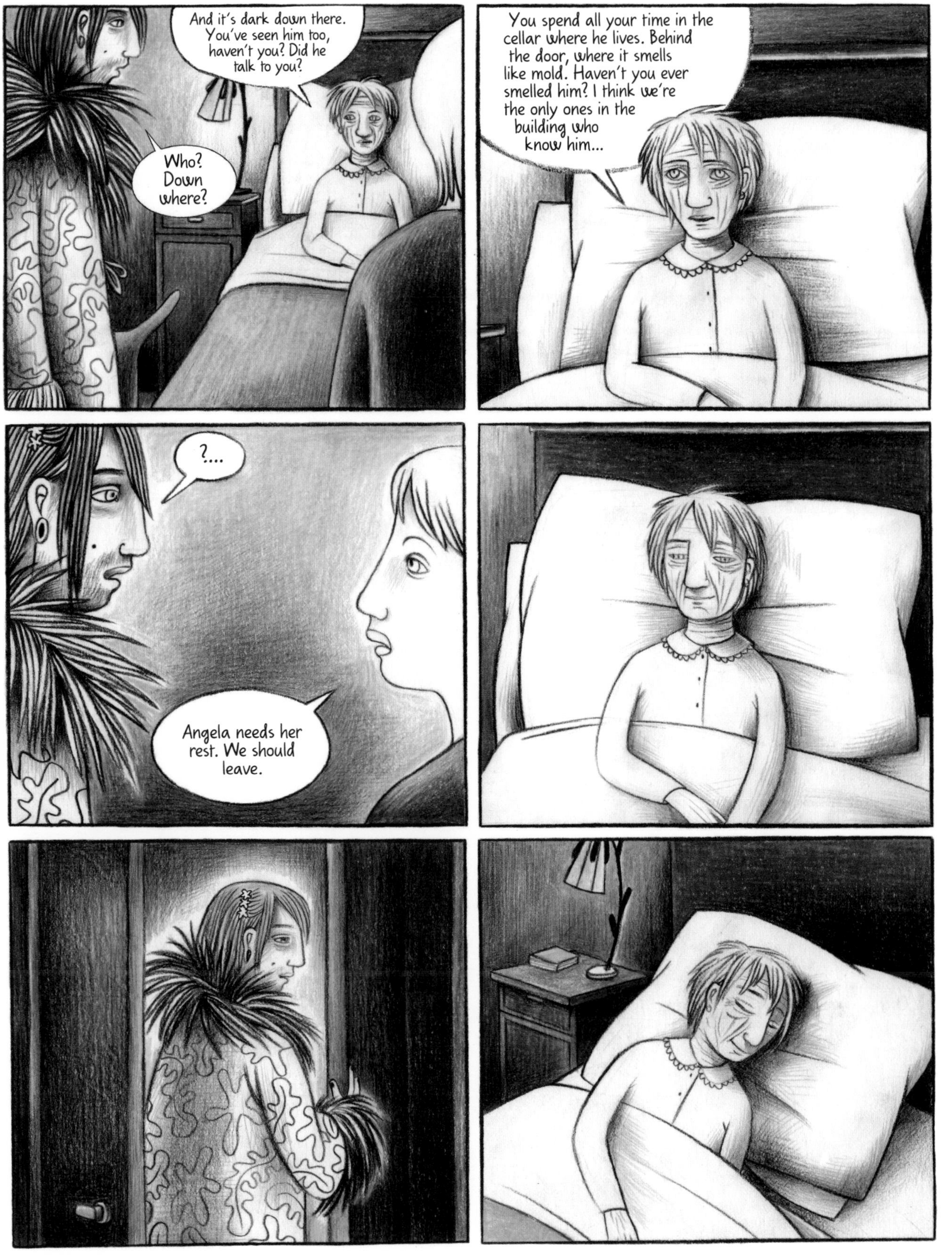
And it's dark down there. You've seen him too, haven't you? Did he talk to you?
Who? Down where?
You spend all your time in the cellar where he lives. Behind the door, where it smells like mold. Haven't you ever smelled him? I think we're the only ones in the building who know him...
?....
Angela needs her rest. We should leave.

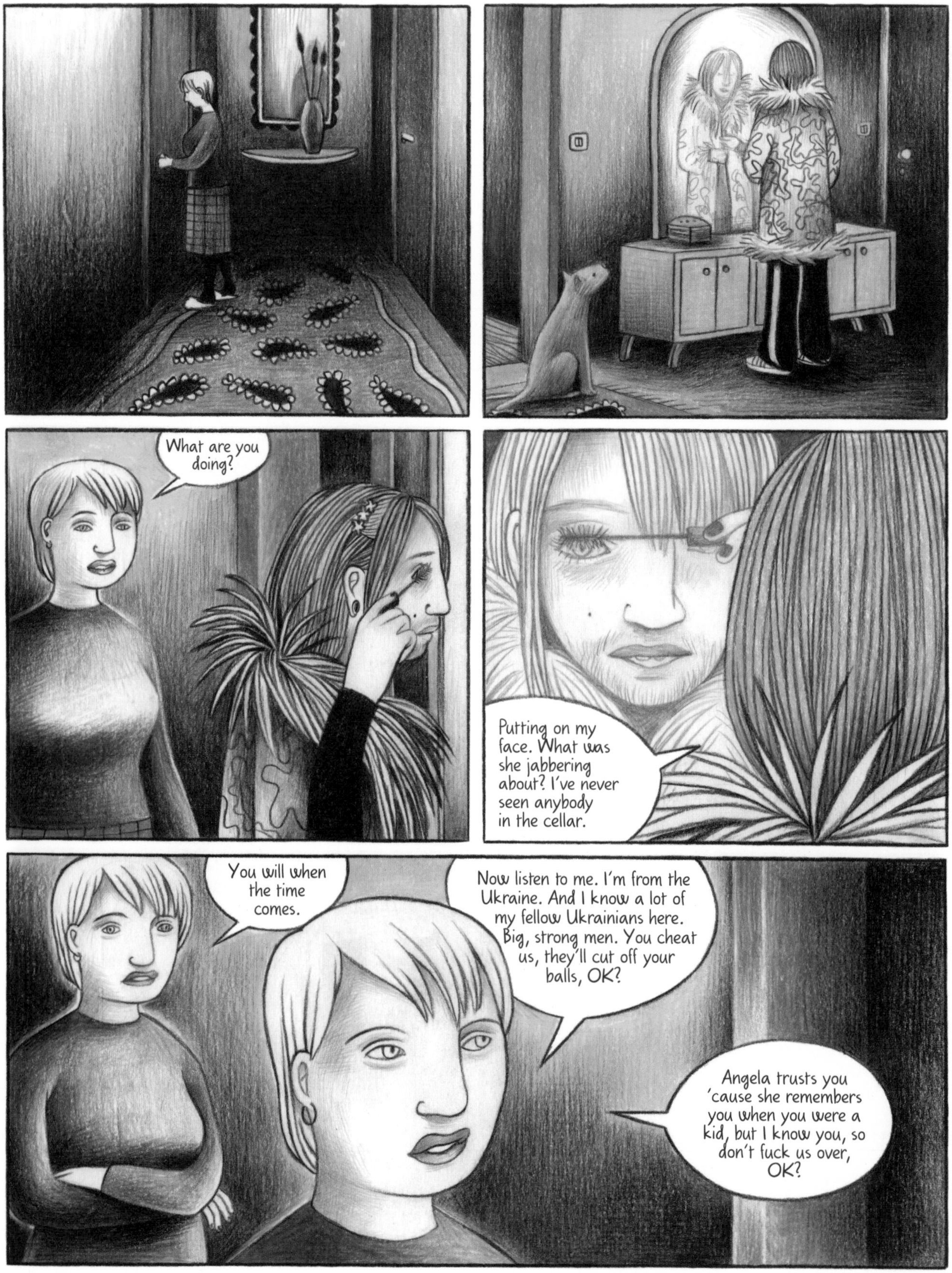
What are you doing?
Putting on my face. What was she jabbering about? I've never seen anybody in the cellar.
You will when the time comes.
Now listen to me. I'm from the Ukraine. And I know a lot of my fellow Ukrainians here. Big, strong men. You cheat us, they'll cut off your balls, OK?
Angela trusts you 'cause she remembers you when you were a kid, but I know you, so don't fuck us over, OK?

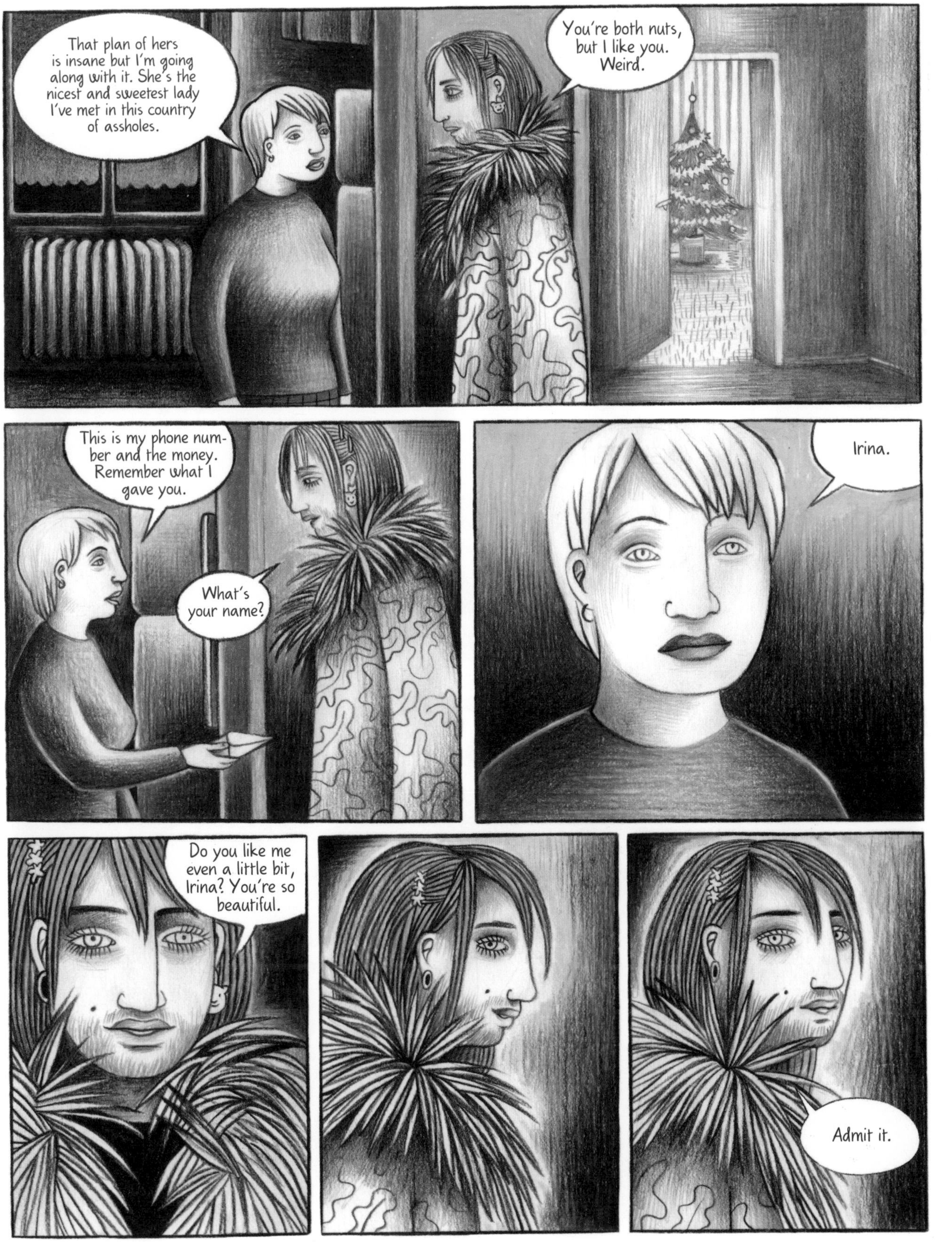
That plan of hers is insane but I'm going along with it. She's the nicest and sweetest lady I've met in this country of assholes.
You're both nuts, but I like you. Weird.
This is my phone number and the money. Remember what I gave you.
What's your name?
Irina.
Do you like me even a little bit, Irina? You're so beautiful.
Admit it.

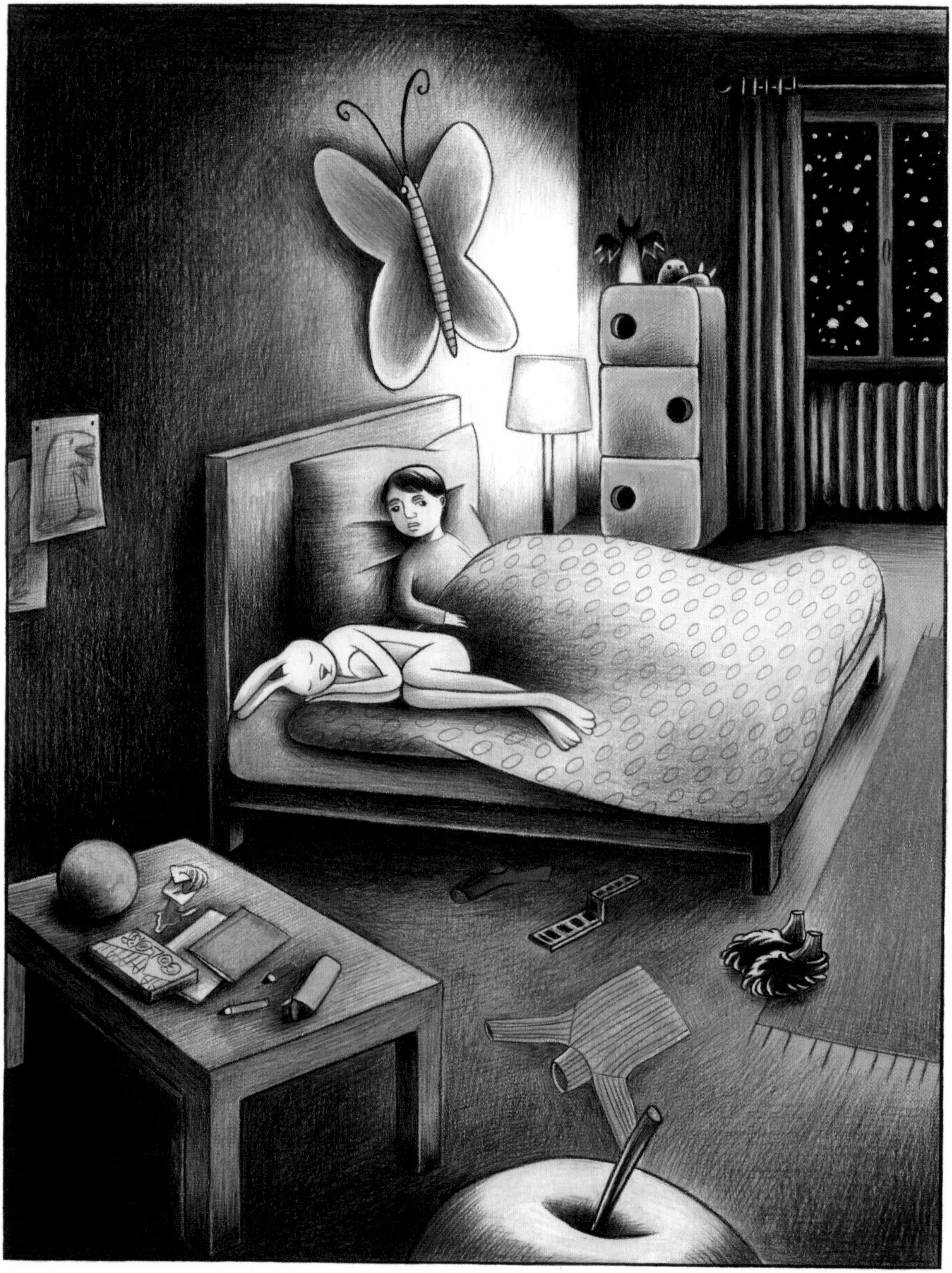

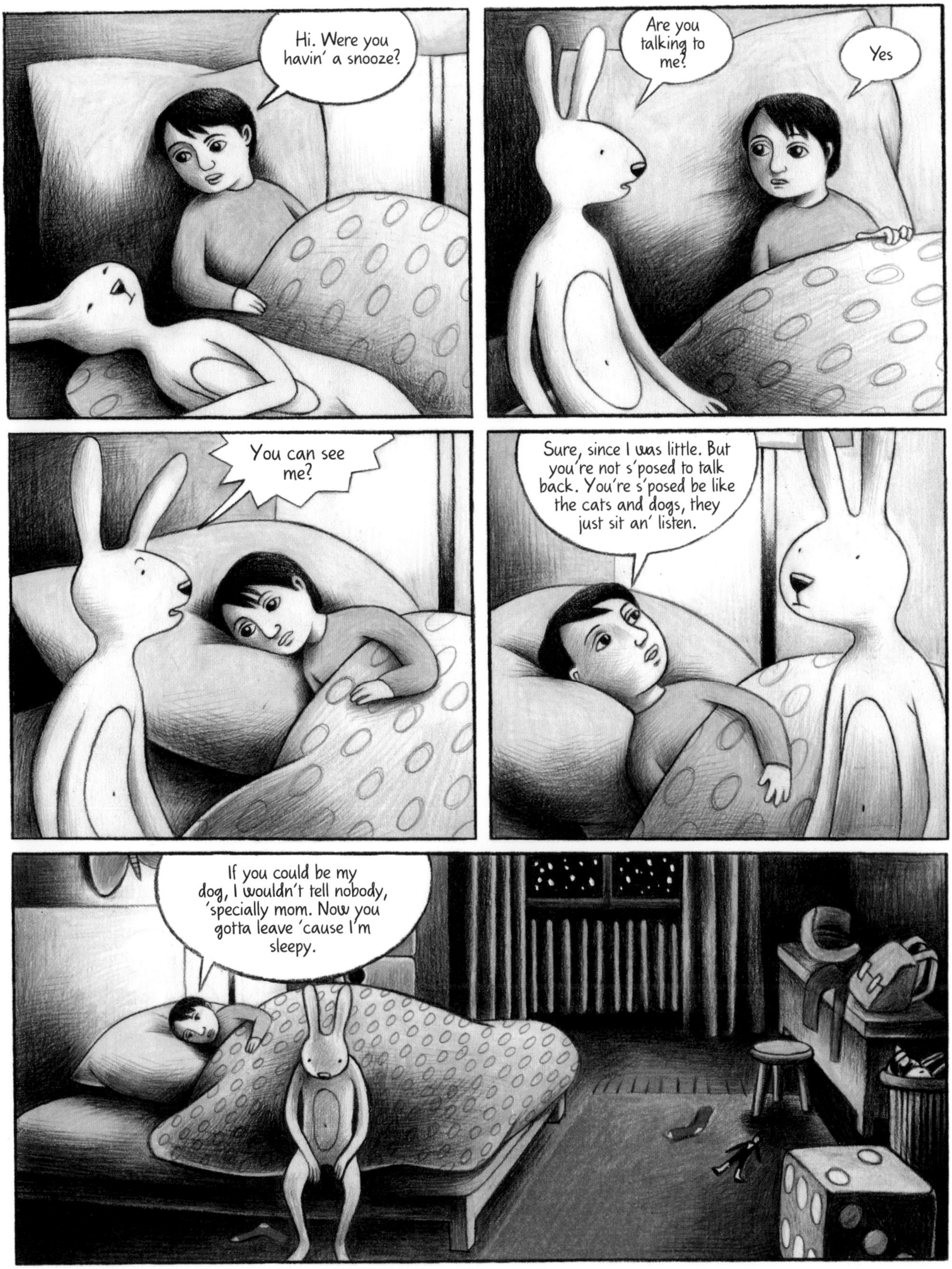
Hi. Were you havin' a snooze?
Are you talking to me?
Yes
You can see me?
Sure, since I was little. But you're not s'posed to talk back. You're s'posed be like the cats and dogs, they just sit an' listen.
If you could be my dog, I wouldn't tell nobody, 'specially mom. Now you gotta leave 'cause I'm sleepy.

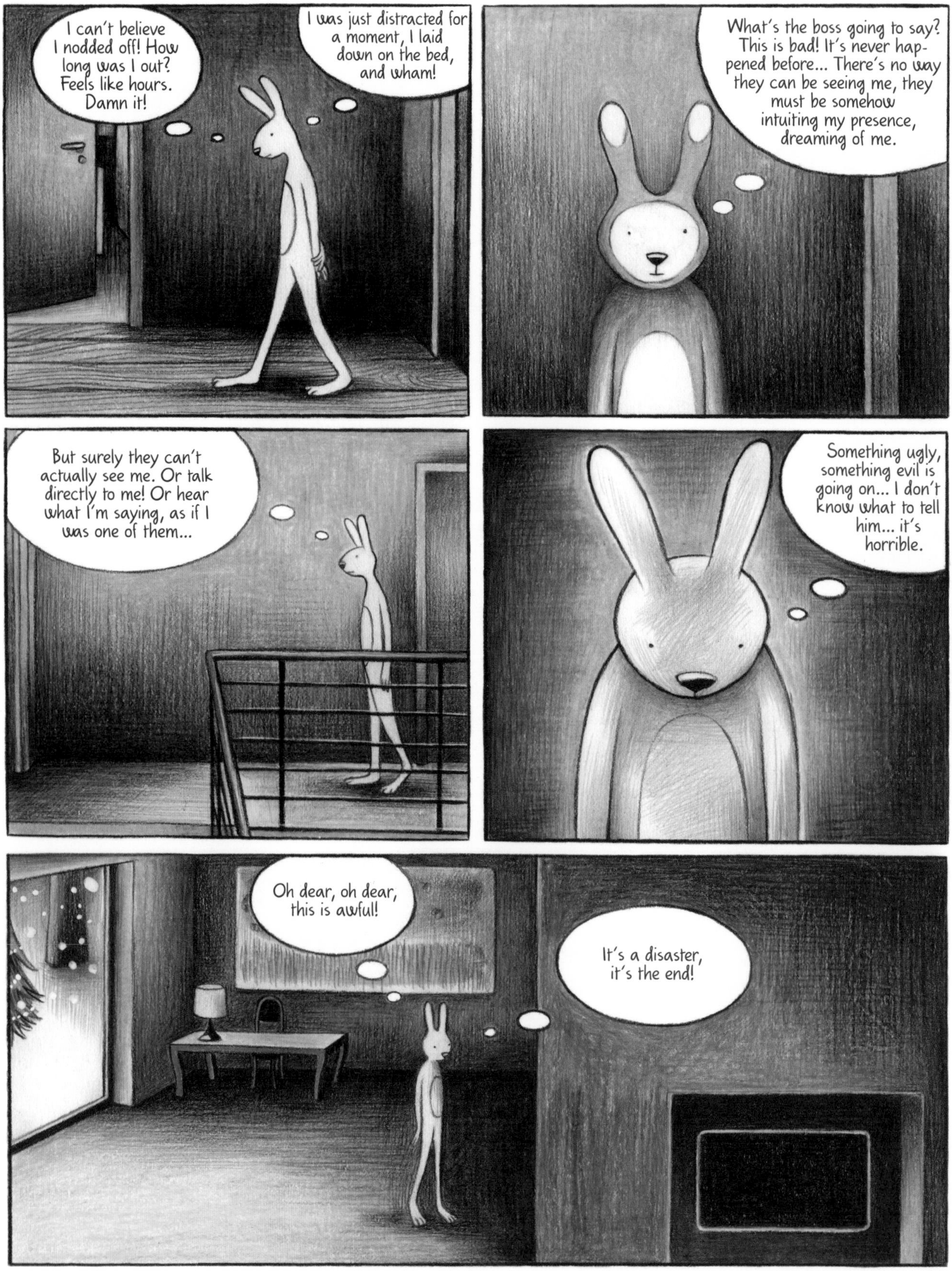
I can't believe I nodded off! How long was I out? Feels like hours. Damn it!
I was just distracted for a moment, I laid down on the bed, and wham!
What's the boss going to say? This is bad! It's never happened before... There's no way they can be seeing me, they must be somehow intuiting my presence, dreaming of me.
But surely they can't actually see me. Or talk directly to me! Or hear what I'm saying, as if I was one of them...
Something ugly, something evil is going on... I don't know what to tell him... it's horrible.
Oh dear, oh dear, this is awful!
It's a disaster, it's the end!

Yes, darling. I lost track of the time too. I miss you so much!

Uh... no, tonight's no good for me. My girlfriend Lisa is coming over. Remember her? I told you about Lisa. So when exactly does your wife leave?

Oh, I bought these rockin' shoes. I got them for when I see you on Thursday. You're gonna love 'em. They're really hot.

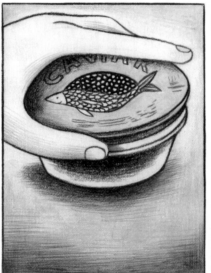

Okay then, good night. I miss you so much, you can't imagine.

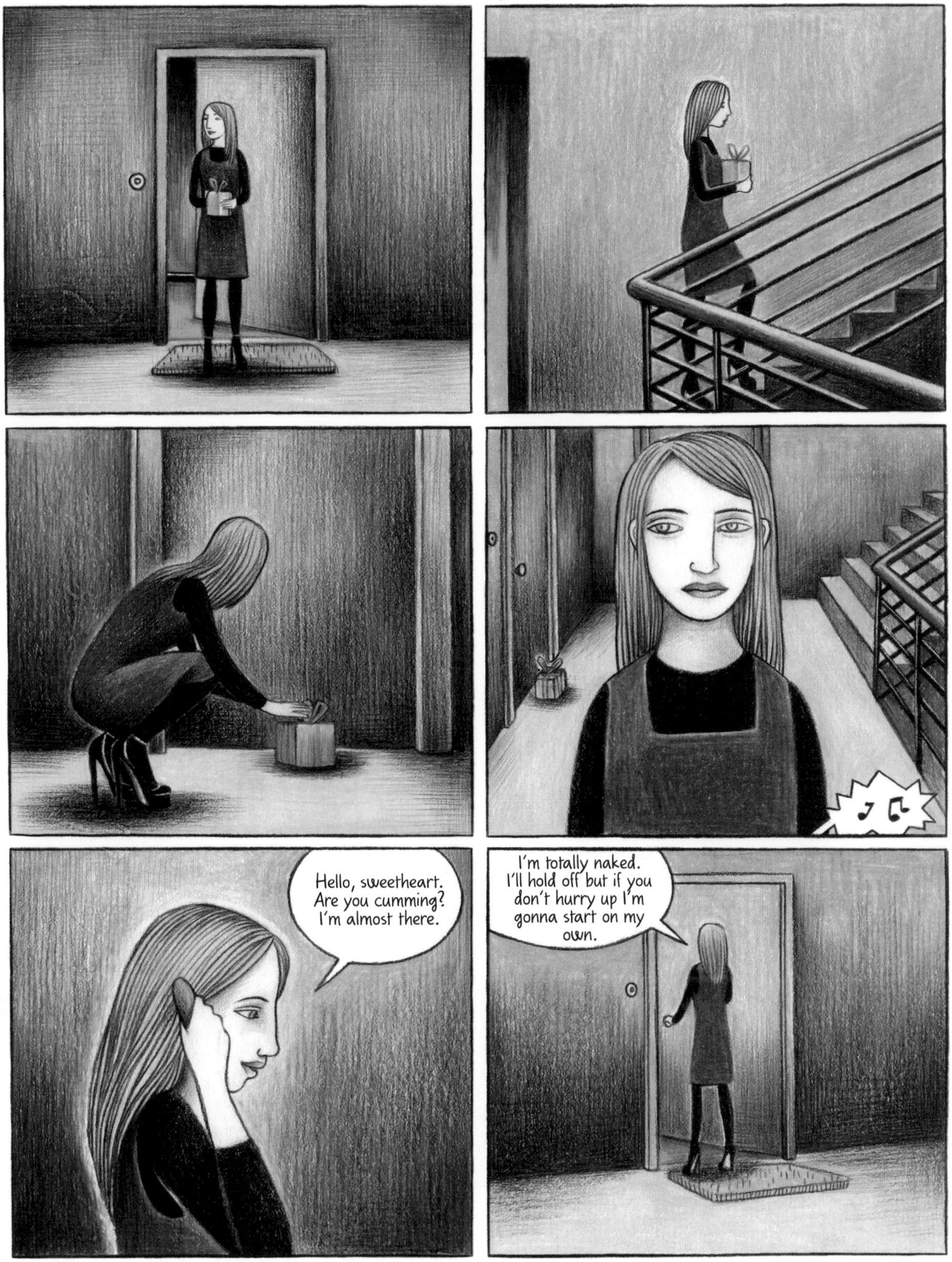
Hello, sweetheart. Are you cumming? I'm almost there.
I'm totally naked. I'll hold off but if you don't hurry up I'm gonna start on my own.

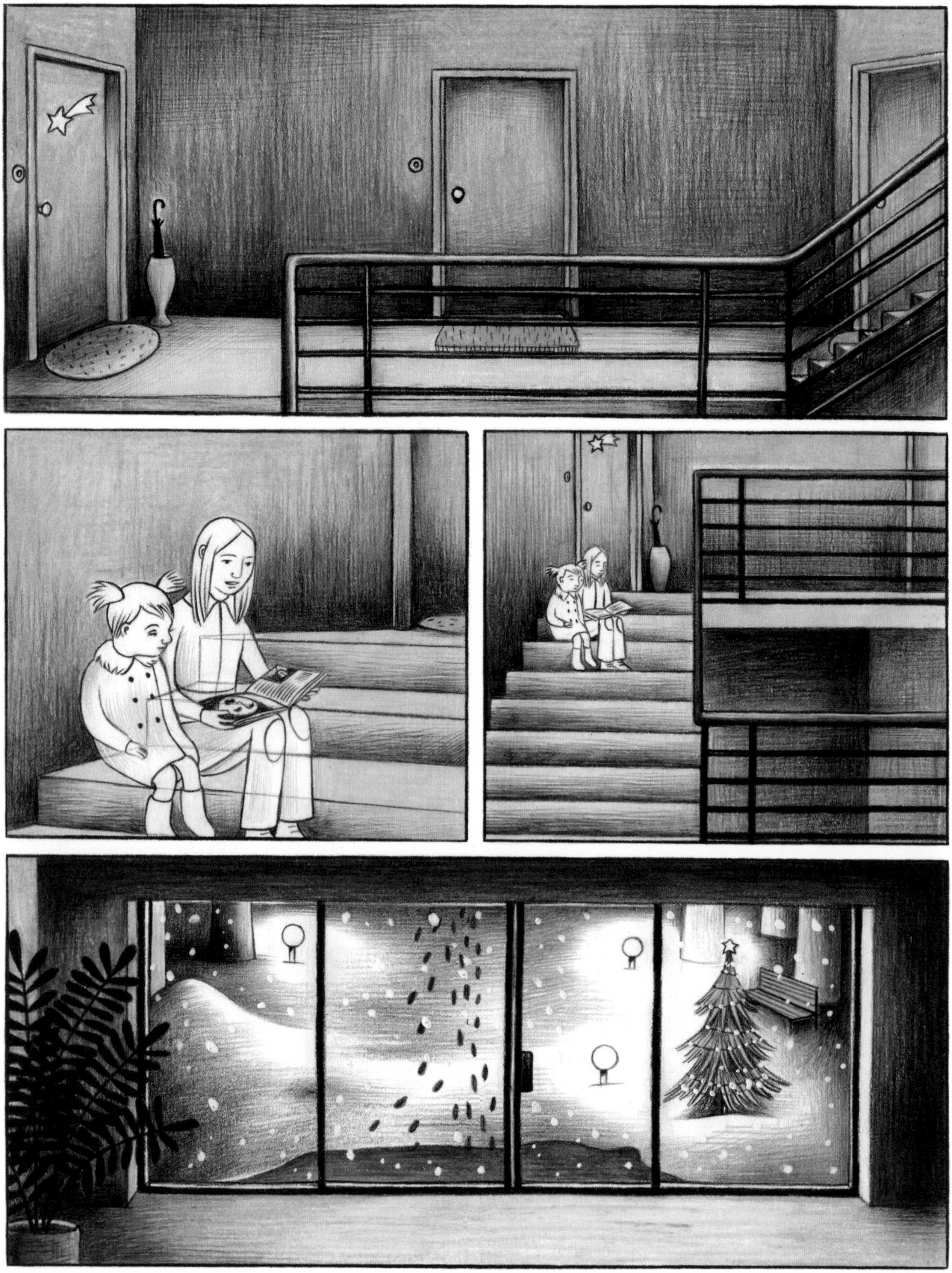

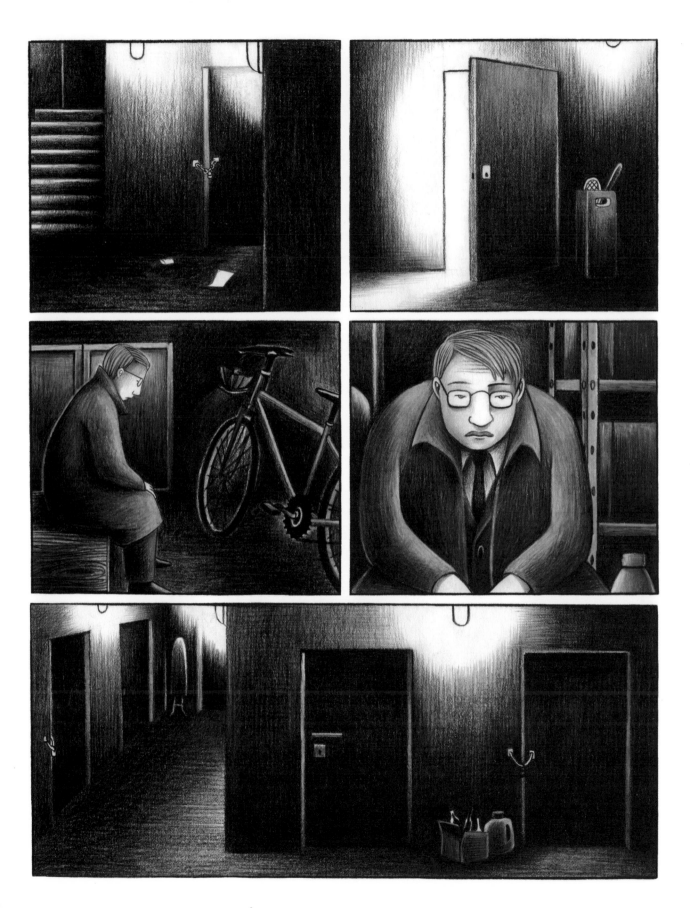

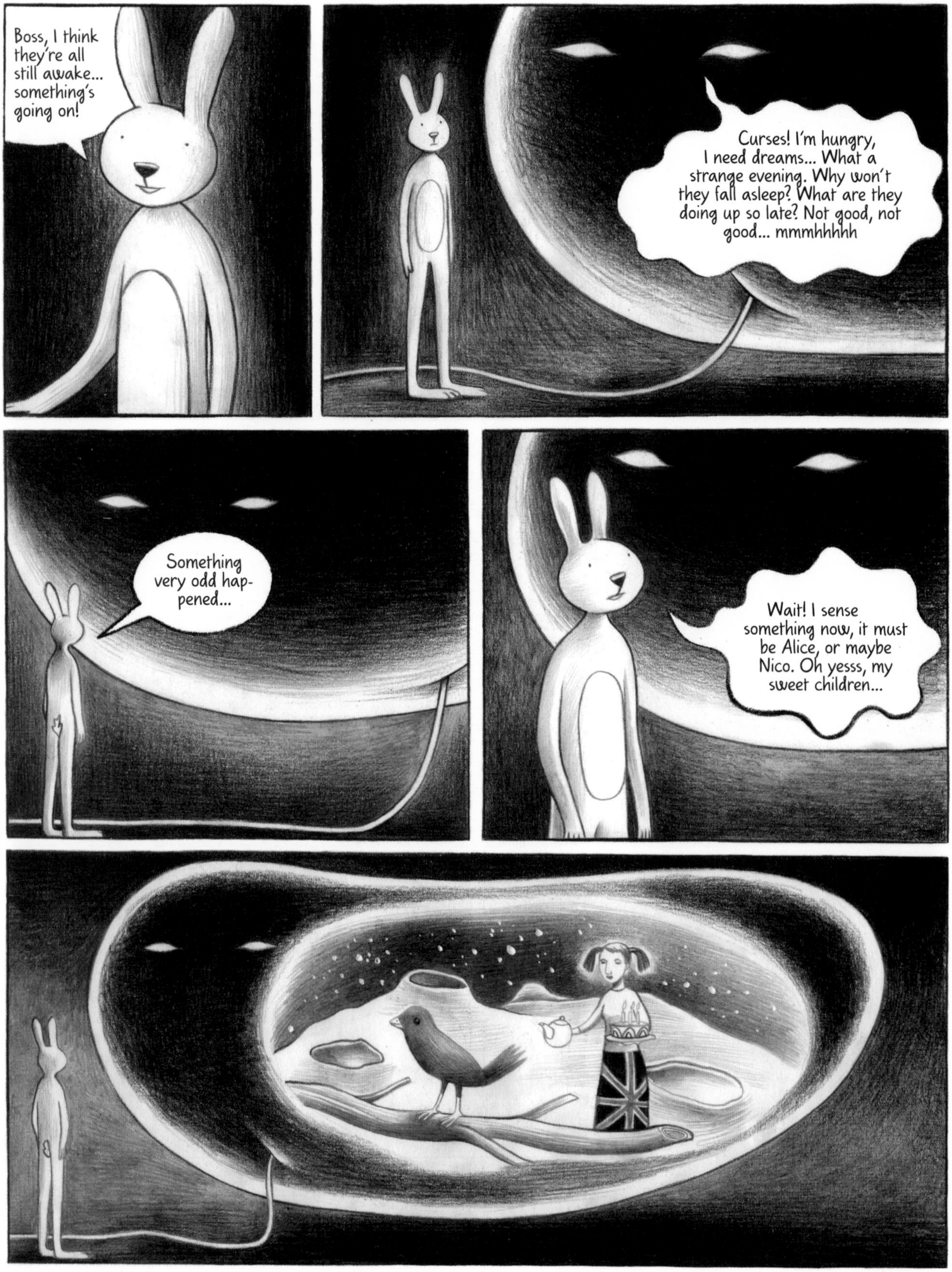

Boss, I think they're all still awake... something's going on!
Curses! I'm hungry, I need dreams... What a strange evening. Why won't they fall asleep? What are they doing up so late? Not good, not good... mmmhhhhh
Something very odd hap-pened...
Wait! I sense something now, it must be Alice, or maybe Nico. Oh yesss, my sweet children...

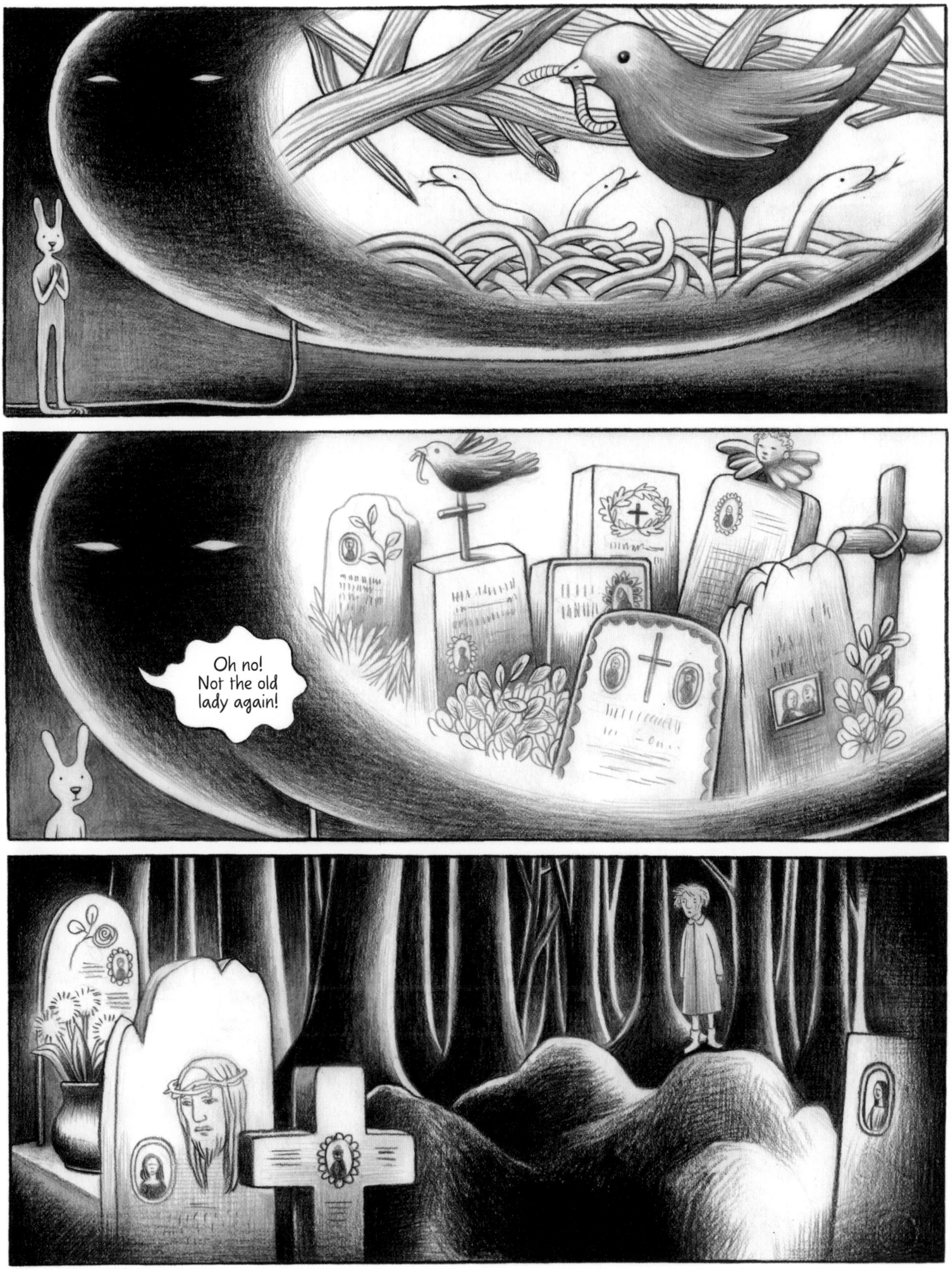
Oh no! Not the old lady again!

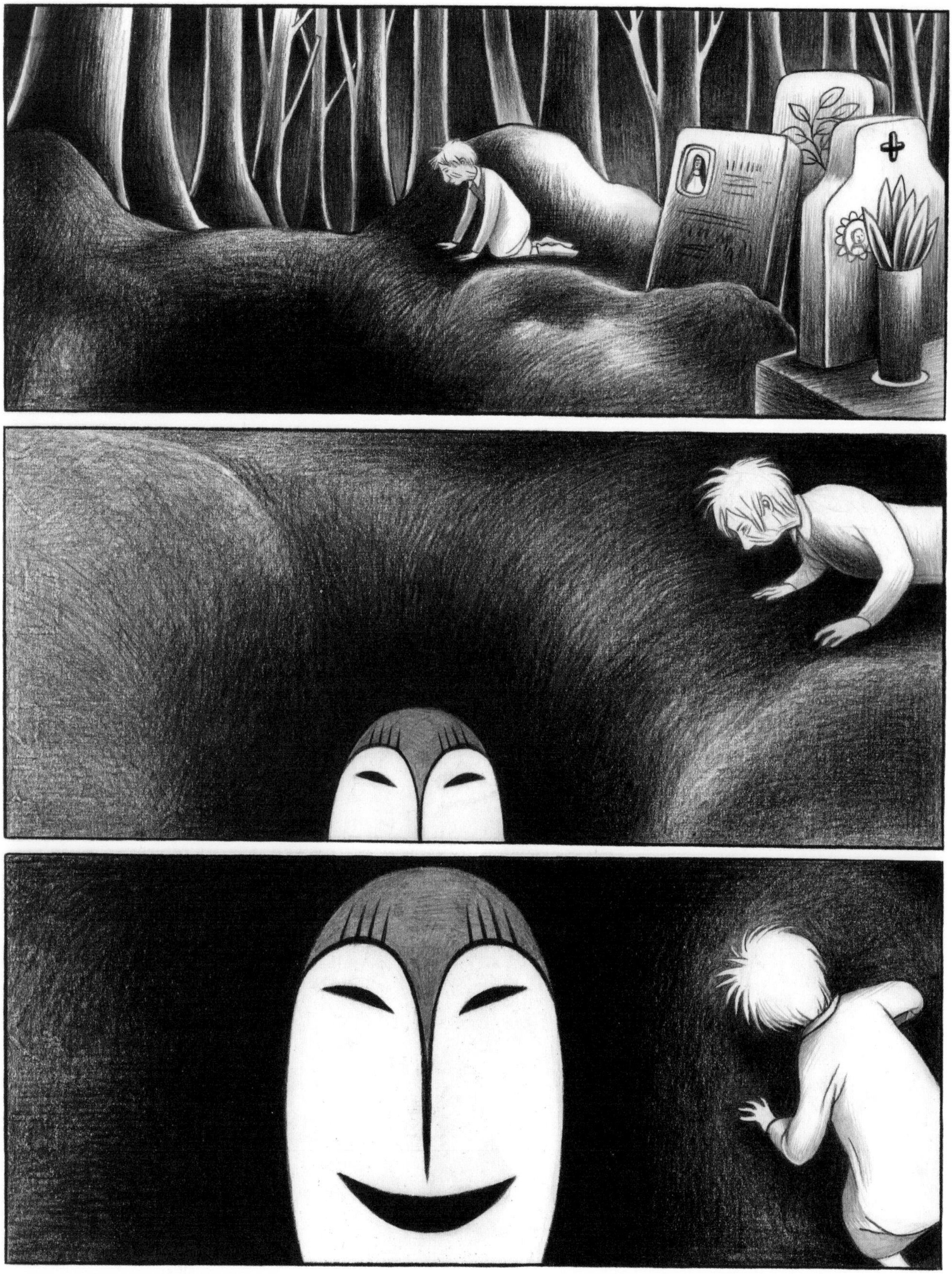

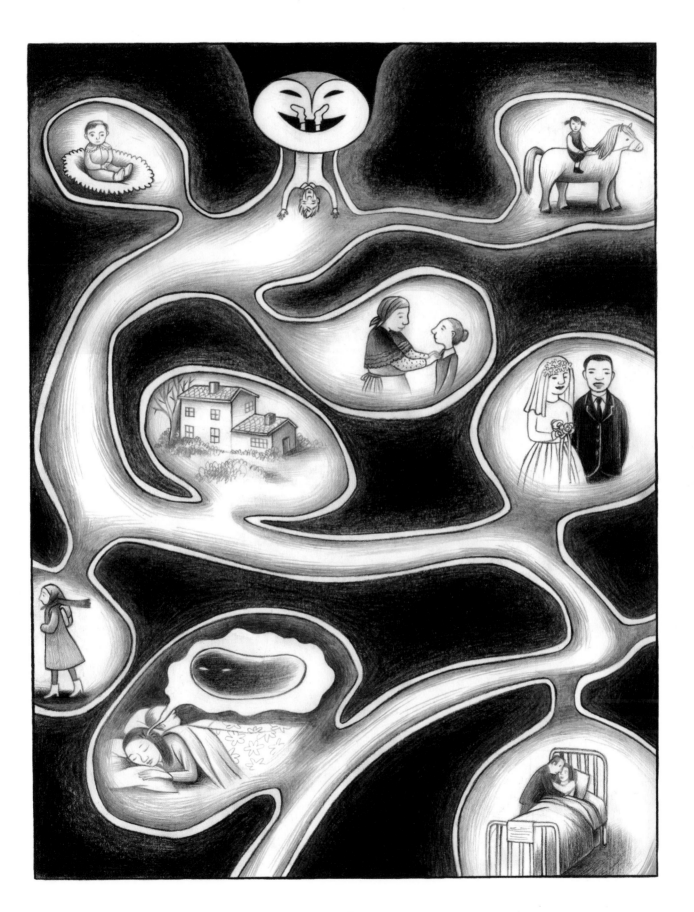

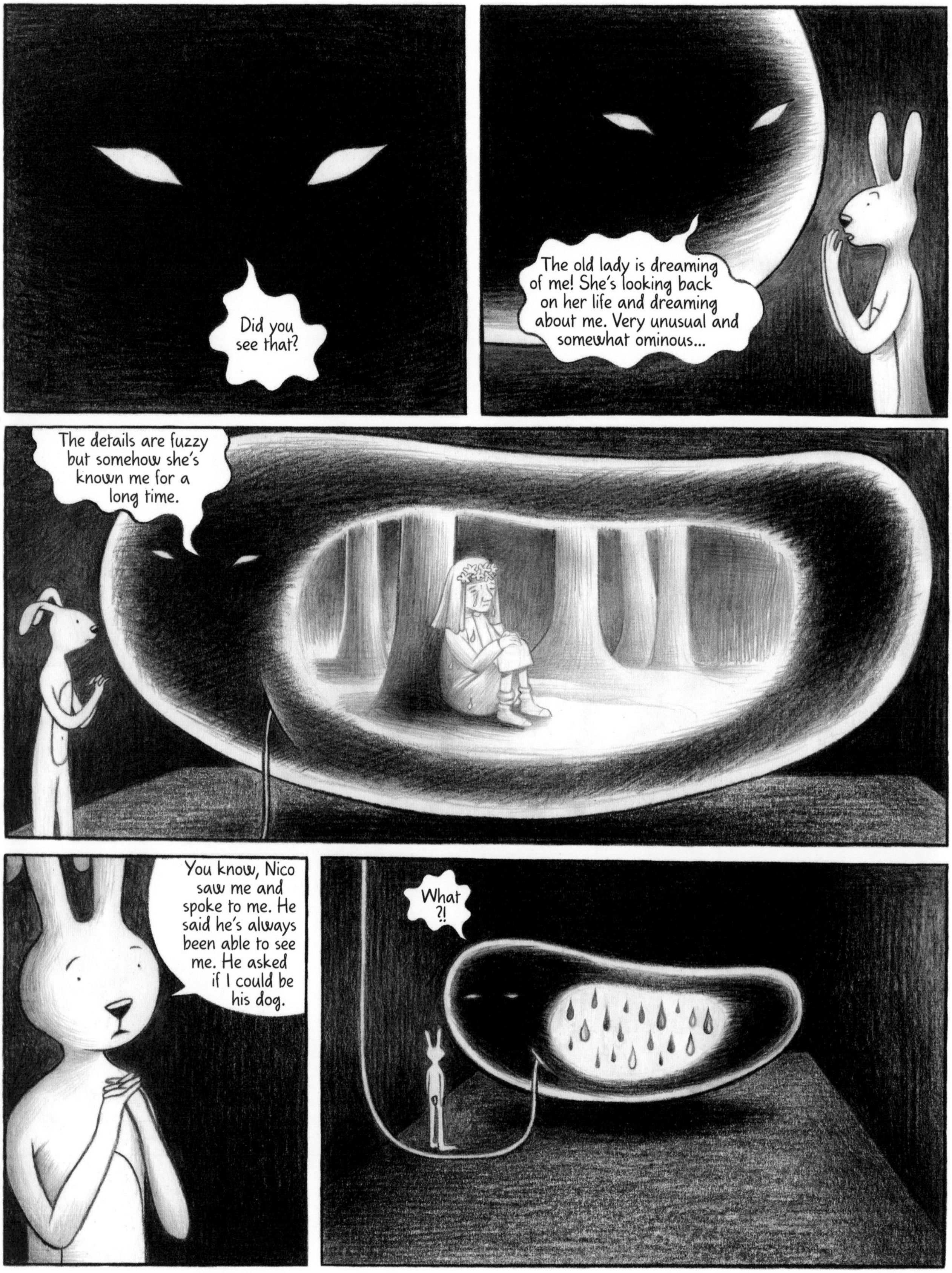
Did you see that?
The old lady is dreaming of me! She's looking back on her life and dreaming about me. Very unusual and somewhat ominous...
The details are fuzzy but somehow she's known me for a long time.
You know, Nico saw me and spoke to me. He said he's always been able to see me. He asked if I could be his dog.
What ?!

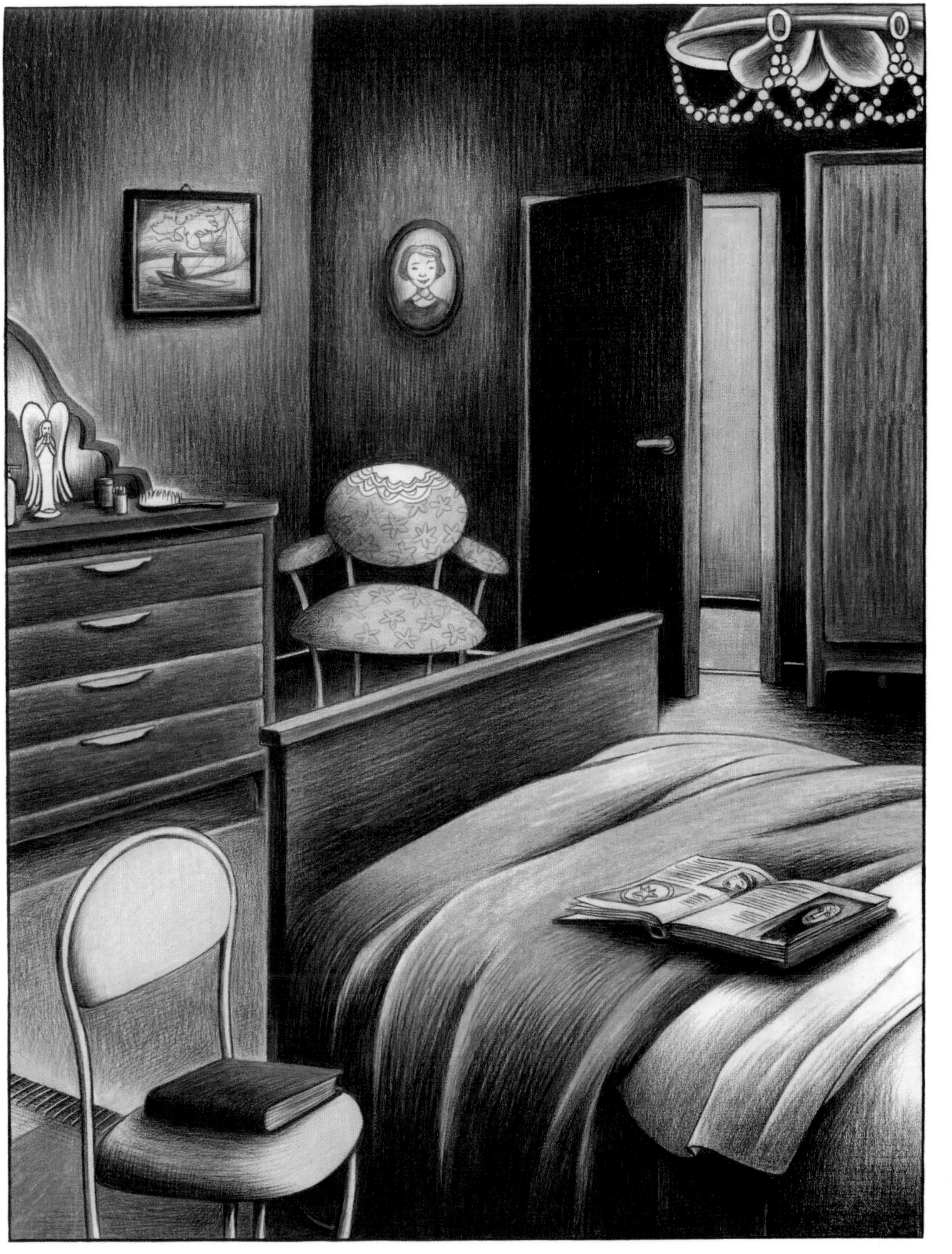

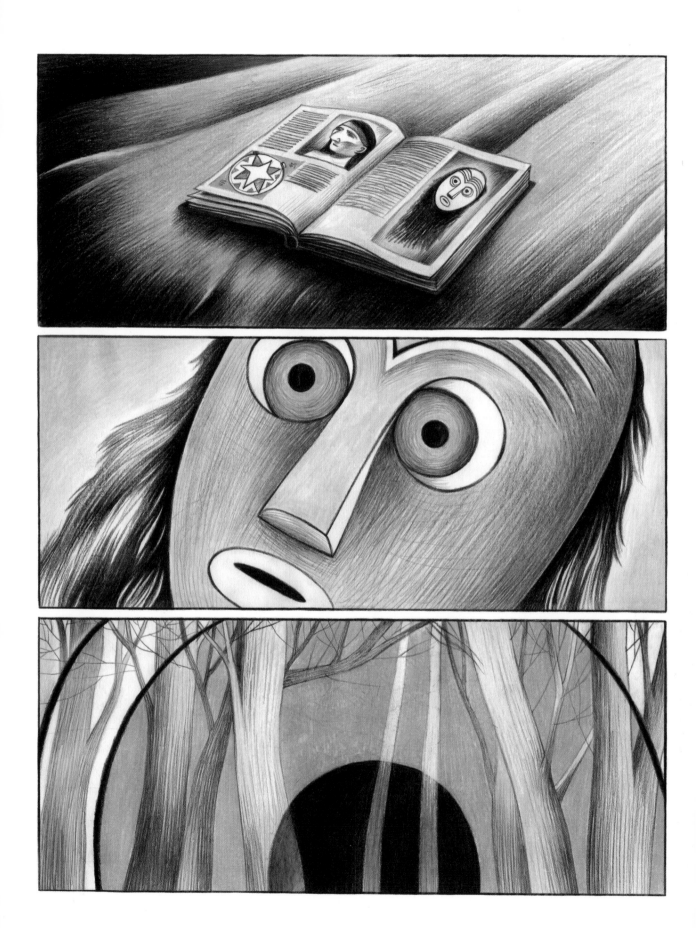

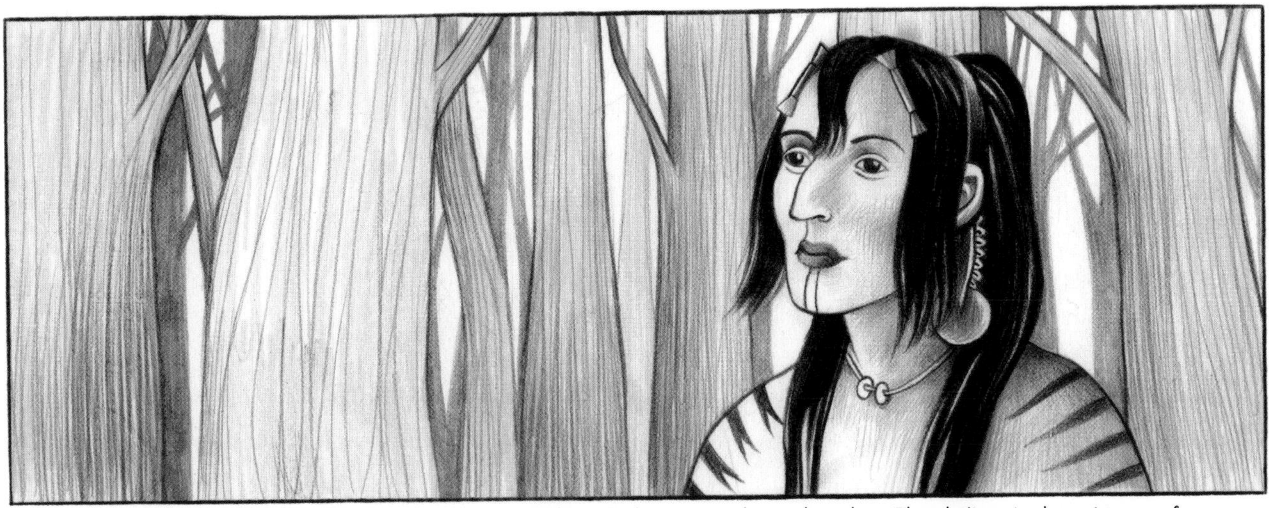

"The Algonquin's religious beliefs don't vary significantly from one tribe to the other. They believe in the existence of a Supreme Being, creator of everything, the 'Gitche Manitou' or 'Great Power,' never to be named or invoked directly.

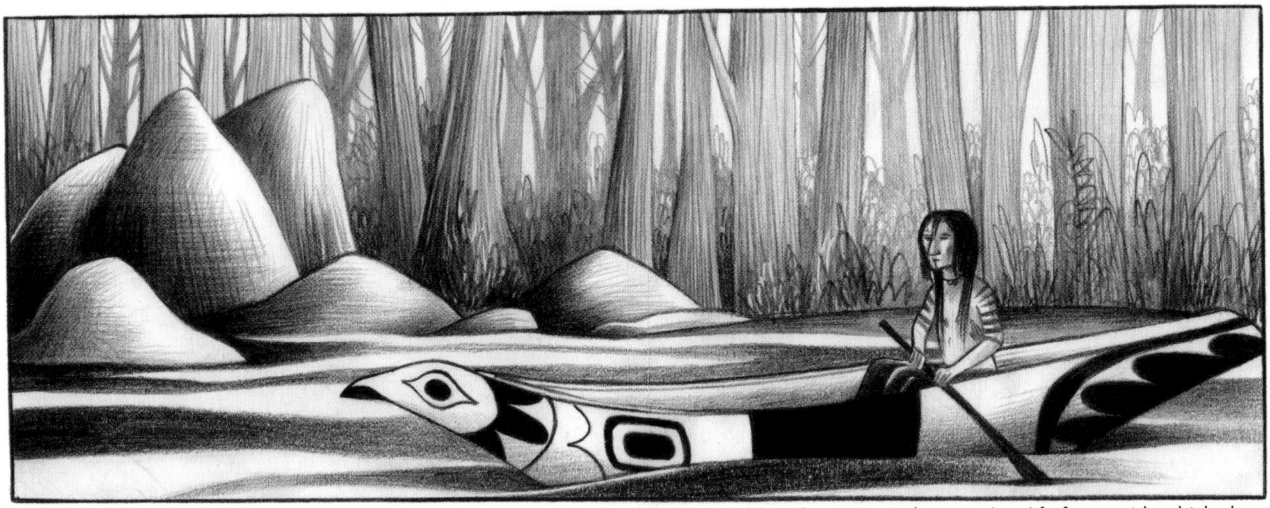

"The 'Manitou,' far from being the actual name of the deity, is in fact one of his physical attributes. It's a life force with which the Supreme Being descends from the sky and spreads among men, animals and objects.

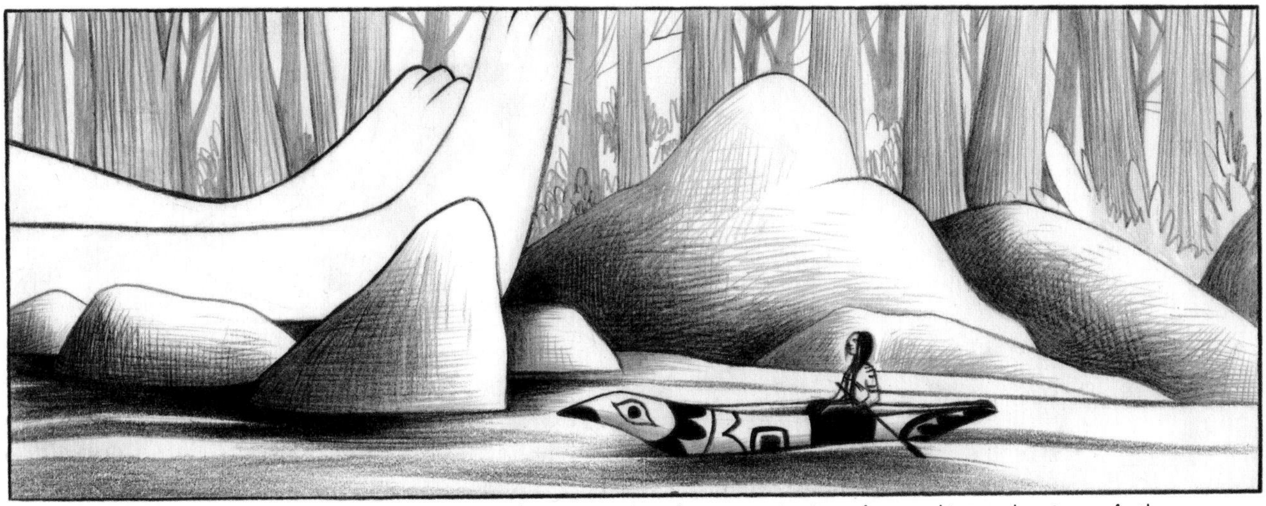

"Leaders, wizards, and shamans possess much 'Manitou,' as do some animals and some objects; the pipe and other ceremonial instruments, for instance, contain a significant amount.

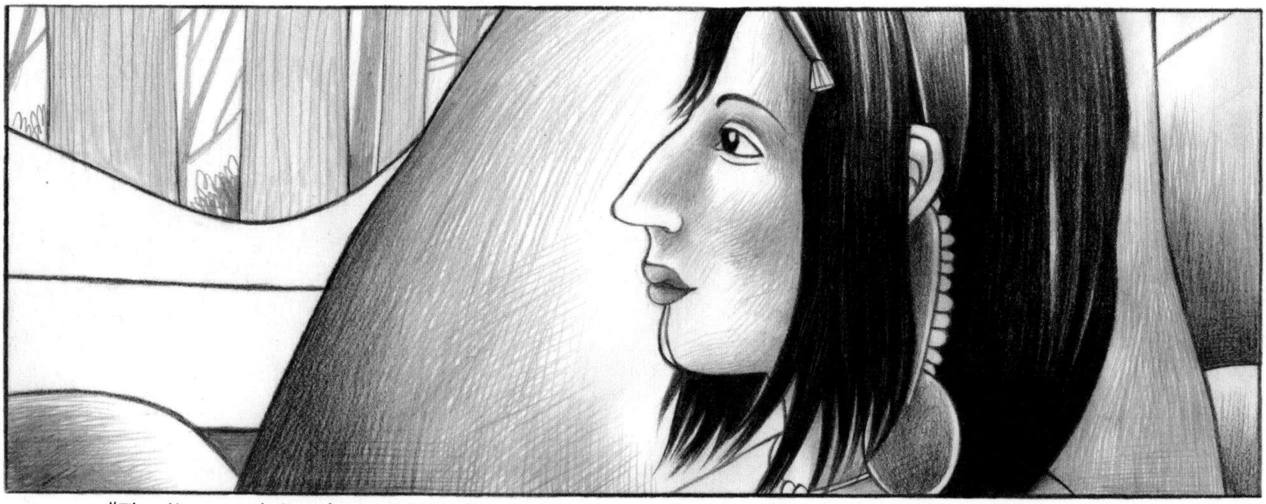

"The Algonquin believed in a civilizing hero, a go-between who linked the corporeal world to the Supreme Being.

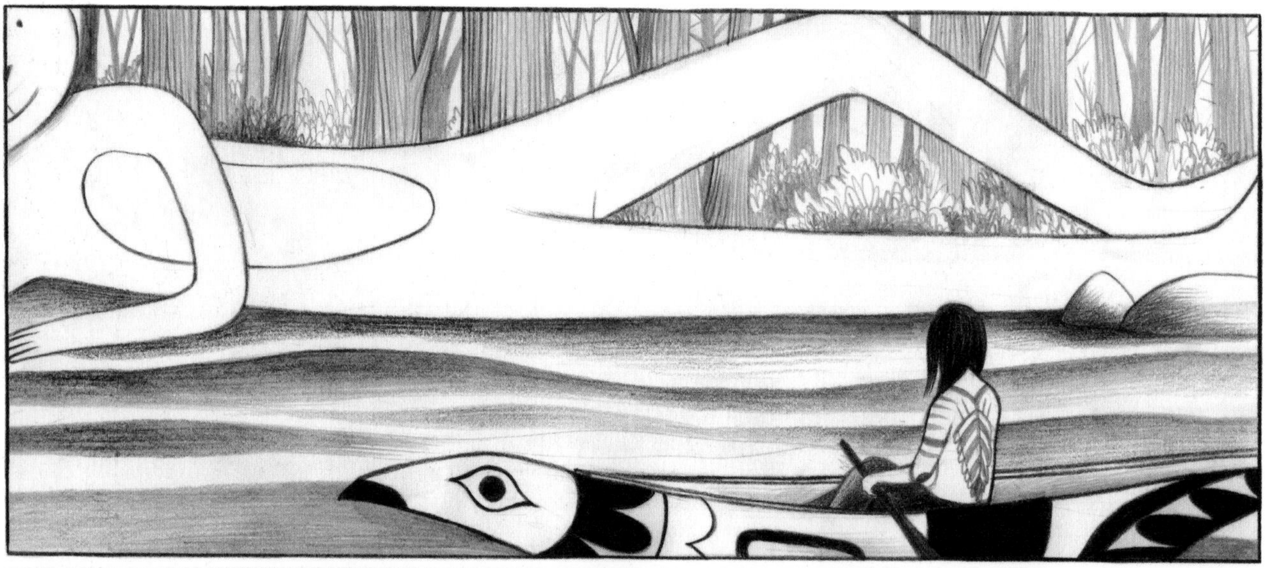

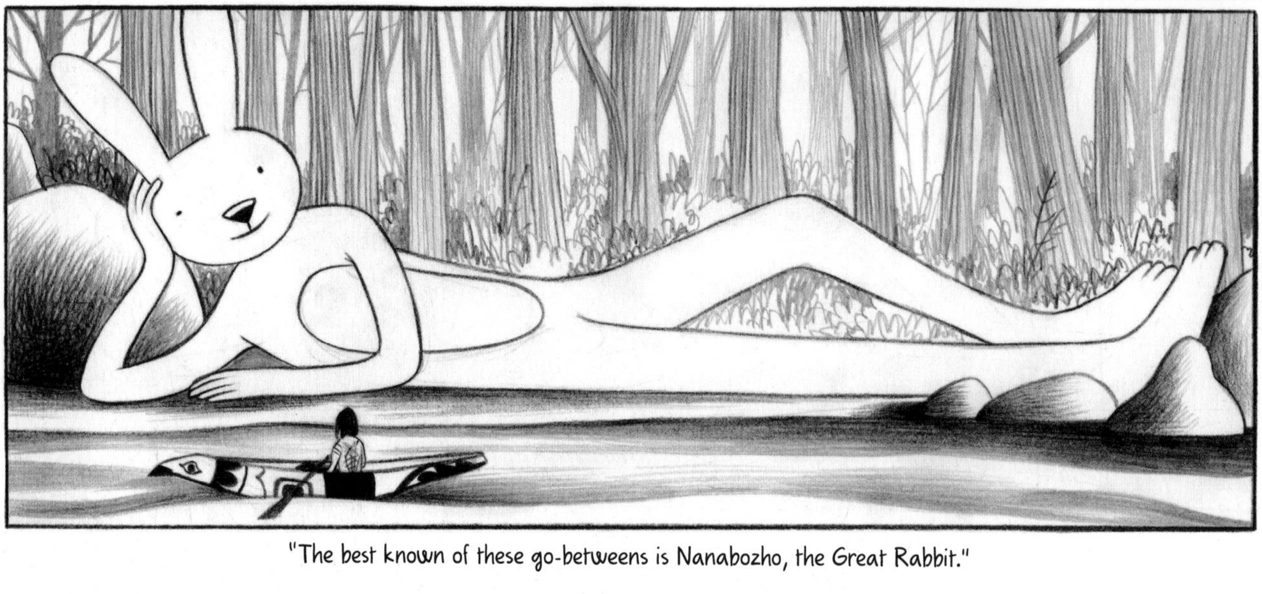

"The best known of these go-betweens is Nanabozho, the Great Rabbit."

THURSDAY, DECEMBER 21

---

01 hour, 56 minutes, 22 seconds

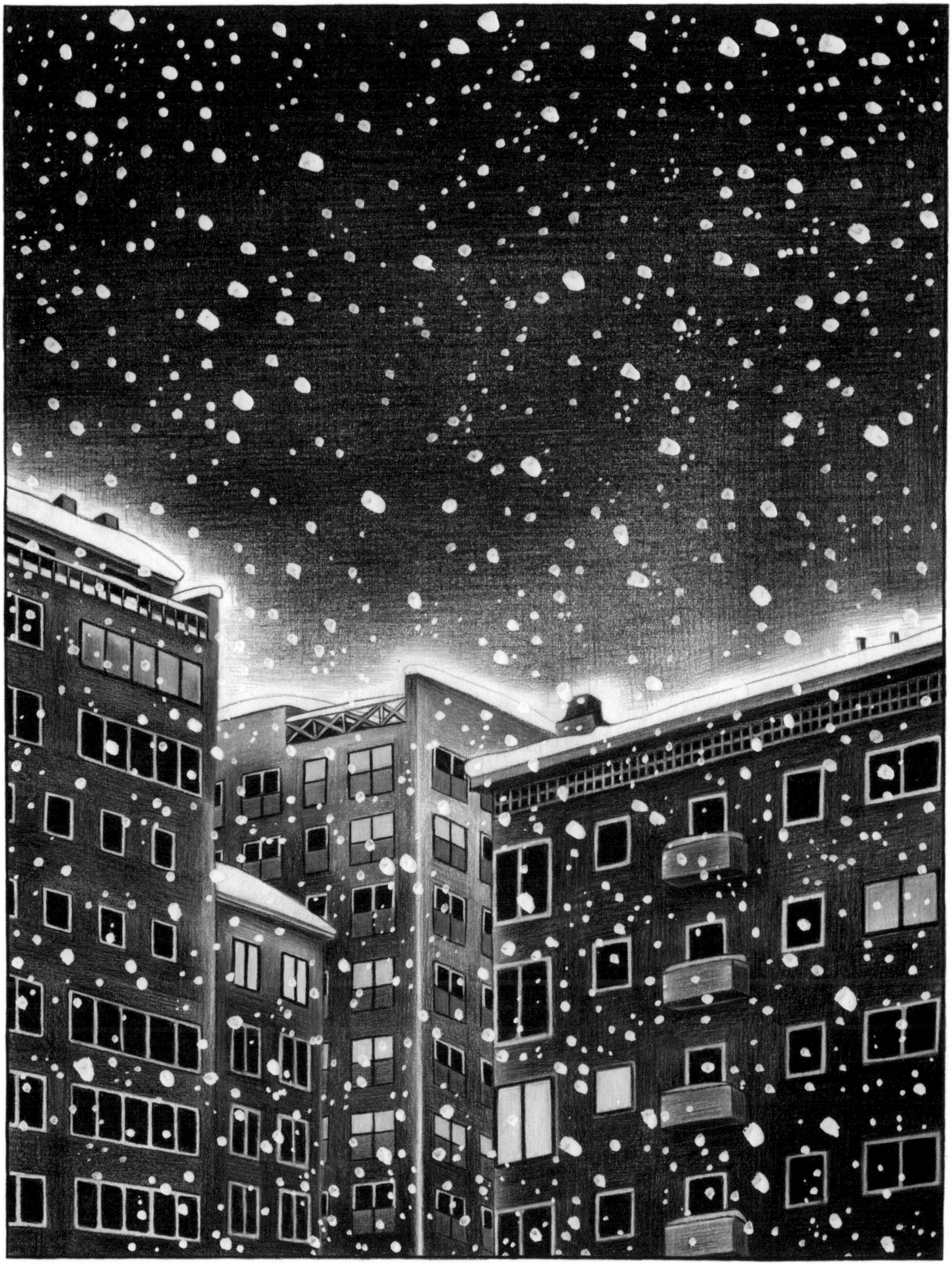

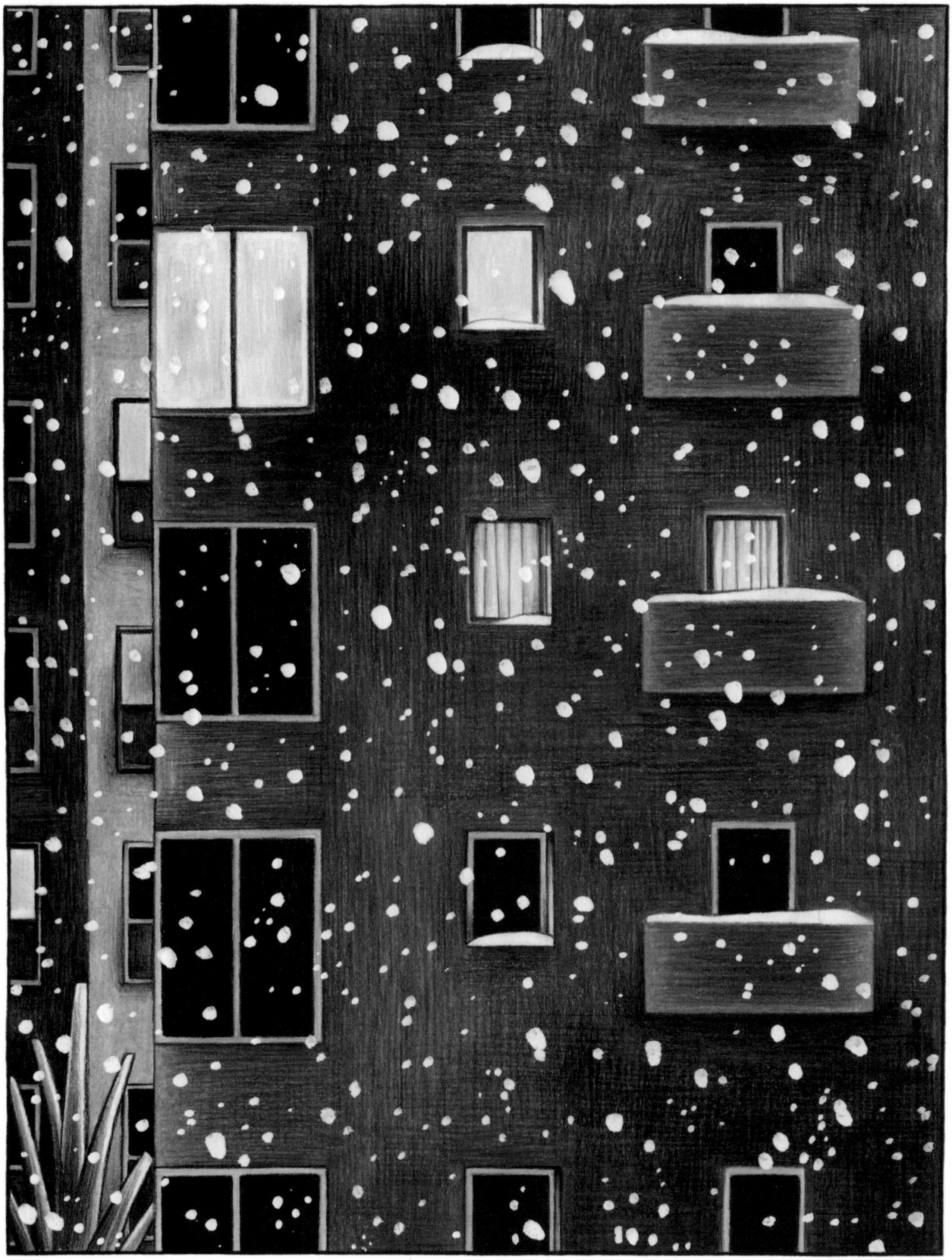

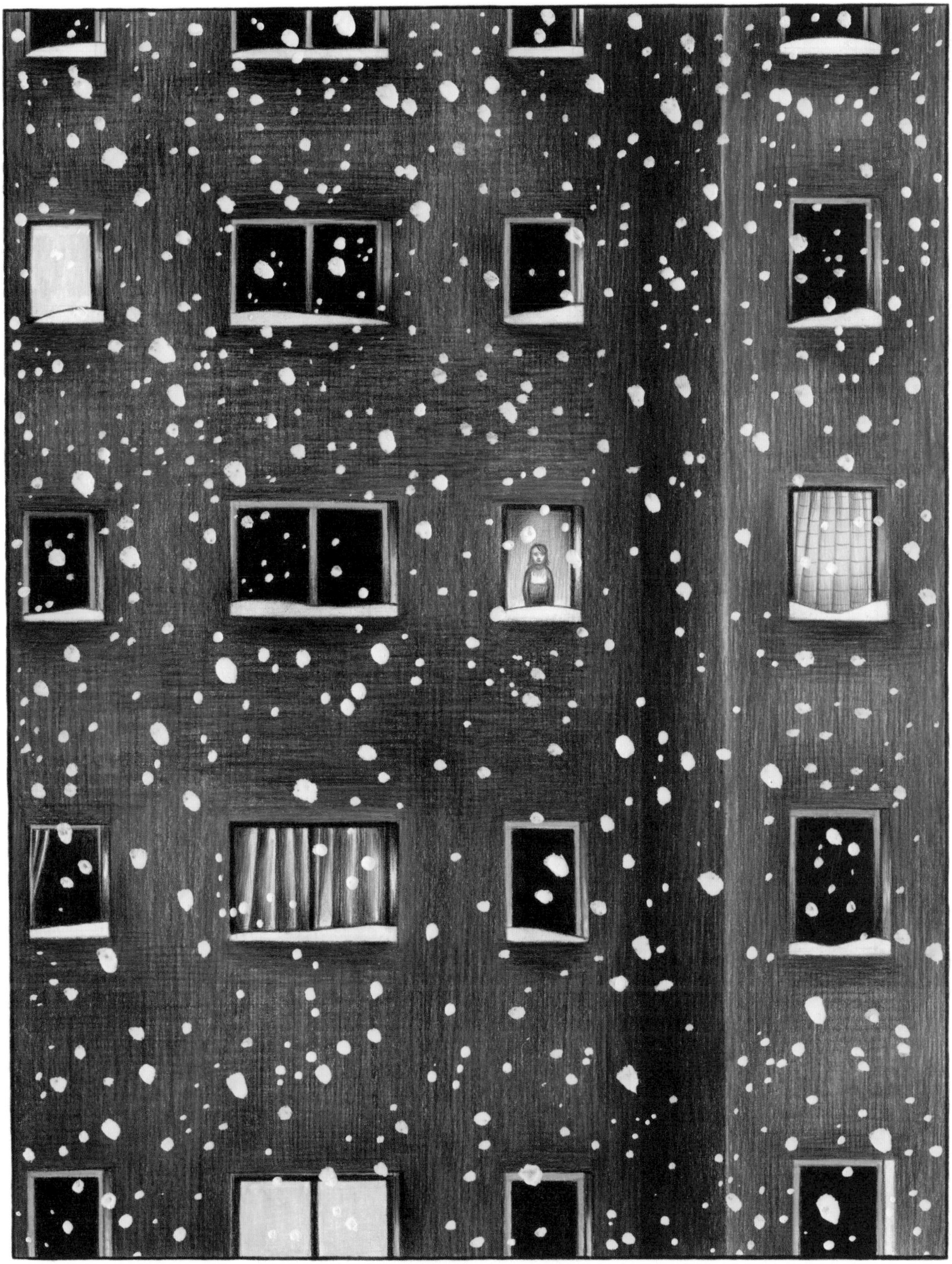

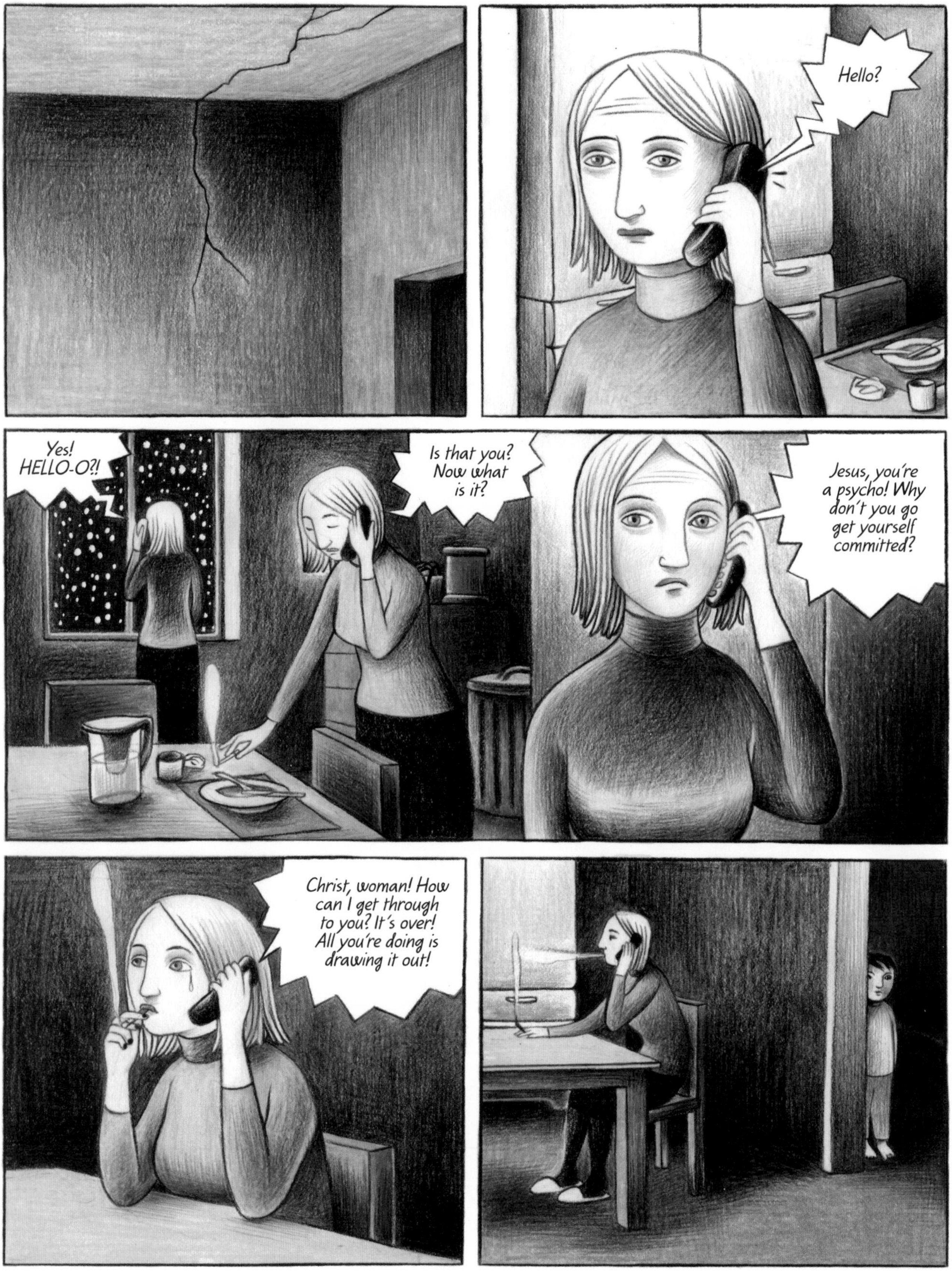
Hello?
Yes! HELLO-O?!
Is that you? Now what is it?
Jesus, you're a psycho! Why don't you go get yourself committed?
Christ, woman! How can I get through to you? It's over! All you're doing is drawing it out!

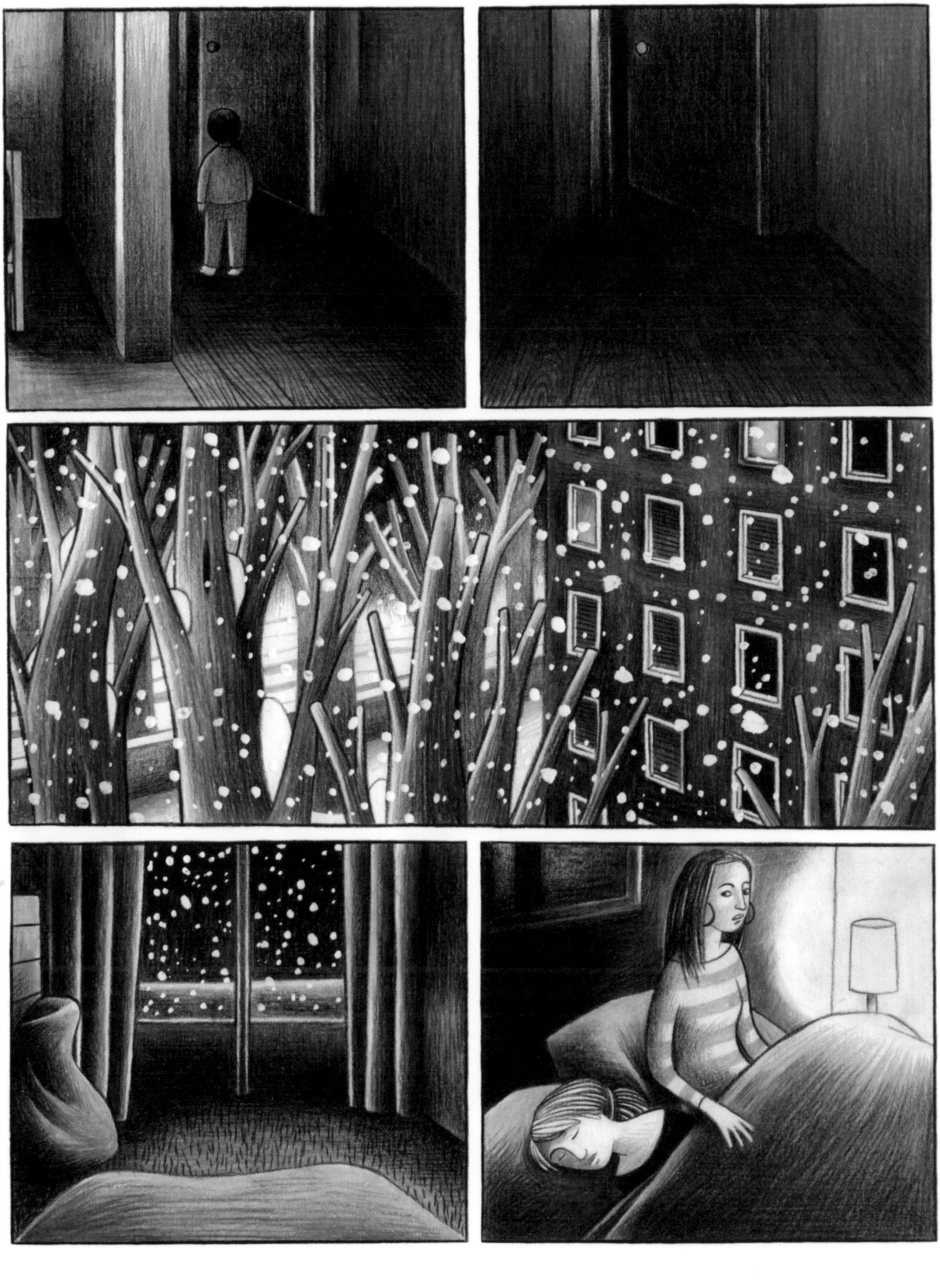

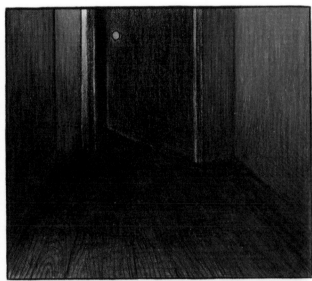

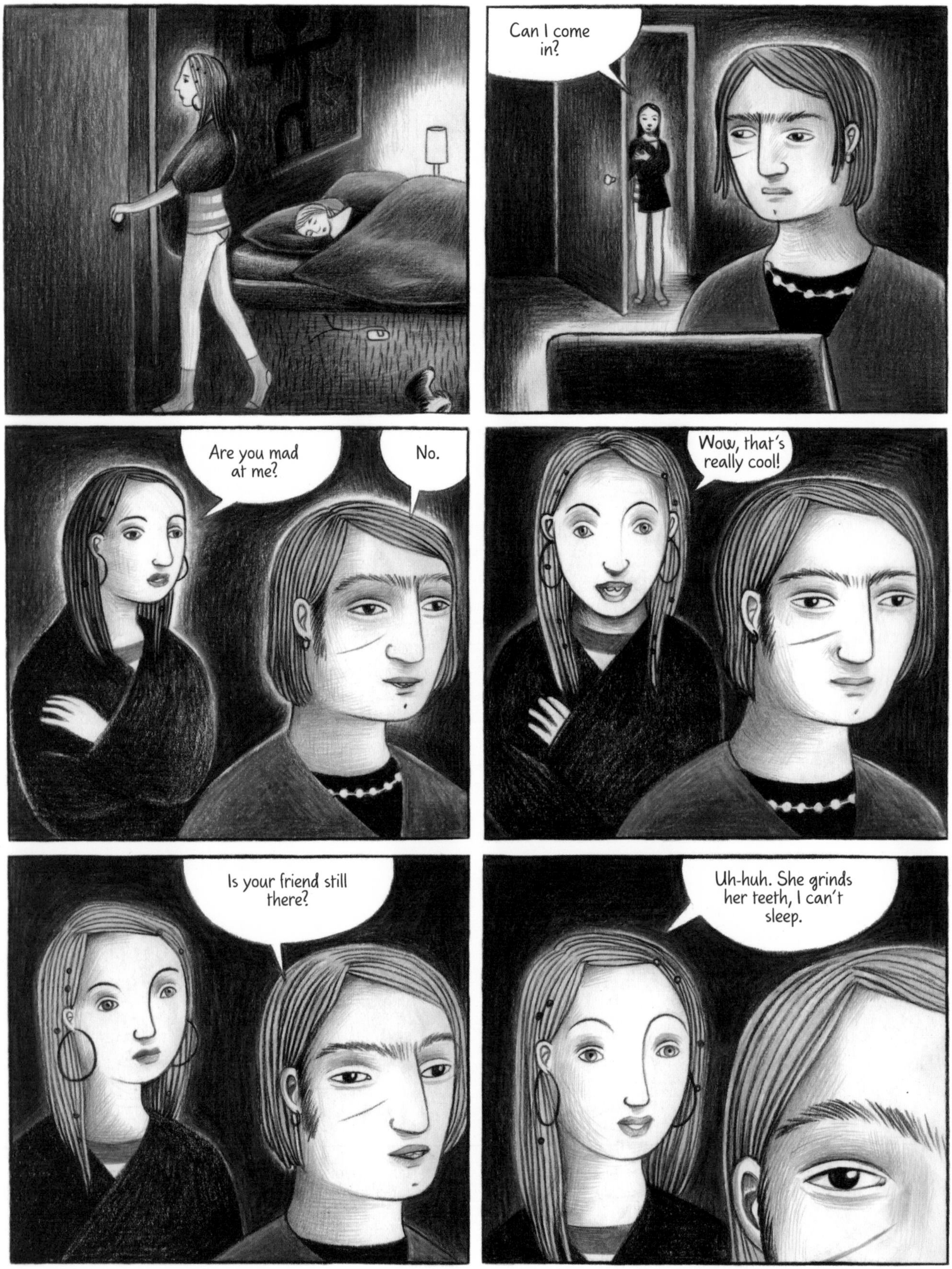
Can I come in?
Are you mad at me?
No.
Wow, that's really cool!
Is your friend still there?
Uh-huh. She grinds her teeth, I can't sleep.

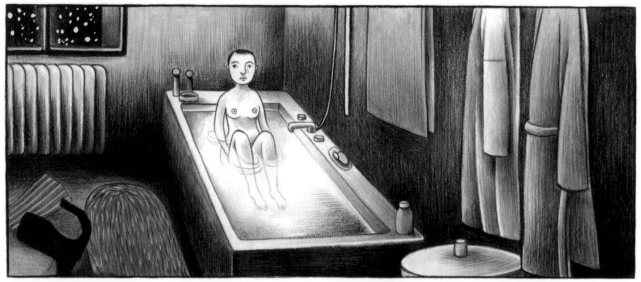

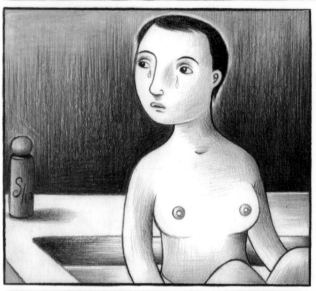

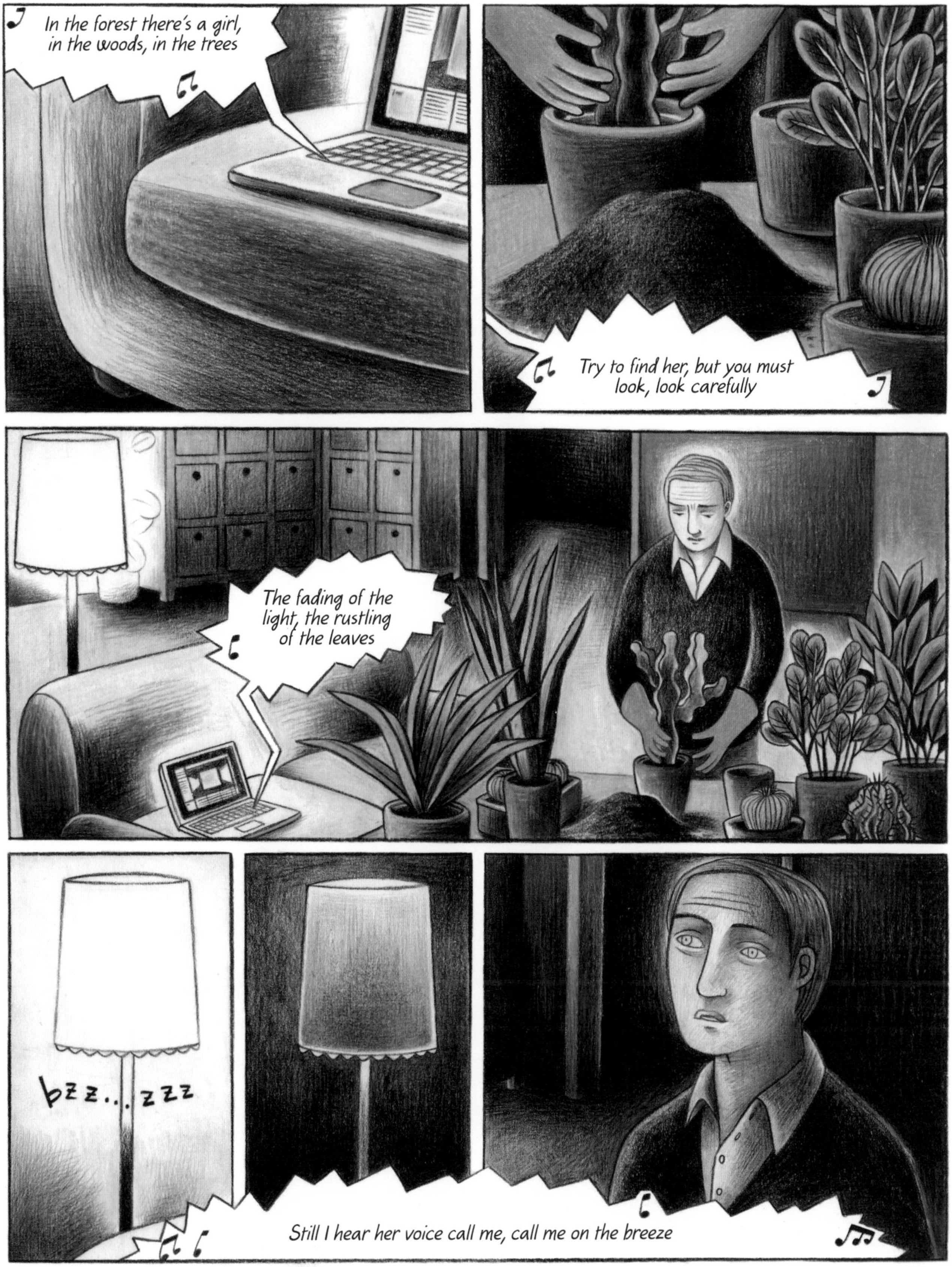
In the forest there's a girl, in the woods, in the trees
Try to find her, but you must look, look carefully
The fading of the light, the rustling of the leaves
bzz...zzz
Still I hear her voice call me, call me on the breeze

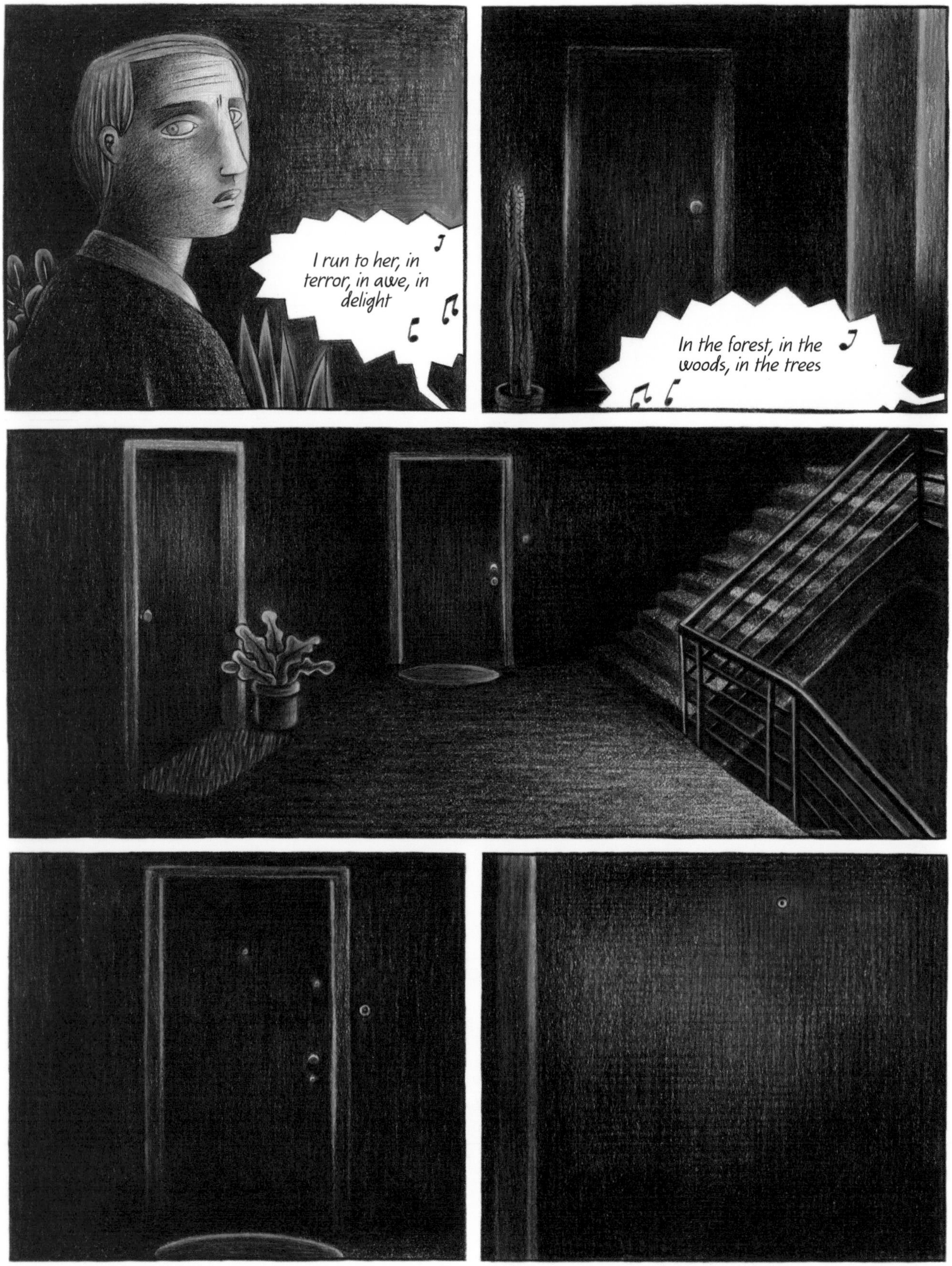
I run to her, in terror, in awe, in delight
In the forest, in the woods, in the trees

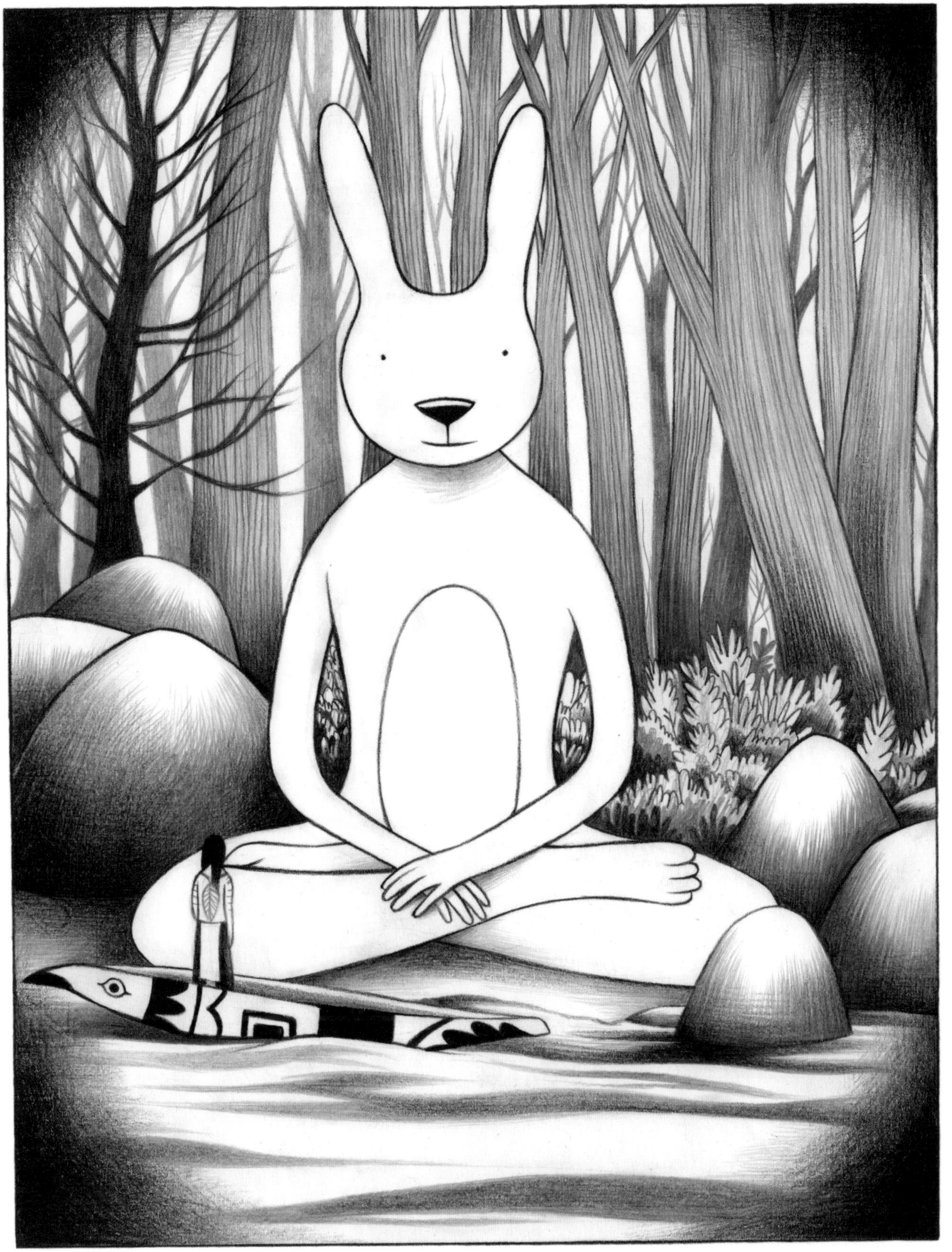

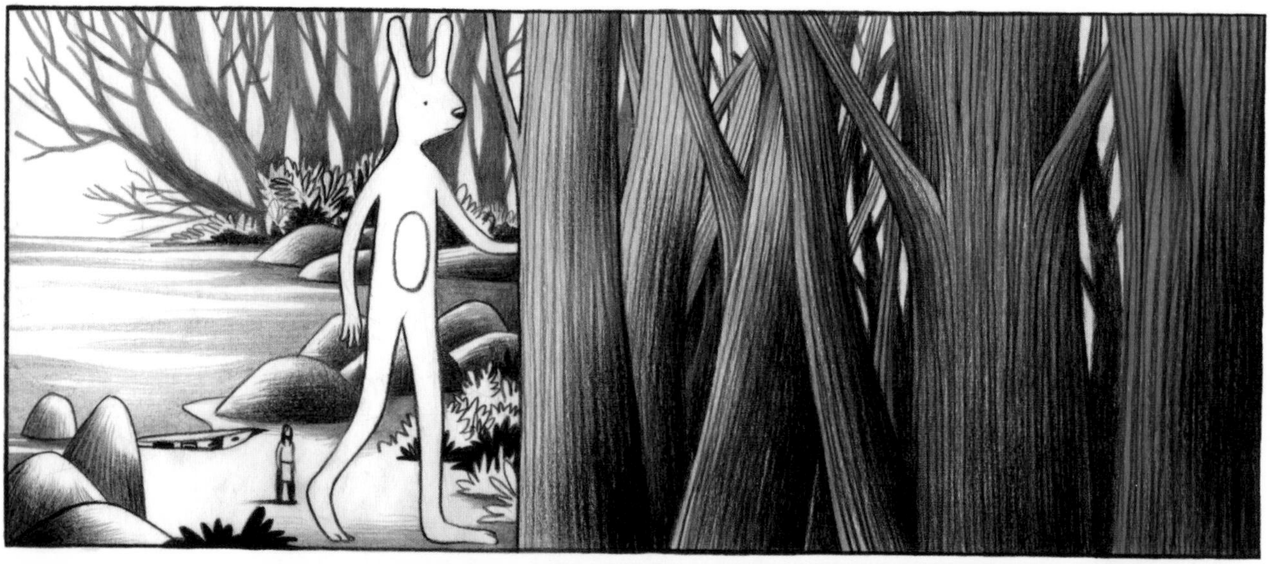

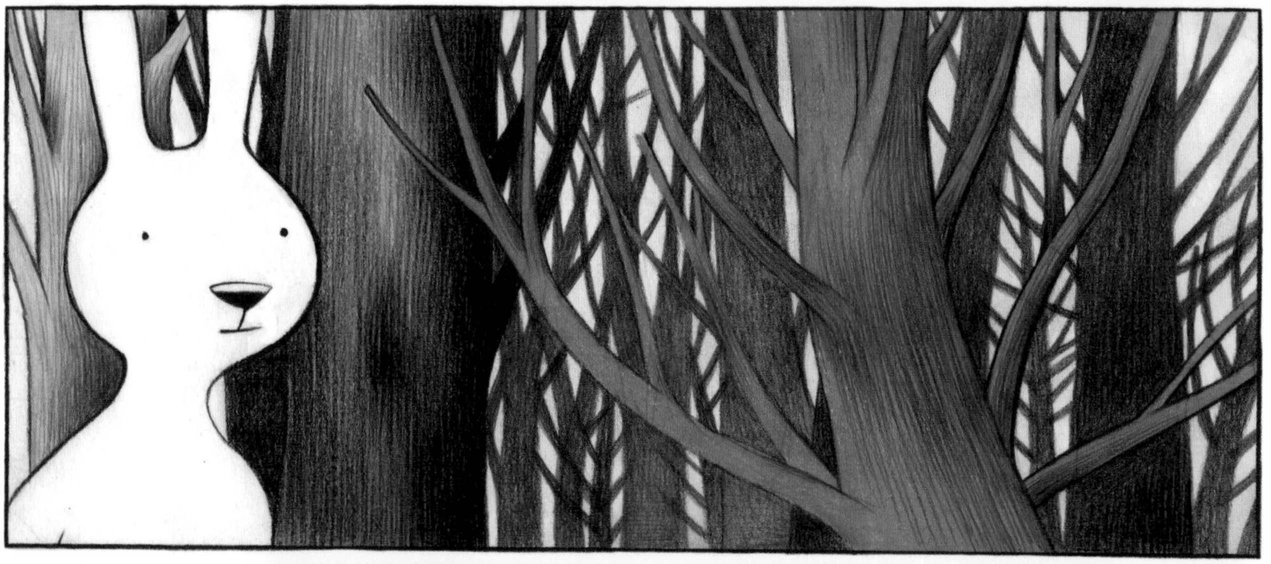

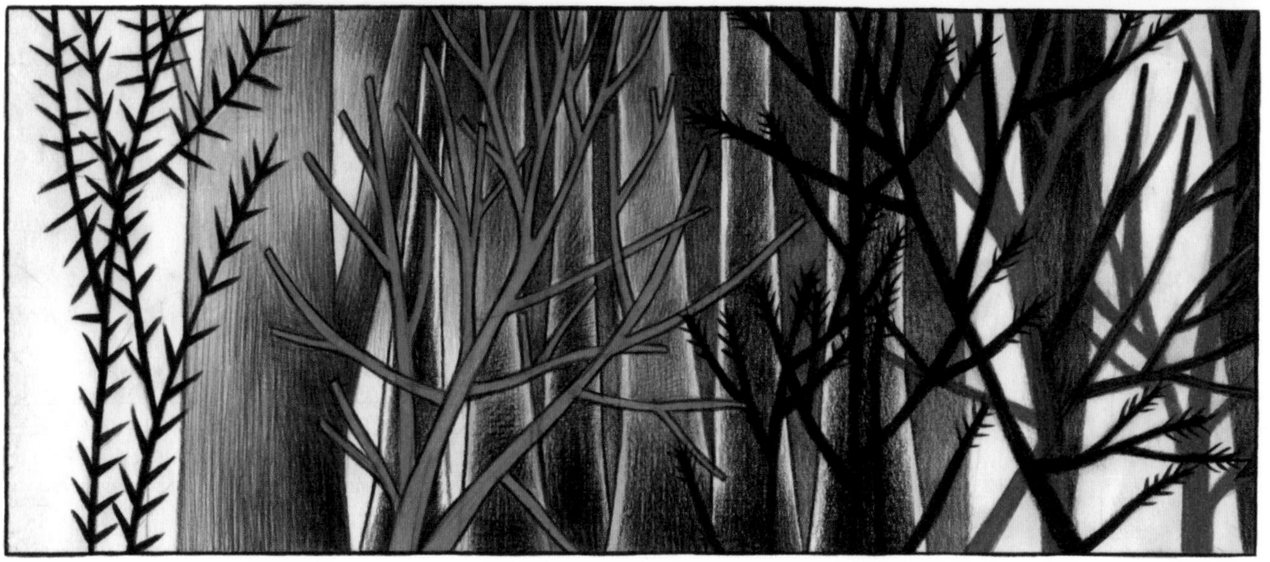

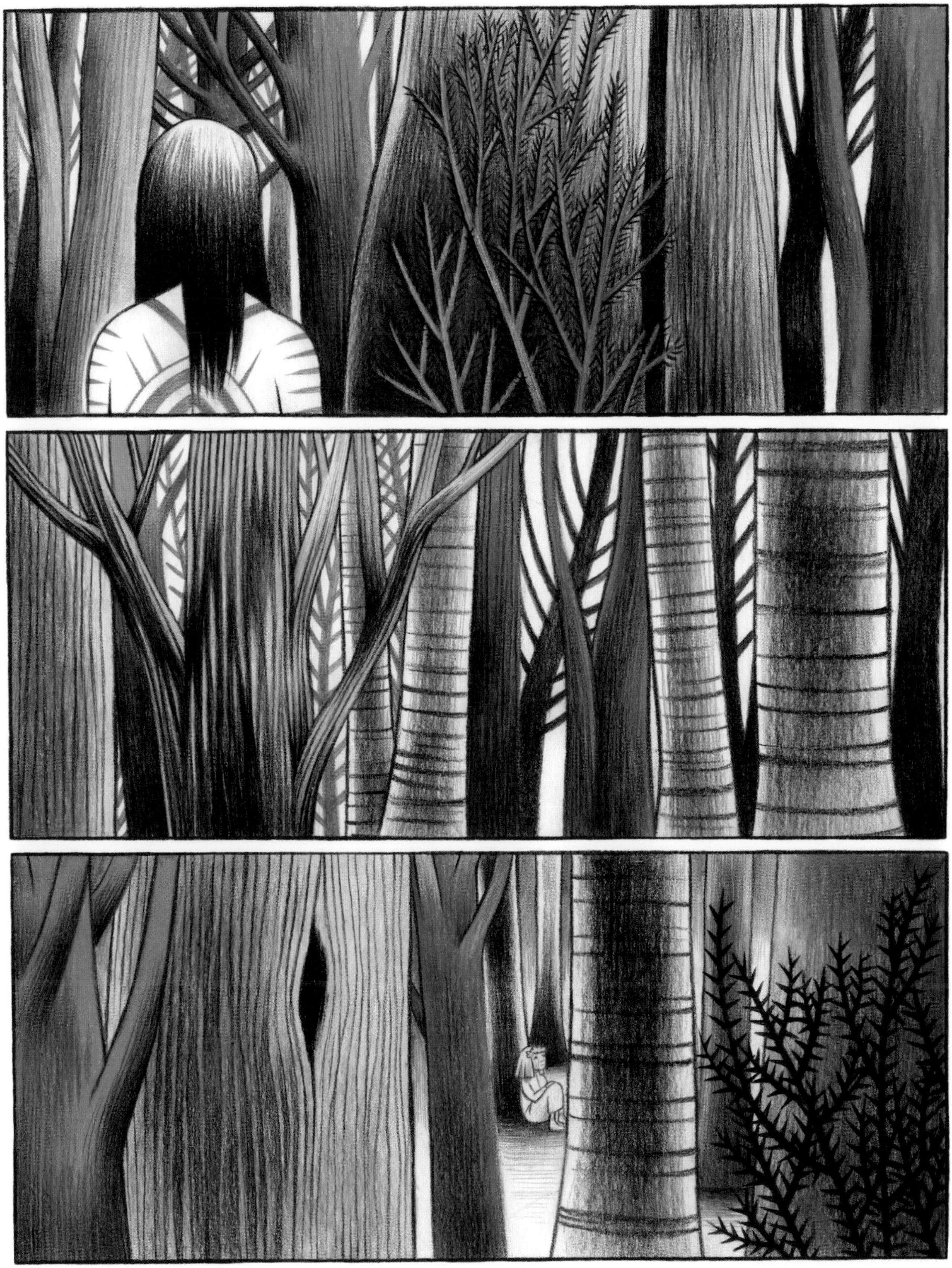

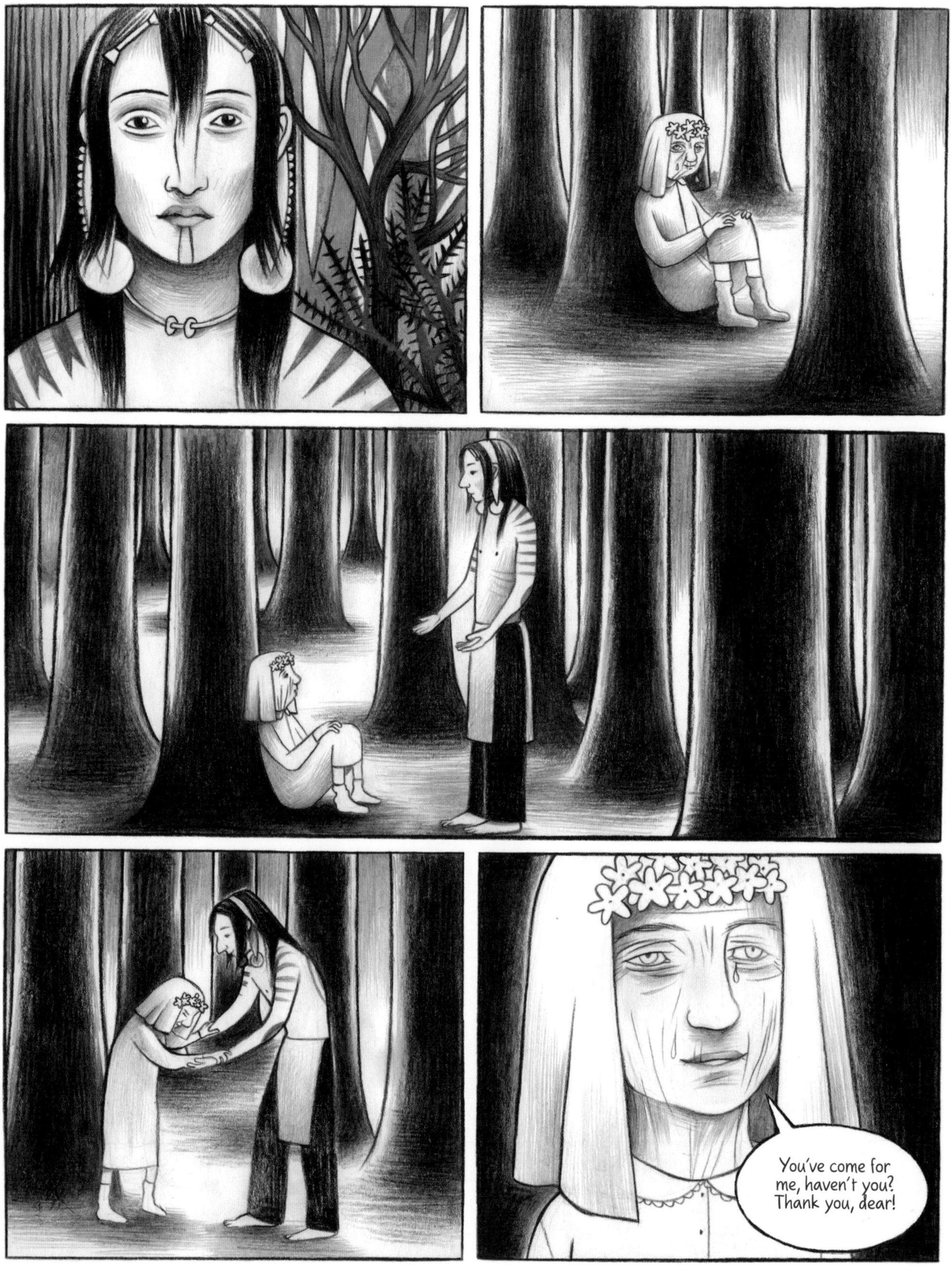
You've come for me, haven't you? Thank you, dear!

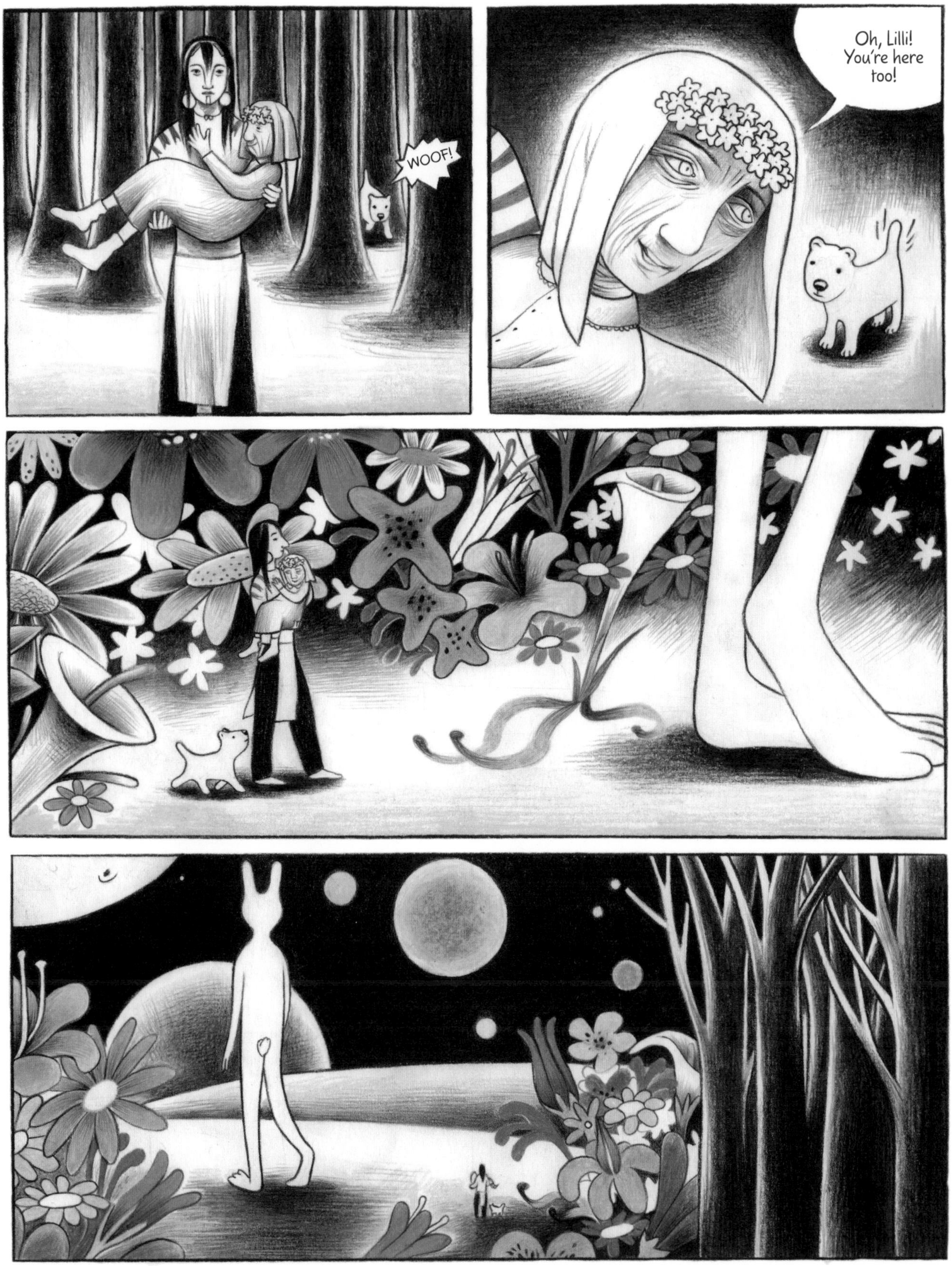
WOOF!
Oh, Lilli! You're here too!

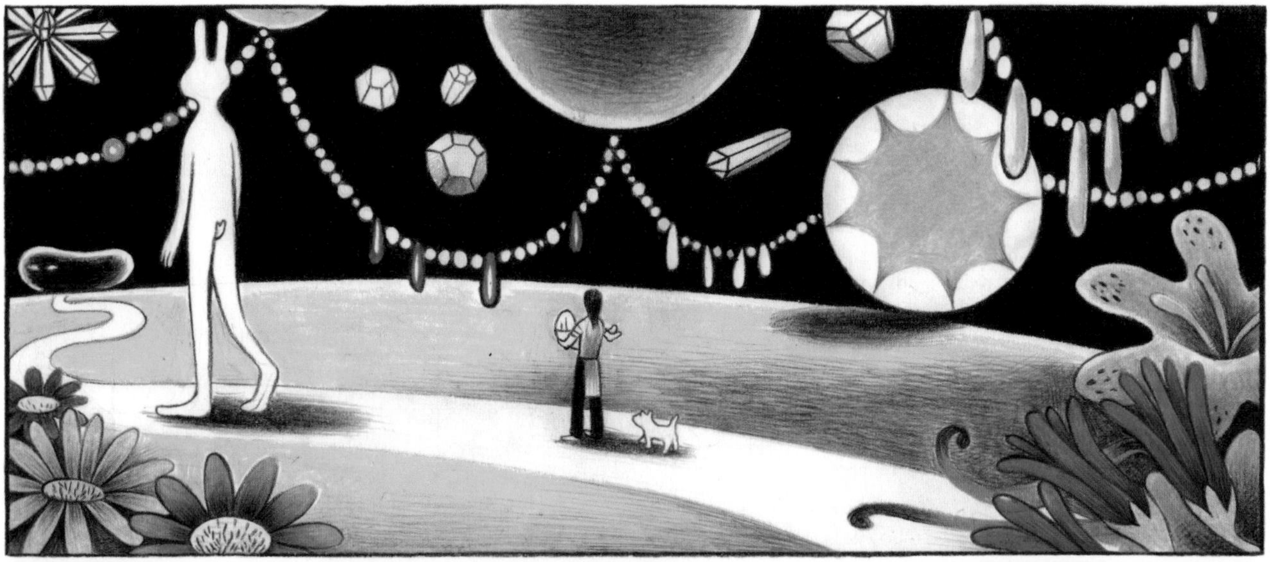

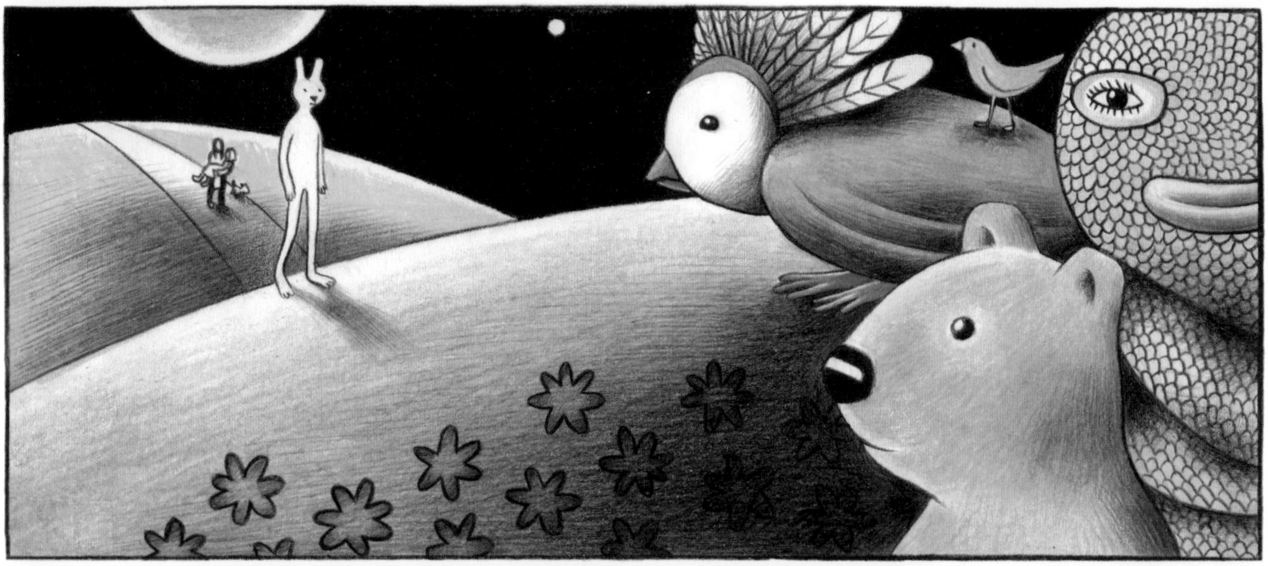

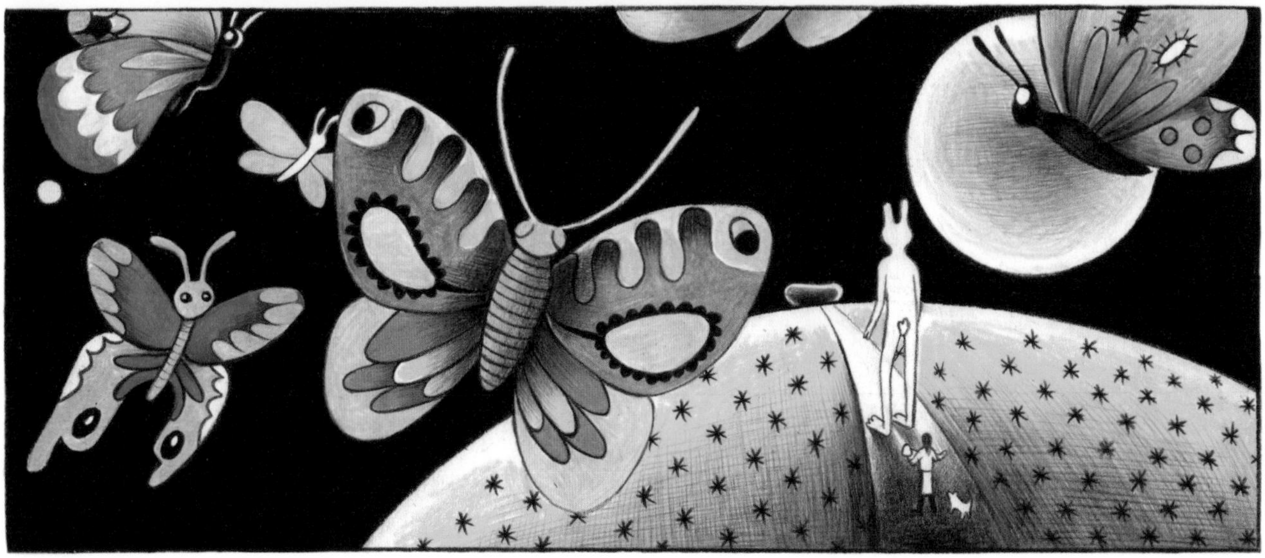

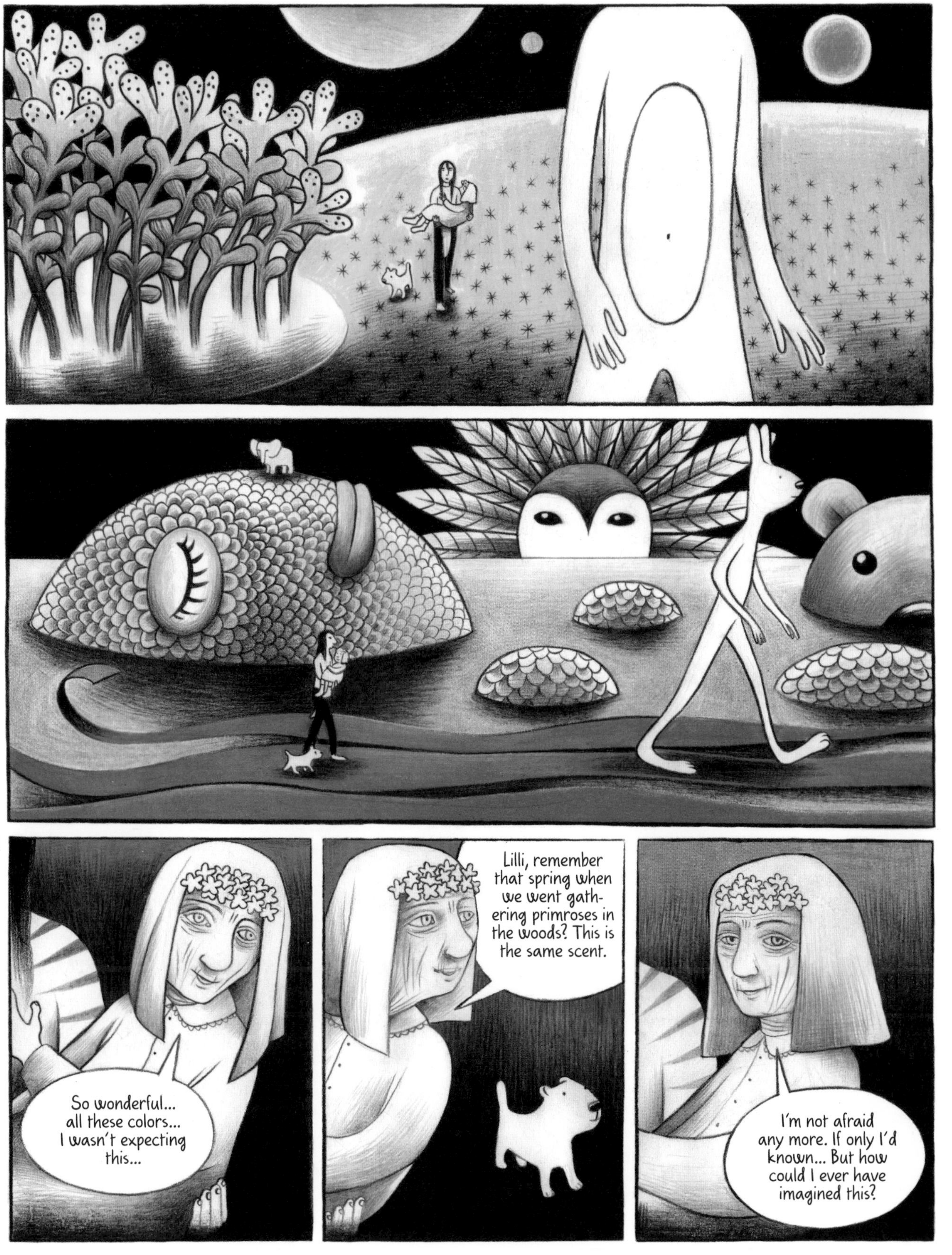
So wonderful... all these colors... I wasn't expecting this...
Lilli, remember that spring when we went gathering primroses in the woods? This is the same scent.
I'm not afraid any more. If only I'd known... But how could I ever have imagined this?

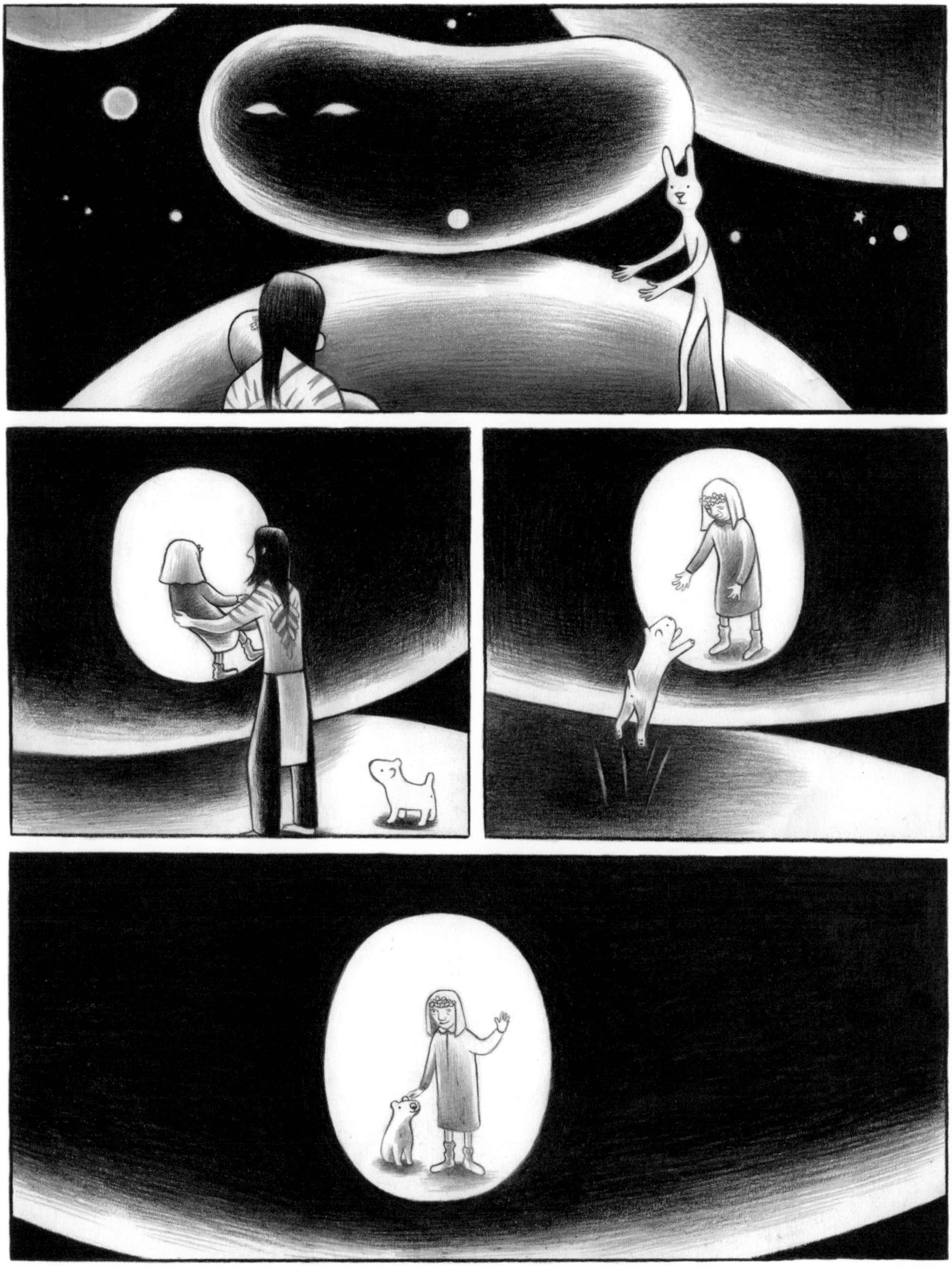

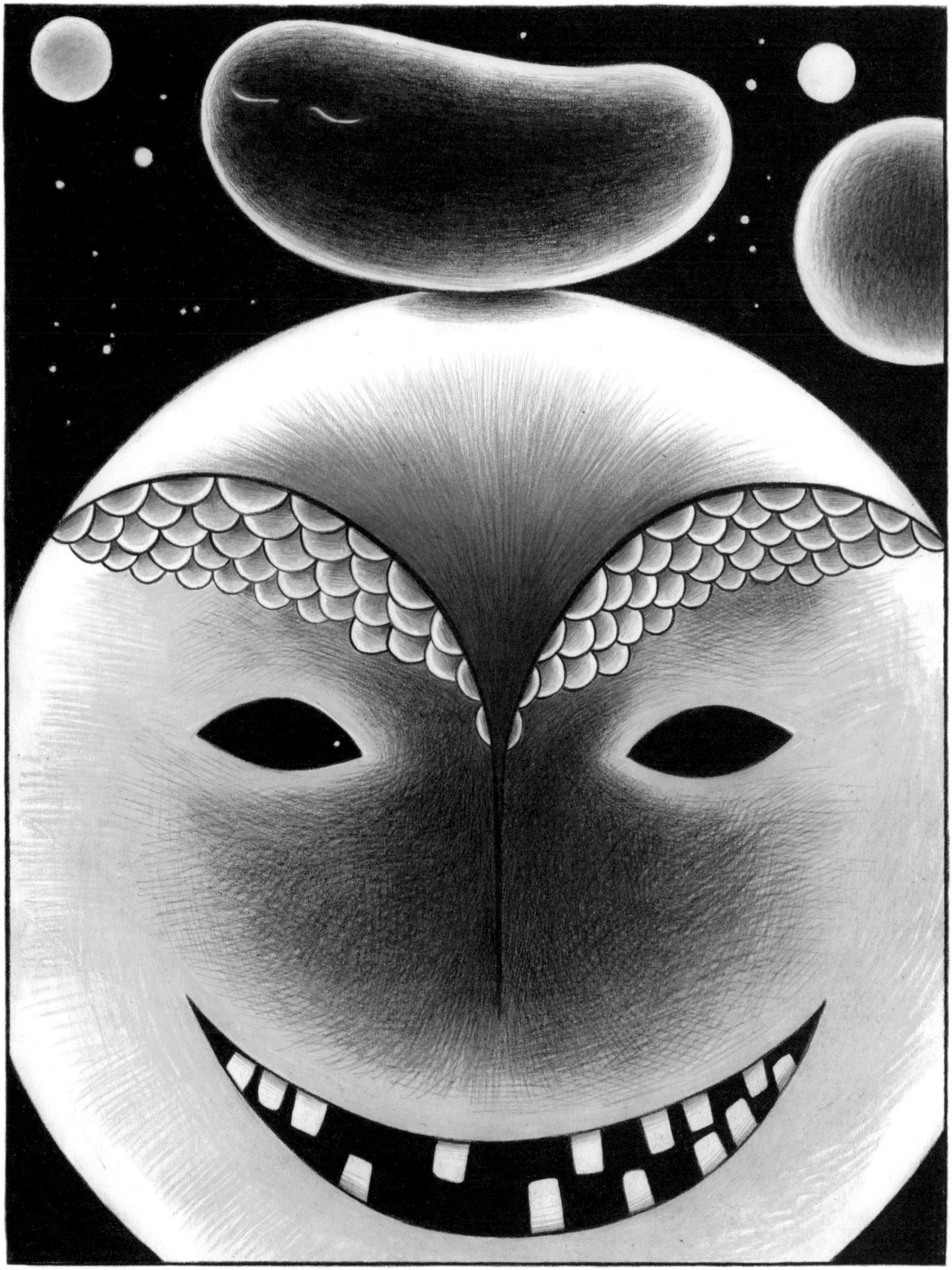

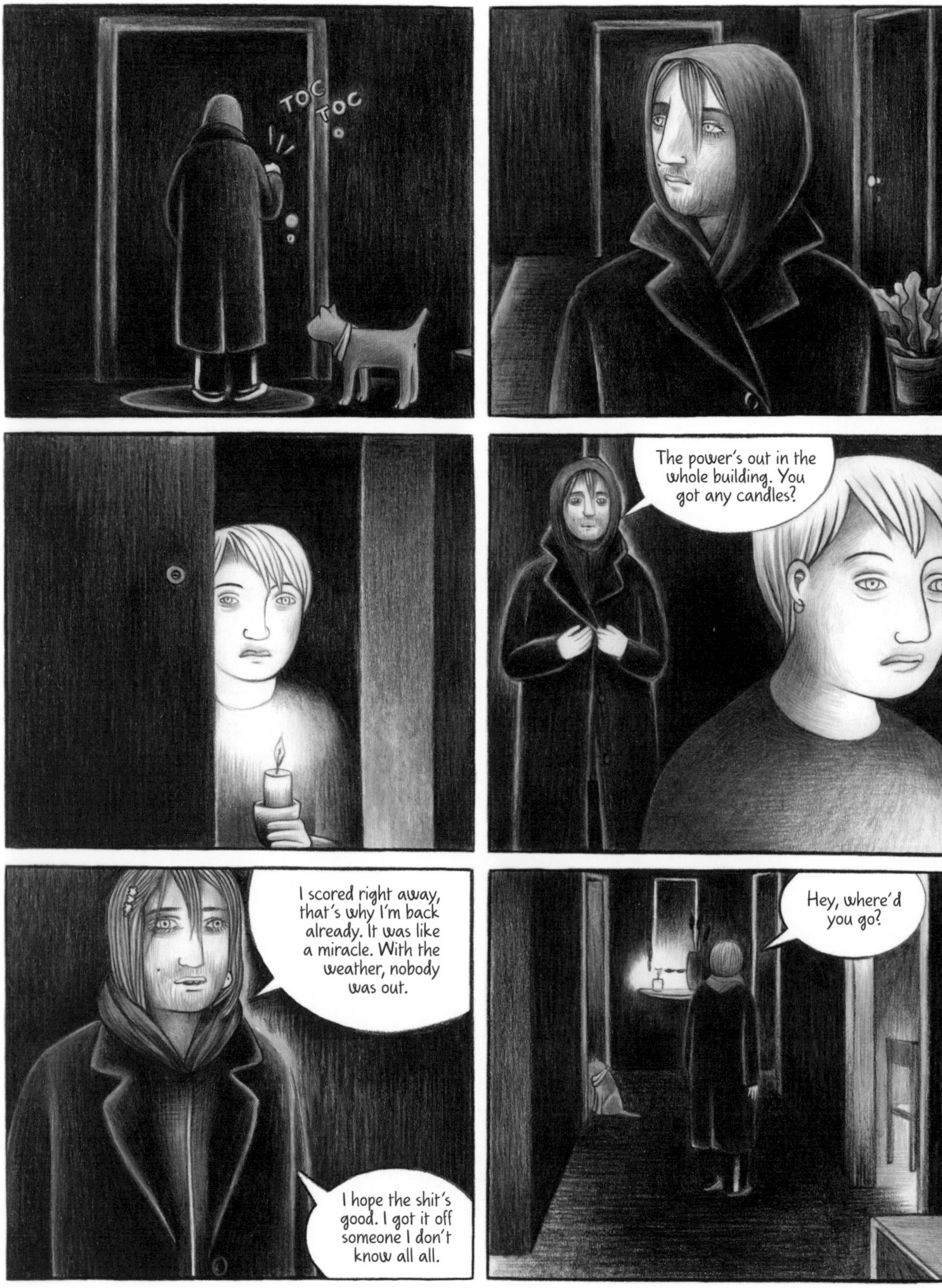
TOC
TOC
The power's out in the whole building. You got any candles?
I scored right away, that's why I'm back already. It was like a miracle. With the weather, nobody was out.
I hope the shit's good. I got it off someone I don't know all all.
Hey, where'd you go?

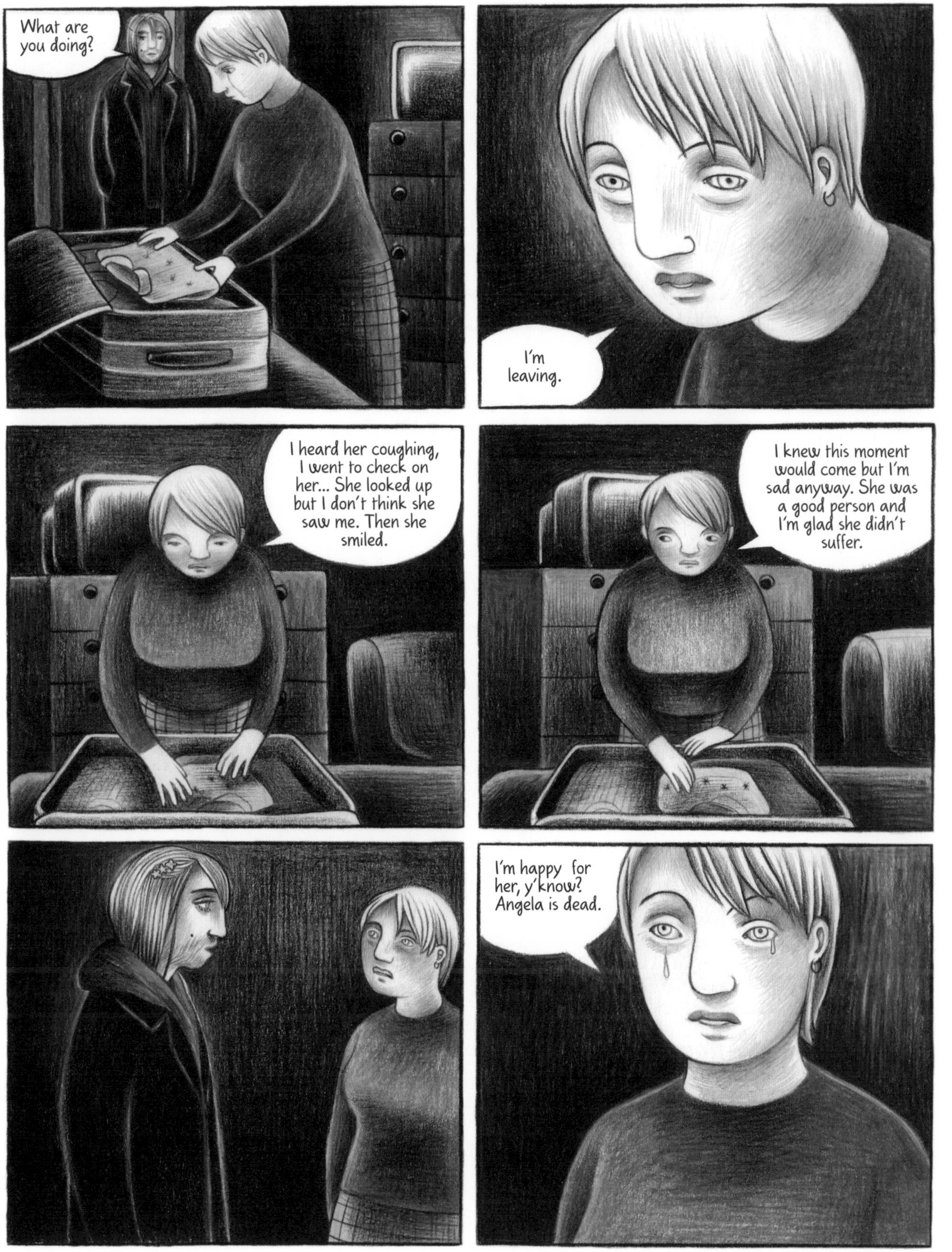
What are you doing?
I'm leaving.
I heard her coughing, I went to check on her... She looked up but I don't think she saw me. Then she smiled.
I knew this moment would come but I'm sad anyway. She was a good person and I'm glad she didn't suffer.
I'm happy for her, y'know? Angela is dead.

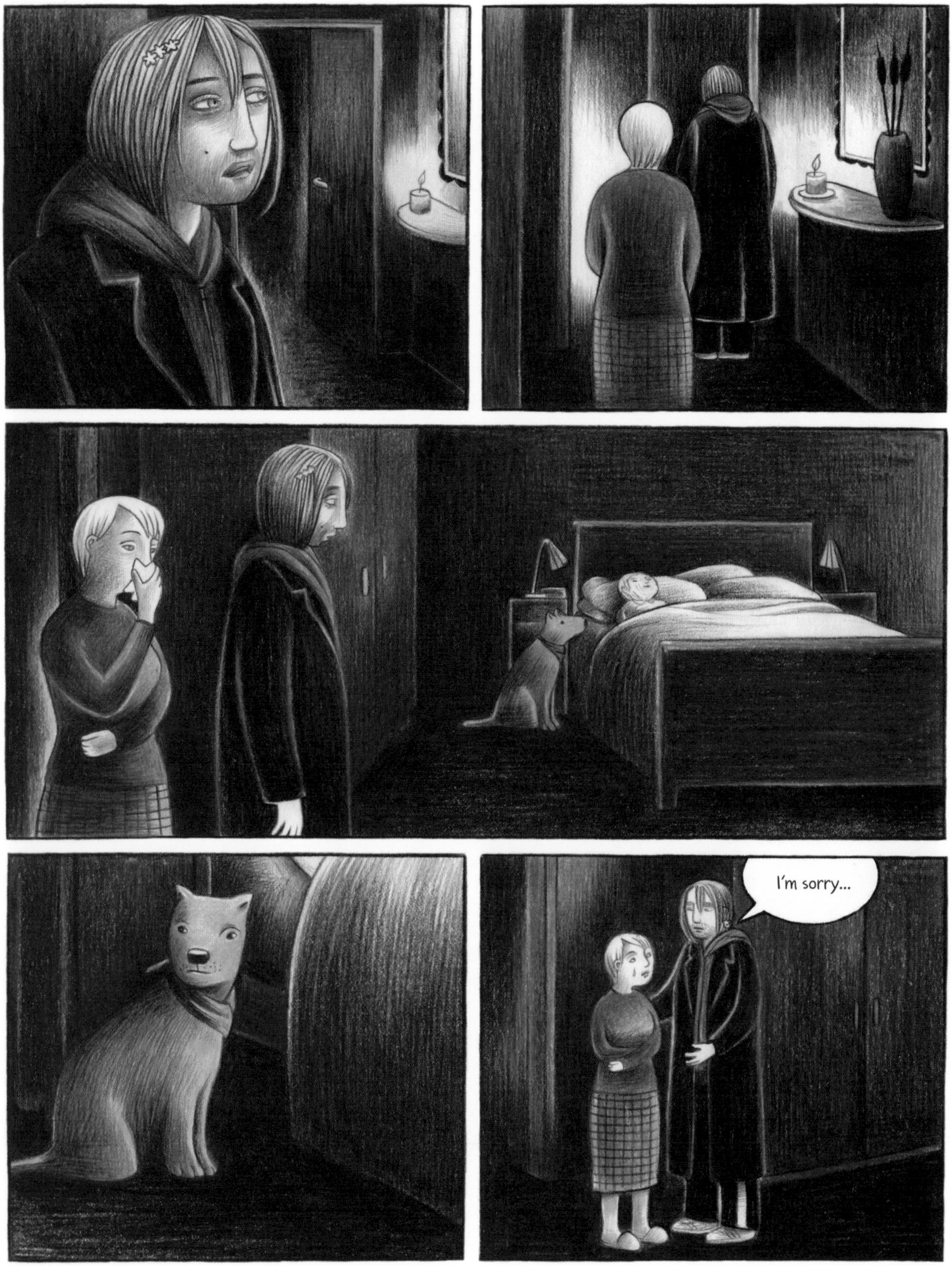
I'm sorry...

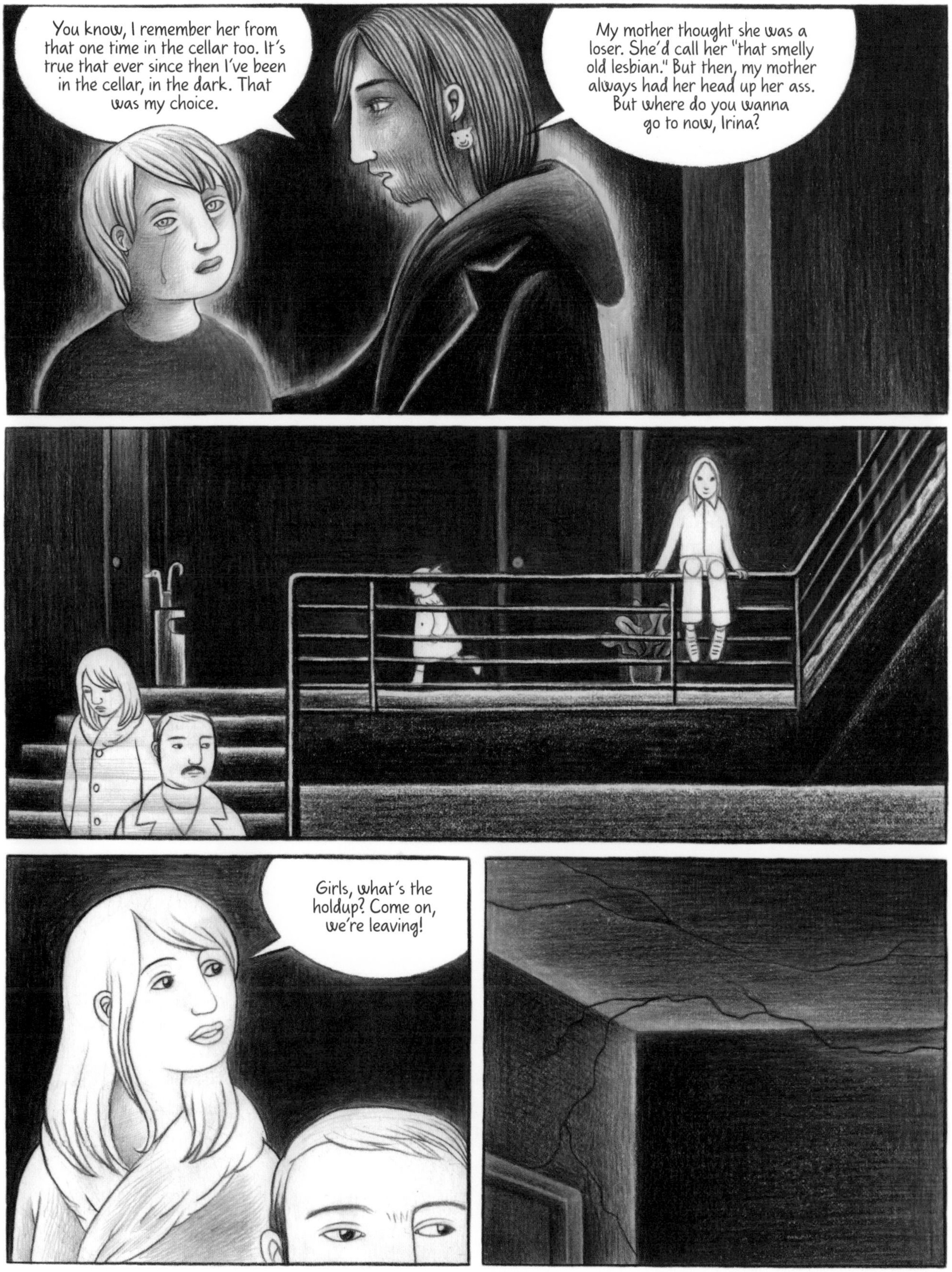
You know, I remember her from that one time in the cellar too. It's true that ever since then I've been in the cellar, in the dark. That was my choice.
My mother thought she was a loser. She'd call her "that smelly old lesbian." But then, my mother always had her head up her ass. But where do you wanna go to now, Irina?
Girls, what's the holdup? Come on, we're leaving!

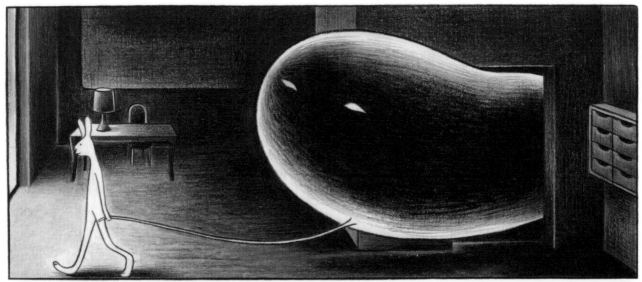

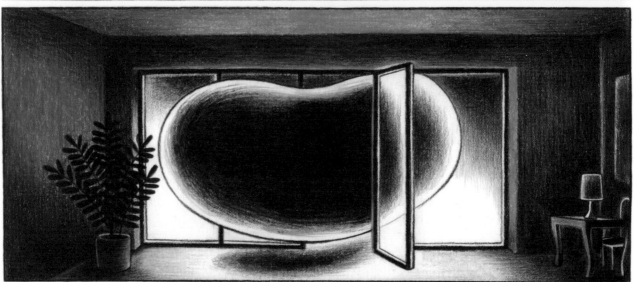

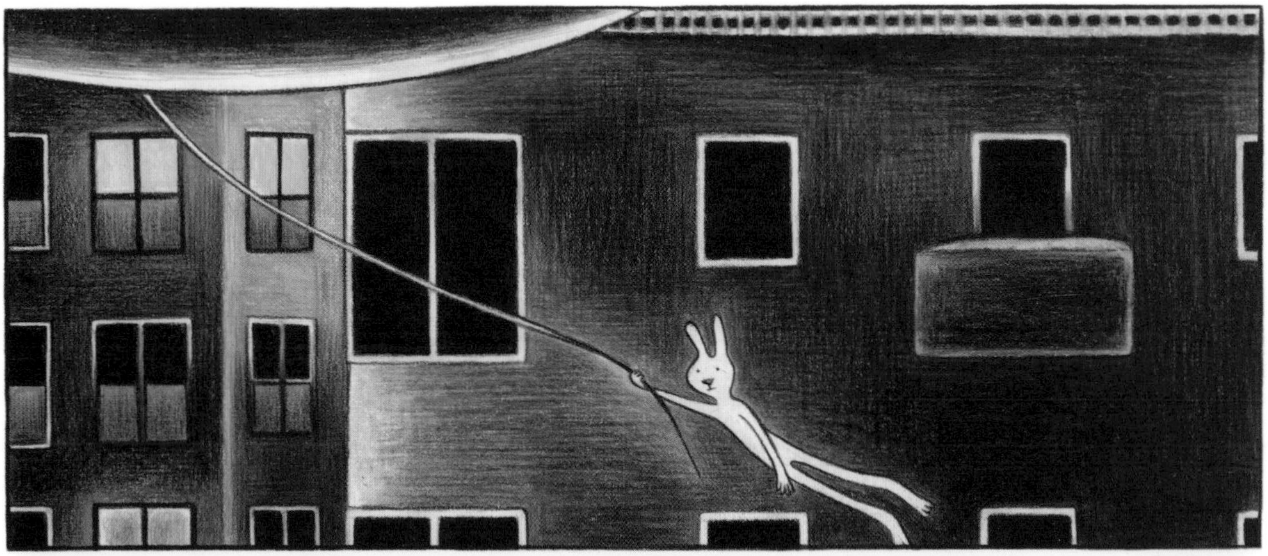

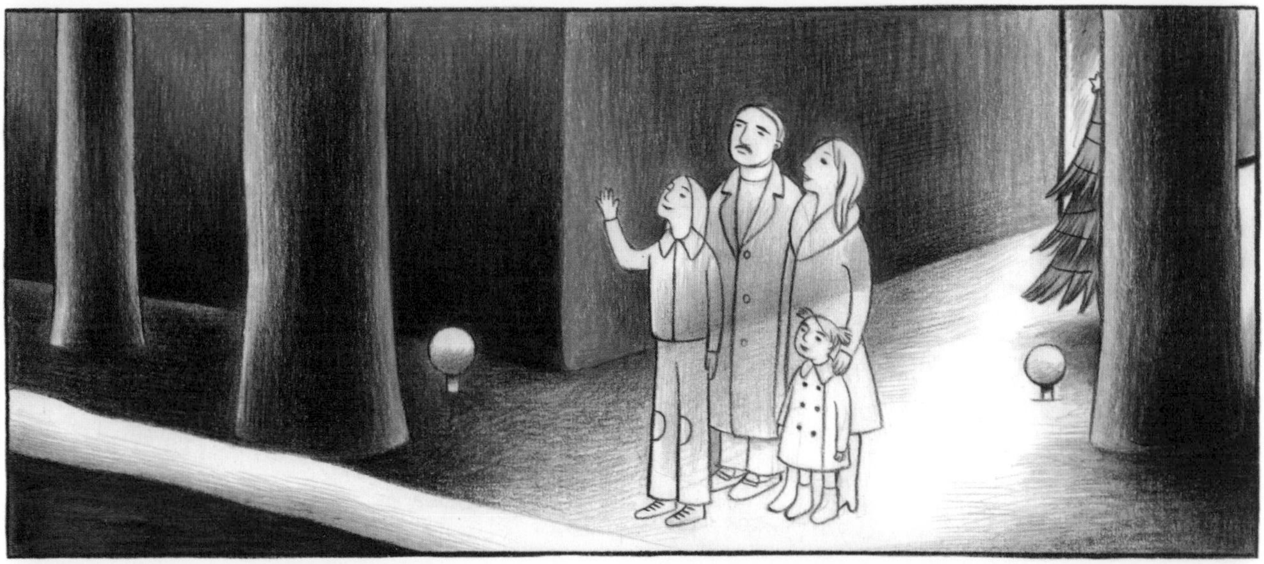

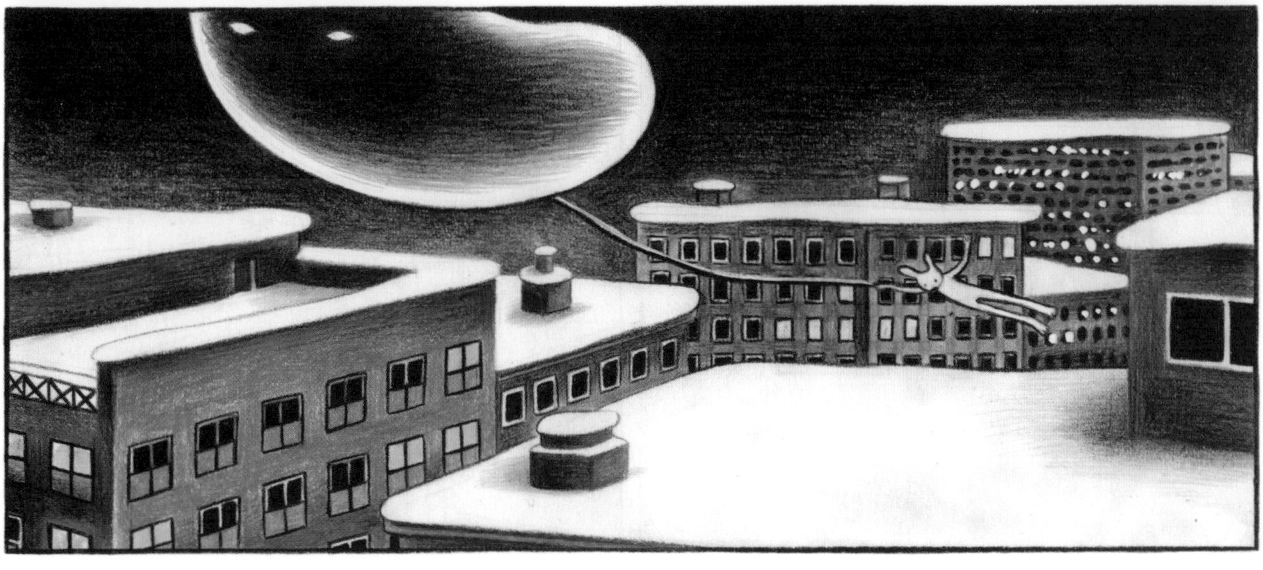

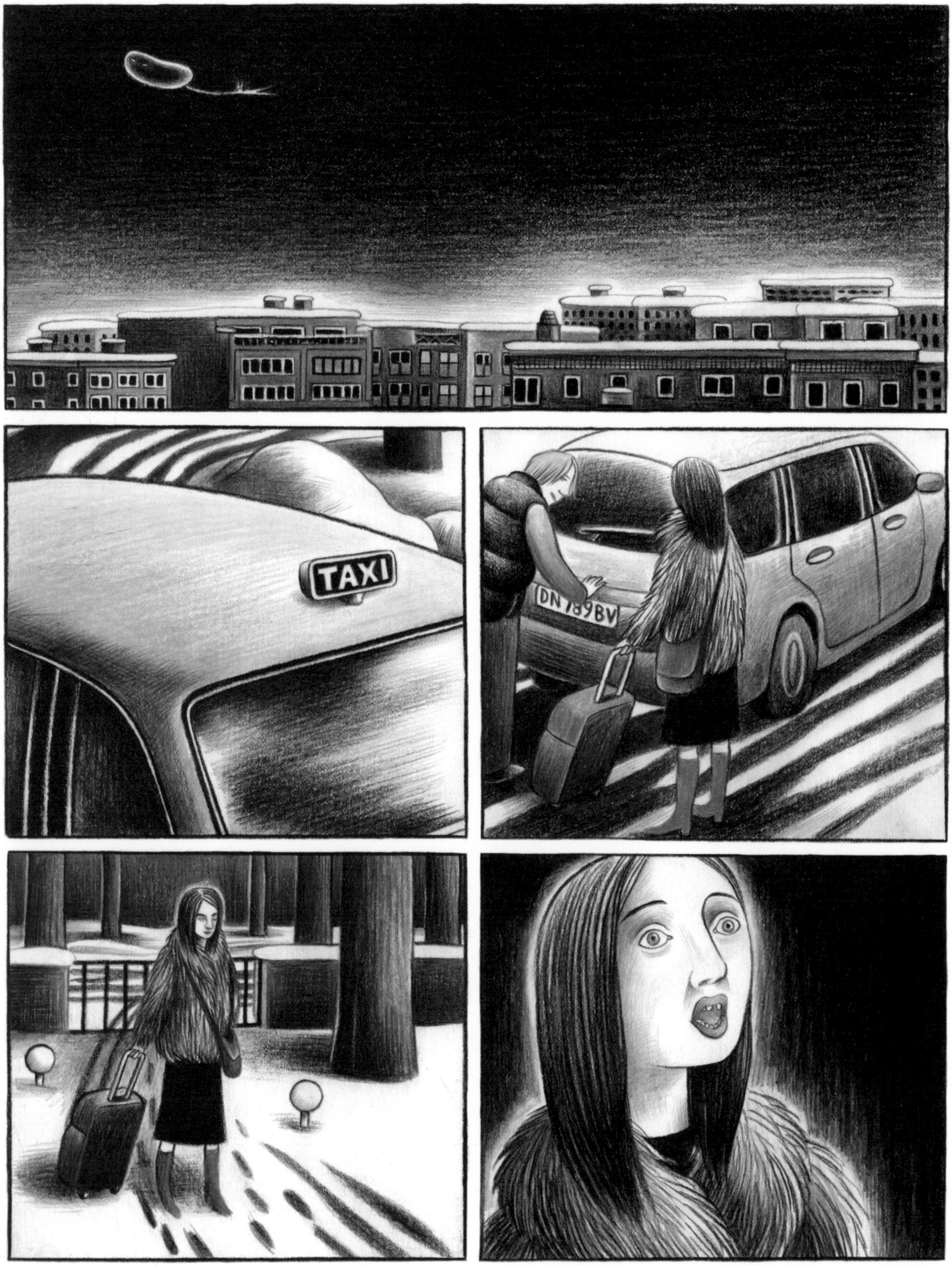
TAXI

THURSDAY, DECEMBER 21

---

01 minute, 09 seconds

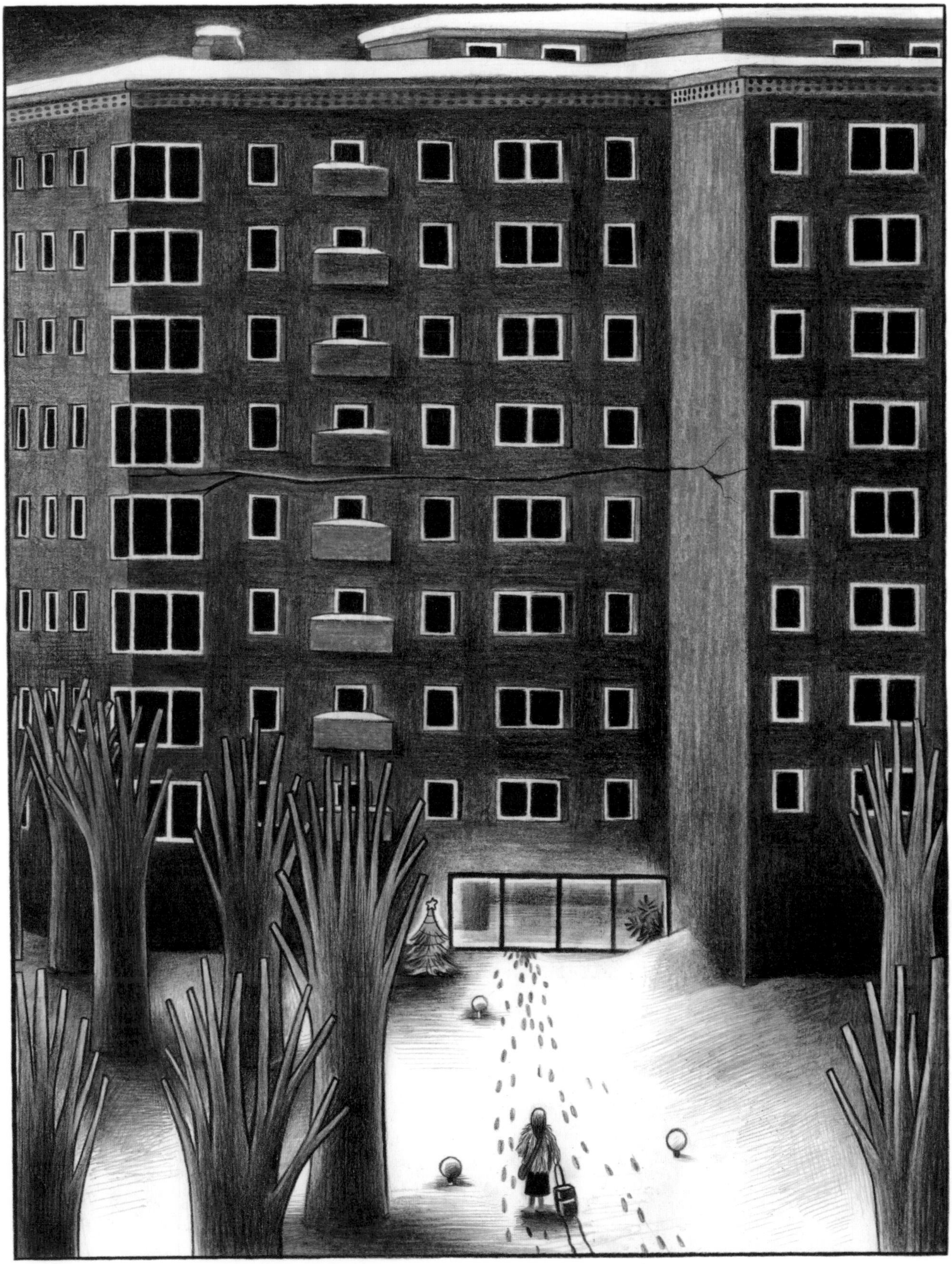

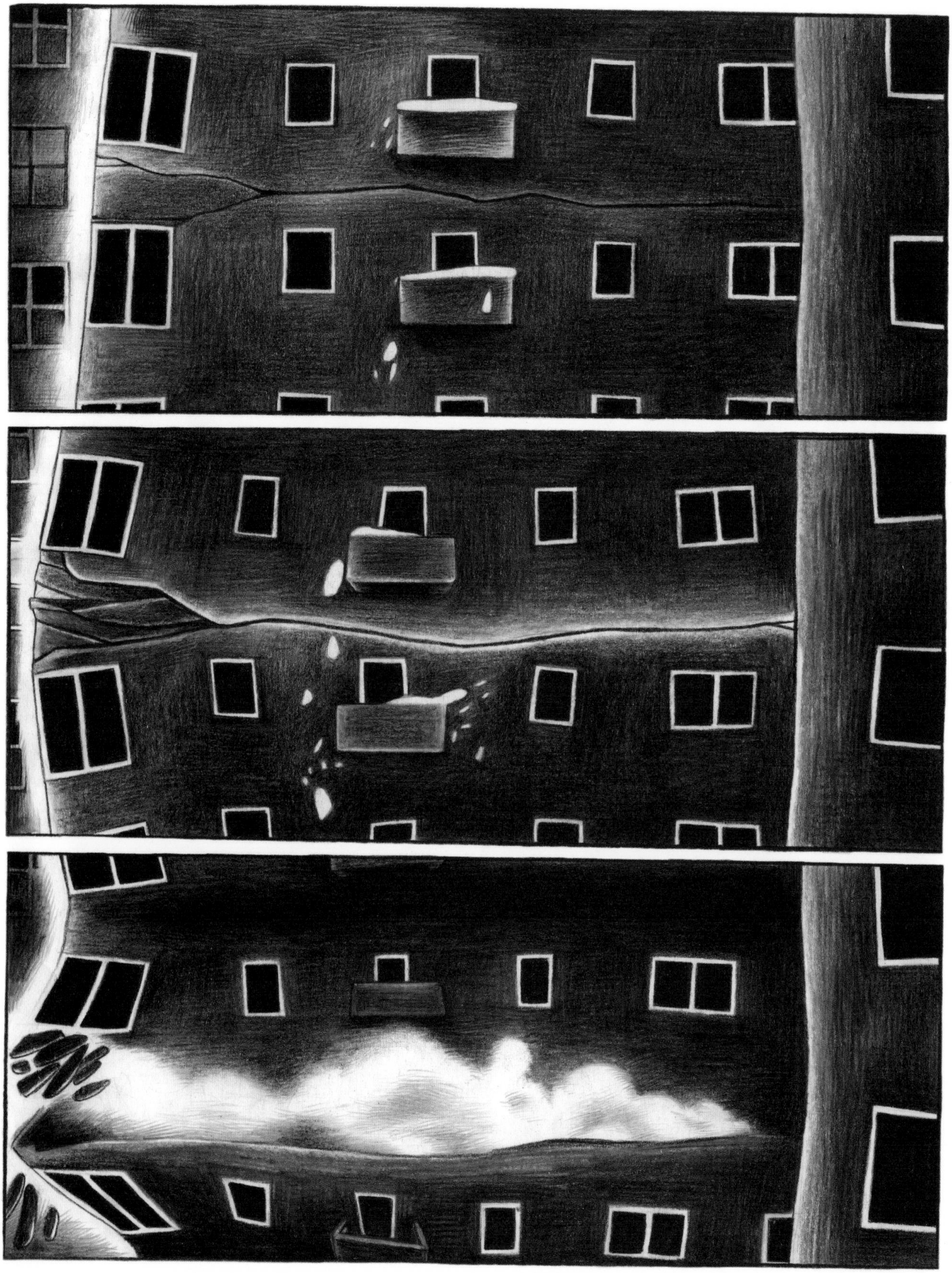

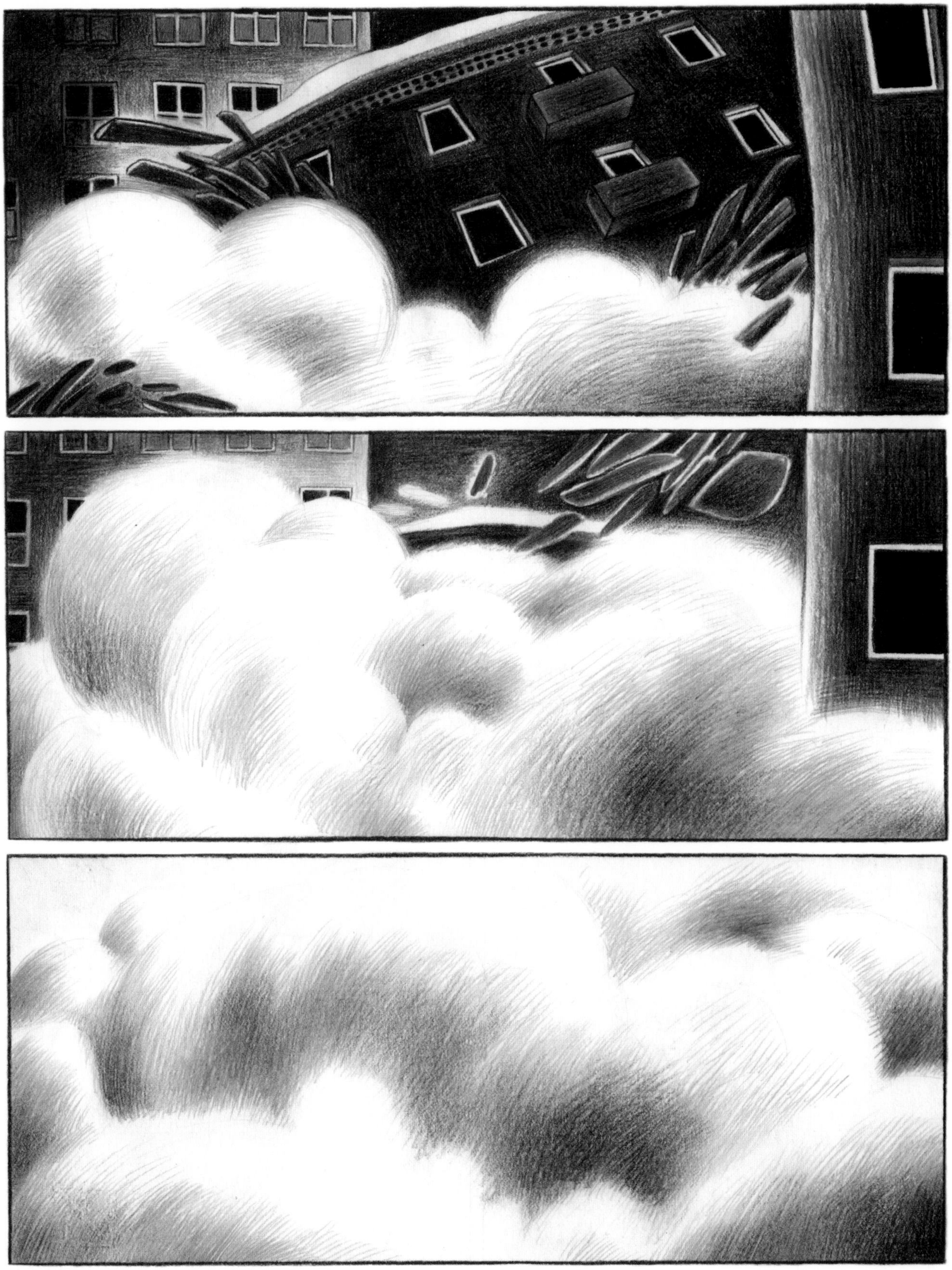

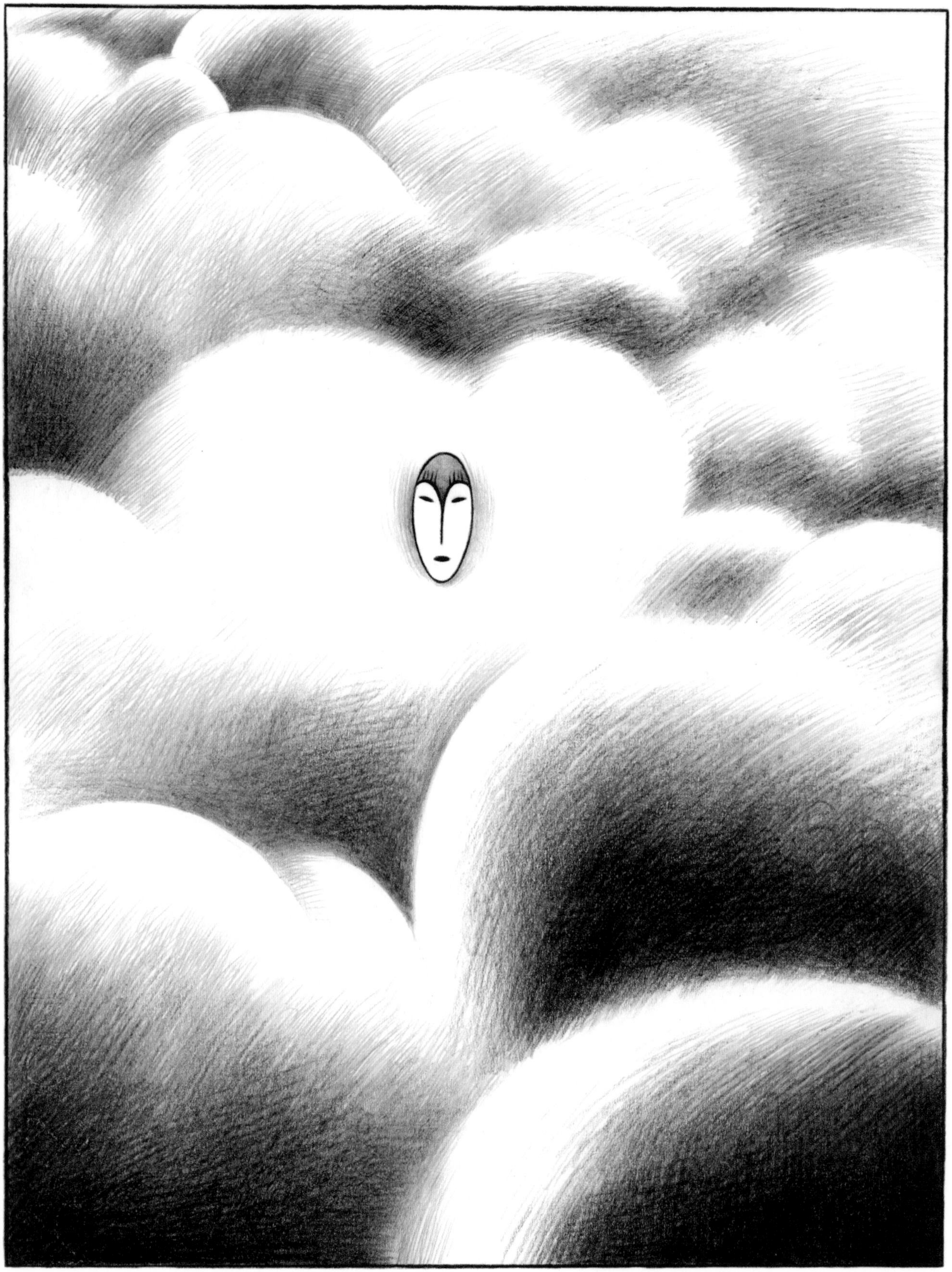

A few weeks later...

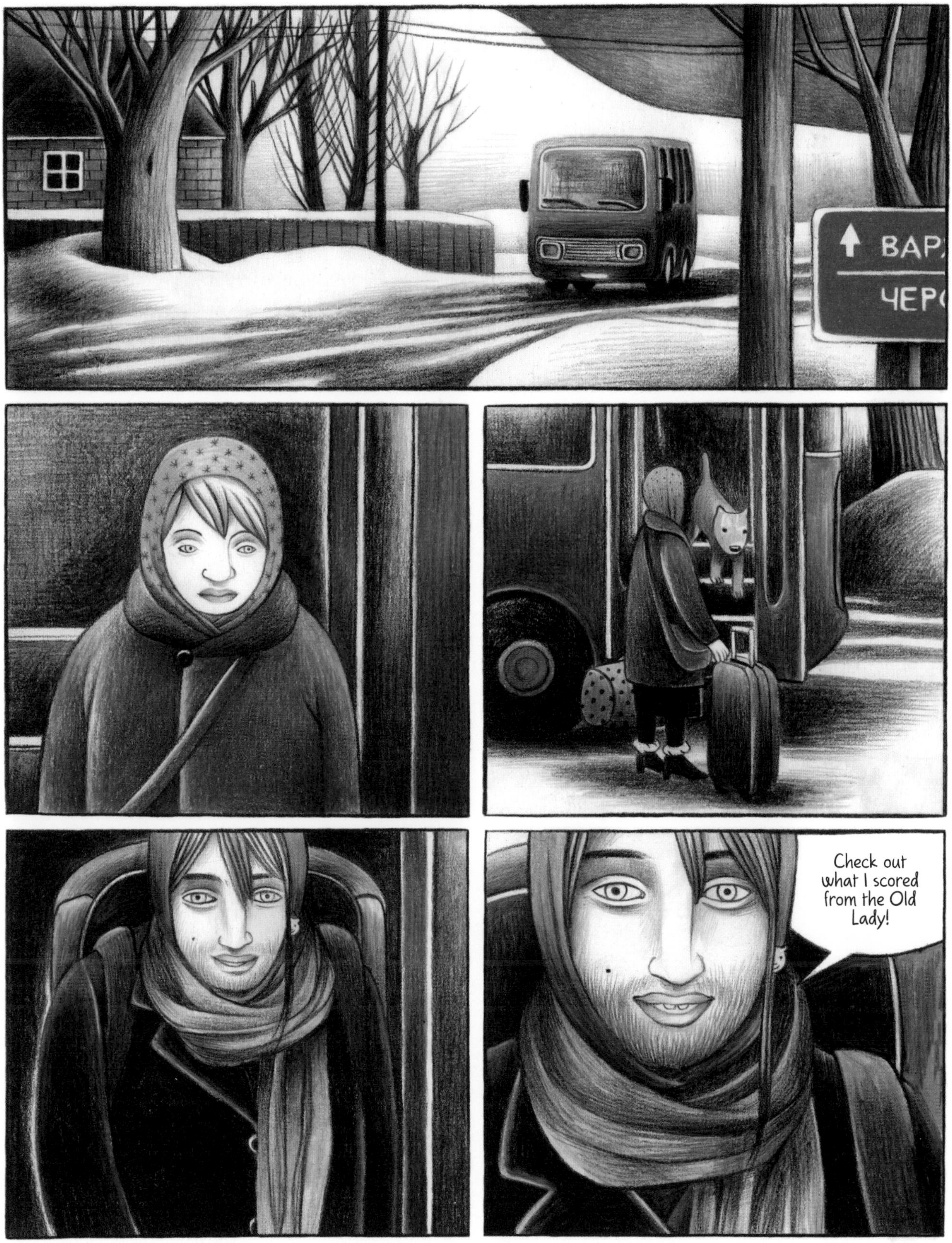
Check out what I scored from the Old Lady!

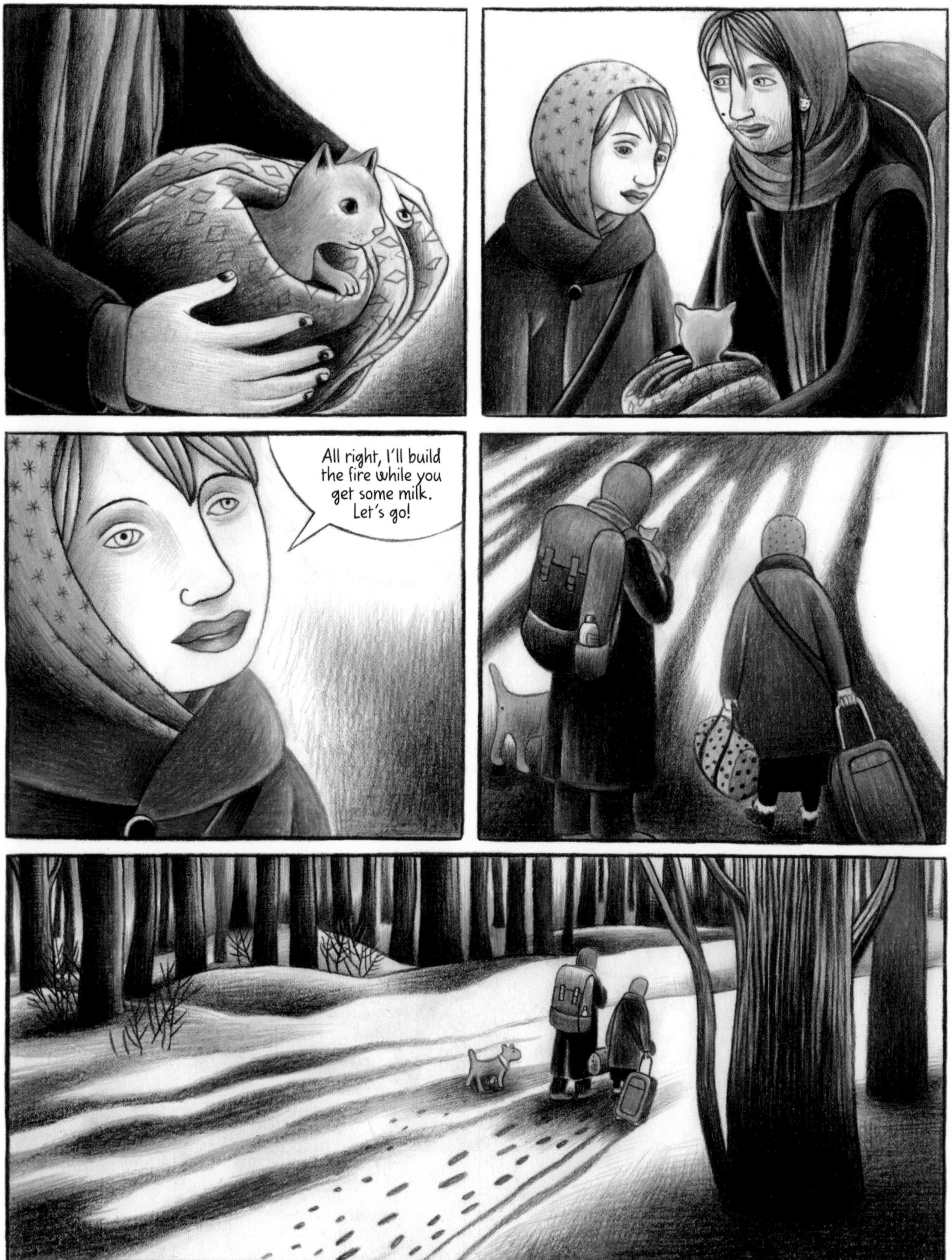
All right, I'll build the fire while you get some milk. Let's go!